About the author

Roger Howard is a British freelance journalist who has travelled widely throughout Iran. He has written extensively on issues of defence and international relations for many newspapers and journals. His work has appeared in the *Daily Mail*, for which he covered the US-led war in Afghanistan, the *New Statesman*, the *Spectator, Middle East International, Jane's Intelligence Review* and the US journal *In the National Interest*. He has also broadcast for BBC World Service and for television networks. He took a First in Modern History from Cambridge in 1988.

About this book

Is Iran at a crossroads? The recent US-led wars in Iraq and Afghanistan have brought new opportunities and dangers that could conceivably either herald a new rapprochement between Tehran and Washington or else bring a sharp detorioration that might perhaps spill over into confrontation. At home, profound demographic changes would seem to make far-reaching political changes appear inevitable in a country whose young population is alienated from the clerical elite that pulls the strings of power.

This book looks at some of the causes of these domestic international tensions and considers some of the possible outcomes. In particular, it asks:

- Is Iran really on the way to developing nuclear weapons?
- What is the Iranian 'Qods Force' doing in Iraq and Afghanistan? And why?
- What are Iran's connections with Middle East terror groups?
- Could Iran disintegrate if the current regime crumbles?
- How much of a threat to the regime do dissident organisations pose?

The book explains the likely course of events in Iran and the region for both general readers and specialists.

ROGER HOWARD

Iran in Crisis?
Nuclear ambitions and the American response

Zed Books
LONDON · NEW YORK

Iran in Crisis? Nuclear ambitions and the American response was first published by Zed Books Ltd, 7 Cynthia Street, London N1 9JF, UK and Room 400, 175 Fifth Avenue, New York, NY 10010, USA in 2004.

www.zedbooks.co.uk

Cover designed by Andrew Corbett
Set in Monotype Dante and Gill Sans Heavy by Ewan Smith, London
Printed and bound in Malta by Gutenberg Press Ltd

Distributed in the USA exclusively by Palgrave Macmillan, a division of St Martin's Press, LLC, 175 Fifth Avenue, New York, NY 10010.

A catalogue record for this book is available from the British Library.
US CIP data is available from the Library of Congress.

ISBN 1 84277 474 3 hb
ISBN 1 84277 475 1 pb

Contents

Acknowledgements

The author would like to thank Professor Sohrab Behdad, Mr Mehrdad Farahmand, Sir David Gore-Booth, Lord Gilmour of Craigmillar, Mr Nigel Laird, Dr Ali Nourizadeh, Mr Ahmed Rashid, Mr David Reddaway, Sir Alfred Sherman and Mr Michael Thomas. I am also particularly grateful to Mr Alan George, author of *Syria: Neither Bread Nor Freedom*, and to my editors at Zed, Dr Anna Hardman and Mr Robert Molteno, for commissioning the project and for their comments on parts of the draft text. But I am grateful above all to my parents for their unfailing support and encouragement.

Roger Howard
Oxford, February 2004

Abbreviations and acronyms

AEAI	Atomic Energy Association of Iran
AEI	American Enterprise Institute
AFP	Agence France Presse
AP	Associated Press
APOC	Anglo-Persian Oil Company
BBG	Broadcasting Board of Governors (USA)
CIA	Central Intelligence Agency
CIS	Commonwealth of Independent States (former Soviet Union)
CSIS	Center for Strategic and International Studies
DIO	Defence Industries Organization (Iran)
EU	European Union
FBI	Federal Bureau of Investigation
FYDP	Five-Year Development Plan (Iran)
GDP	Gross Domestic Product
HEU	heavily enriched uranium
IAEA	International Atomic Energy Agency
IAF	Israeli Air Force
ICO	Islamic Conference Organization
IDF	Israeli Defence Force
IELTS	Internal English Language Testing System
IFM	Iran's Freedom Movement
ILSA	Iran–Libya Sanctions Act
IMF	International Monetary Fund
IRGC	Iranian Revolutionary Guard Corps
IRNA	Iranian Republic News Agency
ISI	Inter-Services Intelligence (Pakistan)
ISP	Internet Service Provider
JINSA	Jewish Institute of National Security Affairs
KDP	Kurdistan Democracy Party
KDPI	Kurdish Democratic Party of Iran
LEF	Law Enforcement Forces (Iran)
LV	Landesamt für Verfassungsschutz (Germany)
MKO	Mujahideen-e Khalq Organization
MOIS	Ministry of Intelligence and Security (Iran)

NAM	Non-Aligned Movement
NCRI	National Council of Resistance of Iran
NNPT	Nuclear Non-Proliferation Treaty
NYPD	New York Police Department
OCU	Office to Consolidate Unity (Iran)
OPEC	Organization of Petroleum-Exporting Countries
OSP	Office of Special Plans (USA)
PFLP	Popular Front for the Liberation of Palestine
PIJ	Palestinian Islamic Jihad
PKK	Partiya Karkeren Kurdistan (Kurdistan Workers' Party)
PMOI	People's Mujahideen Organization of Iran
PUK	Patriotic Union of Kurdistan
RPG	rocket-propelled grenade
S3	Shahab 3 (Iranian missile)
SANAM	Southern Azerbaijan National Awareness Movement
SCIRI	Supreme Council of Islamic Revolution in Iraq
SNSC	Supreme National Security Council (Iran)
SOE	state-owned enterprises
VEVAK	Vezarat-e Ettel'at va Amniat-e Keshvar (Iran)
VOA	Voice of America
WMD	weapons of mass destruction
WTC	World Trade Center
WTO	World Trade Organization

Introduction

Like many other terms, 'crisis' is an over-used word that has become devalued by its frequent but misplaced reference to any scenario in which an unusual level of drama is played out. In its proper sense, however, it clearly refers to a pivotal moment at which a process of transition climaxes and a future is determined.

Without the benefit of hindsight, it is of course impossible to judge if Iran is indeed fast approaching any such turning point. From the moment of its inception the present regime has often appeared to be in a state of crisis, but has nevertheless defied all predictions by somehow struggling through, just as there have been many other occasions when dramatic, rapid change has eventuated against all expectation: the political turbulence that began in the autumn of 1978 and led to Islamic revolution the following winter, for example, was not widely foreseen in a country that was famously described by President Jimmy Carter in December 1977 as 'an island of stability'. There are, however, convincing reasons to suppose that, at some point in the future, Iran will witness a crisis point at which the present regime will effectively survive or disappear and that its relationship with the United States could change dramatically, either by sharp deterioration or because of a thawing of the ice that has held the two countries apart since the Islamic Revolution.

The most powerful force pressing for sweeping political reforms within the country is demographic change. Iran, in sharp contrast to most Western countries, has a predominantly young population whose values and attitudes differ profoundly from those who pull the strings of political power. Remembering nothing of the events of 1979, much of this upcoming generation shares none of the common memories and experiences that shaped the Revolution but is instead heavily influenced by Western ways of life whose images are broadcast by satellite television and disseminated by the Internet. This generation gap becomes immediately obvious to any Western visitor to the country, for in the streets of today's Iran, Islamic decree is openly defied by young couples who hold hands and by increasing numbers of young women who revealingly push back their traditional headscarf (*hijab*). In the privacy of their homes, many press the case for democratic and secular rule.

At first sight it seems quite likely that such pressures will bring about political reform in the immediate or short term. The prospect of conservative victories in both the parliamentary elections in February 2004 and in the presidential election in 2005 as a result not of popular support but of a lack of public interest in the political processes of the existing regime could lead, as President Bush has argued, to a sudden forfeiture of 'its last claim to legitimacy'[1] and a 'chasm between the authorities and the people'[2] that prompts mass demonstrations on a greater scale than June 2003, when violent student riots rocked the current order. But even such large-scale protests, should they ever eventuate, would still be some way removed from a true political crisis, since to carry real weight such demonstrations need to be led by a respected leadership, in the same way that Ruhollah Khomeini had once orchestrated opposition to the Shah, and have some degree of organization and some political programme, no matter how basic or vague. But these crucial ingredients are, at the time of writing, wholly absent from Iran's political picture.

Equally uncertain is the way in which such a political crisis is likely to be resolved. It is possible that such a transition could be extremely bloody and violent in the same manner as the 1906–09 Constitutional Revolution, when a written constitution was first established in Persia,[3] the political stirrings of 1963, during the protests at the Shah's 'White Revolution', or the winter of 1978–79. But because such an outcome is widely deemed unlikely in a country where the anarchy and disorder of less than a quarter of a century ago are so easily remembered, it is more likely that any such political crisis will be resolved more peacefully and perhaps suddenly, as conservatives effectively dissolve the regime in the same largely unexpected manner in which they agreed in October 2003 to bow to international demands over their nuclear programme. But whenever and however it eventuates, a political crisis in Iran is none the less inevitable at some point.

When viewed from a wider, international perspective, it is also clear that there are other pressures upon the country that could easily lead to a critical juncture at which Iran's relations with the United States could either sharply deteriorate or significantly improve.

As discussed in the subsequent chapter, these pressures are in part a reflection of the newly drawn geopolitical picture that has been created by the War on Terror and the invasion of Iraq by American forces. For while there is nothing new about the hard rhetoric that President Bush had voiced in January 2002, when he famously declared Iran to stand alongside North Korea and Iraq as a member of an 'Axis of Evil', the new geo-strategic map of the Middle East and Central Asia has suddenly realized the worst fears of Iranian security chiefs. Even before President Bush had fired the first shots in the war against Iraq, Iran had already been almost entirely surrounded by US forces based not just in Afghanistan but also in the CIS republics of the former Soviet Union, notably Uzbekistan, Tajikistan, Georgia and Kyrgyzstan, as well as the longer-established bases in most of the Gulf States. Even Russia, long seen by Tehran as both a friend and ally, has at times seemed to be bowing to US pressure, notably in the summer of 2002, when its government agreed to hold joint military exercises in the Caspian region.

Such an overwhelming US regional presence is likely to act as a catalyst to other existing political forces inside Iran. In a positive sense, it could prompt its rulers to co-operate with American demands and thereby foster a new accord between the two countries. Alternatively, it could easily foster an Iranian perception, warranted or otherwise, of imminent American aggression. Convinced of a forthcoming US attack, Tehran could then take the very measures that Washington would regard as hostile and the consequent American reaction would thereby make Iranian fears self-fulfilling. The dangers of such a state of mistrust became clear in the wake of Operation Desert Storm, the allied offensive to drive Iraqi forces out of Kuwait in February 1991. Fearing that they, after Saddam, would be the next targets for the vast US-led army that had assembled in the region, the Iranian rulers had closed ranks and accelerated their arms programme, further fuelling the West's mistrust. In May 1991, as they openly complained about the US presence, Iran's leaders successfully test-fired a modified version of North Korea's Scud missile that demonstrated a capability to hit American bases in both Saudi Arabia and Turkey with a one-ton warhead, accepted deliveries of new Russian submarines and Chinese boats and sharply accelerated their programme to develop their own Shahab 3 missile.

The purpose of this book is to look in more detail at what lies behind the tensions that affect contemporary Iran. At an international level, Iran has courted the particular antipathy of Washington by its sponsorship of international terror (Chapter 2), its alleged interference in the affairs of its neighbours, Afghanistan and Iraq (Chapter 3), and its failure to answer important questions about a nuclear programme that is supposedly intended to supply energy to a fast-growing population but which in practice may well continue to conceal an ambition to build a nuclear warhead (Chapter 4). The Iranians will have to address all of these issues if they are to cement any tentative rapprochement with the USA that could perhaps emerge in the wake of the 'earthquake diplomacy' that followed the humanitarian operation to relieve the stricken city of Bam in southern Iran, devastated by an earthquake on 26 December 2003.

The second part of the book looks at Iran's domestic pressures that exist in their own right. Chapter 5 looks at the struggle for political power between bitterly opposed factions, as conservative defenders of the status quo seek to impede the drive for the rule of law, freedom of speech and democracy in a country where by Western standards, as Washington also emphasizes, they are conspicuously absent. Chapter 6 considers some of the constituents of Iran's economic and social tensions.

The final part of the book looks at some of the different ways these different pressures may in the future be manifested and perhaps merge. It is not inconceivable, for example, that Western rhetoric and media influence, perhaps sponsored by US hawks who want to finance Iranian 'liberation' in the same manner as the Iraqi opposition to Saddam was once funded, will incite popular unrest that will force the Iranian authorities to introduce sweeping political reforms (Chapter 7). But a more radical US or Israeli approach will be to sponsor armed opposition groups, such as the Mujahideen-e Khalq Organization (MKO), that could conceivably wage campaigns of sabotage, bombings and assassination that are calculated to have a similar effect (Chapter 8).

But quite apart from the provocations of the Iranian regime on these and other issues, there can also be no doubt that this state of tension between the two capitals has on occasion also been exacerbated by a sometimes aggressive approach from the White House that reveals more about the American mind than about Iranian policy. This is considered in the chapter that follows.

Notes

1. Speech to the National Endowment for Democracy, Washington, 6 November 2003.

2. The phrase was used by the reformist Islamic Iran Participation Front on 11 November 2003.

3. 'Persia' was officially renamed 'Iran' in 1935.

PART I
Iran and the USA

1 | The American mind

Nearly a quarter of a century after the Islamic Revolution, the subsequent hostage-taking of American diplomats in Tehran and the sudden rupture of diplomatic ties, a new chapter in the story of US–Iranian relations looks ready to begin. It is possible that this chapter will tell a happy tale of a new rapprochement, an easing of American economic sanctions and perhaps a more peaceful and stable Middle East. But it is also at least as likely that relations will deteriorate even further as continuing mistrust, hostility and acrimony threaten to spill over into confrontation.

The possibility that US–Iranian relations may be reaching a new juncture reflects several recent developments. The near completion of Iran's nuclear programme – supposedly carried out only for civilian energy – will force its international critics either to take unilateral action against the reactors at Arak and Bushehr or instead decisively to put their faith in the snap inspections of the International Atomic Energy Agency (IAEA) that the Iranian authorities, in a deal struck on 21 October 2003, agreed to respect. While Tehran's compromise was greeted warmly in European capitals, it has been viewed with overt scepticism by many in Tel Aviv and Washington: leading hawk John Bolton quickly pointed out that 'even if Iran follows through with its promises, many further steps are required in order to prove beyond doubt that Iran is foreswearing the pursuit of nuclear weapons',[1] while the CIA informed Congress, in a report made public on 8 November, that 'even with intrusive IAEA safeguards inspections at Natanz, there is a serious risk that Iran could use its enrichment technology in covert activities'.

Major changes in the wider geopolitical picture have also created new opportunities and dangers. In particular, because the US administration is now highly dependent upon neighbourly co-operation in stabilizing the highly turbulent regions of Afghanistan and Iraq, it is ready to reward any Iranian support or to penalize any disruption. Correspondingly, this US military presence in the region will either prompt the Iranian authorities to co-operate with the initiatives to rebuild the new political orders or to obstruct such efforts. Moreover, the highly flammable condition of both Iraq and Afghanistan, and of much of the wider world since the rise of Al Qaeda, has also meant that Washington can easily pin responsibility for terrorist outrages upon Iran, no matter how unwarranted such charges may in fact be: a car bombing in Riyadh on 12 May 2003 had prompted the US government to break off unofficial dialogue with Iranian representatives, even though there was no firm evidence of their regime's complicity.

At a more general level, the military assaults on Iraq and Afghanistan have also either vindicated or challenged the highly assertive US foreign policy advocated by 'aggressive nationalists' such as Donald Rumsfeld and Dick Cheney and the 'neo-conservatives' such as Paul Wolfowitz and Richard Perle. At the time of writing, it appears that the White House has retreated from its policy of regime change and pre-emptive military action in order to return to a more traditional diplomatic style that would repackage President Bush as a man of peace: Washington's unsuccessful offer of a high-level humanitarian mission to Iran, made in the wake of the massive earthquake in Bam province on 26 December 2003, clearly illustrated this change of tone. But should the US military succeed in effectively pacifying the two countries and impose its own Pax Americana, then the White House could very well resume its earlier stridency and adopt a much aggressive posture that would inevitably square up to the 'dangerous' Tehran regime.

A softer tone is likely to manifest itself in the more moderate voices of the US State Department that have advocated the establishment of new diplomatic channels and the partial lifting of economic sanctions in return for continuing compliance with the demands of the IAEA and co-operation in the efforts to rebuild post-Saddam Iraq and post-Taliban Afghanistan. The State Department had signalled its readiness to explore such moves during 2003, some months before the US humanitarian effort to relieve Bam symbolized hopes that relations between the two countries could finally improve. Any such approach would also be welcomed by politicians in Tehran, mindful that a new accord with the USA, after years of sanctions and isolation, would be widely greeted by ordinary Iranians.

By contrast any dispute between Iran and the USA would be likely to reflect the influence of, or pass the initiative to, hawkish influences whose antipathy to the Tehran regime has long been vociferously expressed. At the same time that the State Department sounded notes of compromise in September 2003, for example, senior figures in the Pentagon were meeting with the cleric Hossein Khomeini, the grandson of the Iranian revolutionary leader, who openly advocated US support for regime change in Iran. Plans 'for an aggressive policy of trying to destabilize the Iranian government', even allowing for the covert support of an exiled militia movement hitherto blacklisted by the State Department as a terrorist organization,[2] are also said to have been actively considered by the same Pentagon figures.[3] And in the offices of its influential think-tanks, where policy proposals are pitched before governmental audiences, some hard-liners have argued a passionate case for 'taking the fight' to Tehran, while on Capitol Hill senators and representatives are sponsoring new legislation to fund Iranian opposition movements with lavish grants similar to those previously provided to Iraqi exiles.[4] The legislation of Senator Sam Brownback, the Iran Democracy Act, for example, seeks to destabilize the Tehran regime by funding dissident organizations inside Iran, an arrangement that would break new ground by contravening an American deal, struck in Algiers in 1981, not to interfere in Iranian domestic affairs.

Such hawkish influences have already strongly influenced US policy. In particular, relations between Tehran and the Bush administration had been badly strained after the President's State of the Union address in January 2002, a speech that even relative Iranian moderates such as President Khatami had furiously denounced as 'threatening and humiliating'. Iran, Bush had famously asserted, was a member of an 'Axis of Evil' that he argued was 'arming to threaten the peace of the world' and thereby posed 'a grave and growing danger' to the United States. Such views had in any case been deeply held by many others within the administration for much longer, including those who had argued ever since the 11 September attacks that the disposal of the Iranian government – its 'mullahcracy' – should be prioritized over the toppling of Saddam's rule. In particular, Tehran had earned a prominent place on the target list produced by an influential pressure group, the Project for the New American Century, forty-one of whose members had addressed an open letter to Bush on 20 September that urged the President to retaliate against Iran if it failed to cut off its support for the Hezbollah movement in Lebanon.

Few would dispute that the potential for any forthcoming confrontation is in part a direct consequence of Iranian provocation. The United States clearly has every reason to fear the proliferation of weapons of mass destruction (WMD) and to insist upon the strict enforcement of the Nuclear Non-Proliferation Treaty and the Additional Protocol that the regime has more recently agreed to respect. In a country where unaccountable, hard-line elites undoubtedly have some scope to pursue their own private agendas, Western fears that Iranian WMD could be secretly passed to third parties, perhaps of suicidal inclination and therefore indifferent to the mutually assured destruction that their own actions would guarantee, hardly seem misplaced. And although the exact amount of influence that Iranian elites hold over some of the militant Palestinian groups is far from clear, there can be no doubt that most hard-liners are strongly hostile to the state of Israel and that some pressure is needed on both sides of the Arab–Israeli dispute if there is to be any lasting peace in the Middle East. Nor does any respected observer seriously dispute that the Iranian people suffer considerable political repression and human rights violation, and that it is within the power of the United States, considered to be the world's only 'hyper-power' since at least 1991, to do something constructive about it.

The Americans have, moreover, on occasion signalled a new willingness to talk, but found Tehran tone-deaf to the overtures they have struck. On 14 March 2002, for example, Senator Joseph Biden of the Senate Foreign Relations Committee made a clear offer to his Iranian counterparts to open a new dialogue that would overcome years of mistrust. But these approaches were rejected by the Supreme Leader Ayatollah Ali Khamenei who was anxious not to let rival politicians steal the credit for any new rapprochement. Biden's approaches, as the influential editor of the conservative paper *Keyhan* argued, were 'aimed at recruiting mercenaries from within the Islamic Republic to advance the US' spiteful objections'.

But such provocation, detailed in subsequent chapters, represents only one side of the coin, for Iran's uneasy relationship with Washington has at times also been fuelled by the particular responses that these provocations have sometimes elicited from the United States. If in January 2002 the US administration had known that Iran had made great efforts to rein in Al Qaeda operatives on its soil and to support the military campaign against the Taliban regime in Afghanistan, why did the President's State of the Union address hit only negative notes at the expense of the more positive? If Iranian co-operation would in future clearly be indispensable to maintain law and order both in post-Taliban Afghanistan and a post-Saddam Iraq, why heighten the sense of mistrust between the capitals? And if Washington really did deem the pursuit of co-operation to be a fruitless task, why publicly condemn Iran, instead of assuming the quieter, less confrontational, tone that characterized EU diplomacy?

Viewed in these terms, the possibility that tension between Iran and the USA might eventuate in the foreseeable future represents a combustible mix of Iranian provocation with sometimes belligerent US reactions. This chapter seeks to examine these American reactions more closely for two reasons. At the time of writing, it appears more likely that this more hawkish mindset will gain the upper hand in formulating US foreign policy towards Iran: not only is American antipathy and mistrust of the mullahs' regime too deeply rooted to be quickly banished, but there is no sign of any compromise on the Middle East peace process and Iranian sponsorship of local 'terror'. And even if Washington does signal a more moderate line towards Iran, then the same voices will continue to hold powerful sway over policy and always be quick to find justification for a more aggressive agenda: as mentioned, there remains the particularly strong possibility of the sudden, devastating terrorist attack for which Tehran will be viewed as the culprit. This chapter seeks to look not at the 'objective' issues that concern Washington, such as Iran's nuclear programme, but rather at the more 'subjective' American mindset that responds to those issues in a distinctive way and which remains essential to understanding relations between the two countries.

The common ground between Iran and the West

At first sight, Iran might seem an unlikely recipient of American antipathy. In clear contrast to North Korea, another member of the 'Axis of Evil', Iran's own history is after all strongly interwoven with that of Western civilization. Ideas, inventions, commerce and migrants had all traditionally flowed to and from Europe through Persia's long and highly porous western border with the Ottoman Empire, ideas such as Manichaeism, inventions that included chess and the stirrup, and commercial artefacts that ranged from ceramics, silk carpets and precious stones in ancient times to oil, tobacco and heroin in the contemporary age. Among these ideas was early Christianity, which was born in the Middle East and spread westwards through the influence of its early converts: at the Council of Nicea in 325 AD, where the words of the Creed were decided, there were more bishops from Persia and India than from Western Europe. Among the most influential migrants, Bernard Lewis has suggested, were the ancient Jews, who had struck up 'a long relationship of mutual exchange' with the Persians that long pre-dated Biblical times. This encounter 'between Iranian religion and the Jewish religion', he continues, was one 'of far-reaching significance' and means that 'we can discern unmistakable traces of Persian influence, both intellectual and material, on the development of post-exilic Jewry, and therefore also of Christendom, and a corresponding influence in the late Greco-Roman and Byzantine world, and therefore ultimately in Europe'.[5]

The West's political influence on Iran has in earlier ages also become evident from the constitutionalism absorbed during spells at European universities by members of some elites, such as Malkum Khan, a chief protagonist for reform during Persia's Constitutional Revolution; Nasir al-Mulk, the Oxford-educated and liberal-minded prime minister of the same time; and, some years later, Mohammed Mossadeq, the nationalist premier who studied extensively in both Paris and Neuchatel in Switzerland. Similar intellectual currents also reached Persia on the printed page, in reformist journals that were smuggled into the country: in the 1890s, for example, *Qanun*, an influential publication that argued the case for the rule of law, was printed in London before being smuggled into Persia, while thirty years later, publications such as *Kaveh*, *Iranshahr* and *Farangistan*, preaching radical messages of socialism, secularism and scientific education, were also either published or edited in the West. Dissident writings and ideas also seeped through Persia's long borders with the states of Central Asia, including the ideas of Marx, Saint Simon and Comte, whose writings deeply impressed a Persian radical, Mirza Adamiyat, during his sojourn in Russia at the turn of the century. And by a curious irony, a term that had been imported into Persian by Western-educated intellectuals, for 'revolution' (*Inqilab*), was adopted by the followers of Ayatollah Khomeini and given more nationalist and Islamist intonations.[6]

Such intellectual influences help to account for the somewhat stronger foundations upon which the freedoms of contemporary Iran – or rather some semblance of such freedoms – are built.[7] In contrast to most Gulf States, ordinary Iranians enjoy at least some freedom at the ballot box. 'President Khatami was elected,' declared Secretary of State Colin Powell, speaking on a Washington radio station in July 2003, 'not in an American kind of election but an election that essentially tapped into the desires of the people.' The Iranian people have a right to vote for their president, for the parties that represent them in the national parliament, the Majles, and for their representatives in the tiers of local government that run cities, towns and villages. In particular, the local elections of 28 February 2003 are widely reckoned the most liberal ever held in post-revolutionary Iran, since the candidates who stood for election were initially selected not by the Guardian Council that has usually shortlisted electoral candidates but by an Election Supervisory Body independent of the country's hard-line institutions and whose choices thereby better reflected the true wishes of opposition members and liberal dissidents.

Because unelected bodies and institutions – the Supreme Leader, the Guardian and Expediency Councils, the judiciary and the military – that are overwhelmingly conservative in orientation continue to hold enough constitutional power to block many of the moves made by the president and the Majles, these arrangements hardly conform to the vision of 'democracy' that the Bush administration has always conjured both as a justification for war against Saddam and as a goal of US foreign policy. But it is none the less difficult to see why the Bush administration has hitherto singled out Iran's track record for condemnation when some of its own regional allies, notably Saudi Arabia, continue to allow their own people far less democratic freedom. 'Iranian students might get beaten up when they go into the streets,' in the words of one former senior Western diplomat, 'but their counterparts in the Gulf States wouldn't even get as far as protesting in the first place.'[8]

There are other liberties, too, that are denied to the people of other Gulf States but which Iranians enjoy, freedoms that help explain why in April 2002 the United Nations Human Rights Commission voted to remove Iran from its blacklist of countries. Despite the closure of numerous reformist journals and newspapers since the reformist president, Muhammed Khatami, was swept into power in 1997, Iran's press is still allowed more freedom of expression than its counterparts in some of these other states and its journalists 'can say more or less what we like about the elected government'.[9]

Women, too, enjoy more social rights than their more repressed regional sisterhood and eleven women MPs were voted to the sixth Majles in February 2000. In 1997 Dr Masoumeh Ebtekar was chosen by Khatami as vice-president with particular responsibility for the environment. A female adviser on women's issues, Zahra Shojaie, was also chosen and entitled to attend cabinet meetings. In general, Iranian women are very well represented in higher education, and in 2002 constituted 63 per cent of university intake. Women's interests also have some legal recognition, notably via Article 21 of the 1989 Constitution, which proclaims the commitment of the Republic to 'the rights of women', and from particular pieces of legislation, such as a new parliamentary law, sponsored by a female MP, Elaheh Kulai, that allows Iranian women greater rights to claim a divorce from their husbands.[10] The regime has also recently introduced other freedoms that are unthinkable in many other parts of the Islamic world, including the liberalization of the dress code for schoolgirls, who are currently no longer compelled to wear headscarves and robes inside schools[11] and the introduction of policewomen into the streets of Tehran. As the Nobel Peace Prize winner, Shirin Ebadi, commented, there has in recent years been some 'success' in promoting the cause of women's right, in a country that is 'on the right path'.[12]

Similar doubts can be raised over Washington's condemnation of

Iran's track record on religious freedoms. When in March 2003 the US State Department continued to designate Iran, alongside five other countries, as a 'country of particular concern' under the International Religious Freedom Act, thereby renewing the status it had acquired two years before, it was difficult to see why Iran merited such a title when other countries, with far more dubious track records on religious freedom, escaped censure altogether. The governments of Turkmenistan and Uzbekistan, for example, have been condemned by the US Commission on International Religious Freedom, and Saudi Arabia by the pressure group Human Rights Watch. 'The Bush administration says it wants to promote human rights in the Muslim world,' said Tom Malinowski, a Washington-based advocacy director for Human Rights Watch, 'but it can hardly say it's trying if it's afraid to state the simple truth about some of its partners.'[13] All three governments have also scored lower marks than Iran on the 'freedom scale' of the US pressure group, Freedom House.[14] In contrast to these other countries, for example, Iran also reserves seats in the elected Majles parliament for all its religious minorities (with the main exception of Bahais), including Christians, Jews, Zoroastrians and Sunni Muslims.

The 'enormous geopolitical importance' of Iran to which President Clinton once referred would also seem to make a convincing reason for any administration to find ways of co-operating with the Tehran regime, not antagonizing it. The US government can hardly afford to watch any future regional competitor holding sway over a region that has a superb strategic position: Iran's warm-water ports on its southern coasts, for example, potentially provide the landlocked states of the former Soviet Union with access to the Gulf or could allow any hostile power to disrupt shipping through the Gulf Straits. But above all the USA could hardly afford to ignore the immense natural resources of a country that draws upon nearly 10 per cent of the world's known oil reserves, produces around 4.2 million barrels of oil every day, mainly from the wells of Khuzestan, where it is easy and cheap to extract, and which in July 2003 announced the new discovery of a 38-billion-barrel oil reserve near the southern port city of Bushehr. Such huge potential prompted many observers to speculate in the summer of 2001 that the new Bush administration would ease up on the issue of sanctions to Iran and thereby allow US oil companies and their subsidiaries, many closely linked with Bush and Cheney, to enter the Iranian market and win highly lucrative contracts. For as President Rafsanjani succinctly expressed the point, when pointing out this symbiosis in a bid to mend relations, it is oil that 'the USA wants to buy ... and we want to sell'.[15]

Washington would certainly have had much to gain if such steps had been taken. When in January 2003 the US Energy Department announced that by 2025 oil imports would account for around 70 per cent of total domestic demand, a vast increase on the current figure of 55 per cent, it seemed that there was therefore little option but to ensure good relations with the few countries that have the capacity to meet long-term Western demand. And in a survey, compiled by Jeremy Rifkin of Hydrogen Economy, that sought to gauge the long-term potential of the world's oil-producing states, Iran scored high marks: at current rates of production, its reserves are expected to last for another fifty-three years, compared with fifty-five years in the case of Saudi Arabia and just ten in the case of the United States.

Iran's strategic location could also allow the huge oil reserves of its landlocked northern Caspian neighbours to be transported either further south, towards the southern ports at Iran's Kharg Island terminal in the Persian Gulf, or westwards into Iraq's existing infrastructure. By September 2003, some initial steps had already been taken towards this end by the construction of a 340-km pipeline between Tehran and Neka that since 2000 had allowed for an 'oil-swap' arrangement between Iran and the Caspian states. Under this agreement, Iranian oil was shipped from Kharg Island to foreign markets in exchange for its replacement with Caspian oil that is brought into the country through the pipeline. All of those who invested in the project, including Russia's Lukoil, the Dublin-based Dragon Oil, BP-controlled Sidanco and the European trader Vitol, were agreed on the huge potential of the pipeline, already expected to move as much as 500,000 barrels of oil per day by the end of 2004.

Besides oil, Iran is also believed to own the second largest reserve of natural gas in the world, a reserve thought to amount to around 20,000 billion cubic metres, much of it concentrated in the massive offshore South Pars field in the Persian Gulf. Standing alongside Russia as potentially the world's biggest supplier of liquefied natural gas, as US Energy Secretary Kyle McSlarrow pointed out in June 2003, Iran is able to play a key part in addressing the world's forthcoming energy crisis, particularly by feeding the ever-growing requirements of America's friends and allies in Western Europe. These needs, also expected to soar in the coming years to around 800–900 billion cubic metres in 2030 from the present figure of 400 billion cubic metres, can potentially be met by vast pipelines that flow from Iran via Turkey to Europe.[16]

Some steps to these ends were taken in December 2001, with the completion of a 2,577-km pipeline from Tabriz to Ankara that, under the terms of a $30 billion deal, allowed Iran initially to export three billion cubic metres of gas every year, a quantity expected to increase gradually to ten billion cubic metres by the end of 2007. In the meantime, EU negotiators have commissioned feasibility studies into the extension of this pipeline further westwards with a view to constructing a huge regional grid that links Europe not only to Iran but also to the huge untapped resources of the southern CIS republics. One important gas pipeline, which in future can form part of this network, has already been recently built between Turkmenistan and Iran, although this pipeline, like all the others that potentially link the country to its foreign markets, has been beset by political dispute and proved hugely expensive. 'It's going to be hard for Iranian gas to reach the large-scale European markets and it won't be quick,' one expert in regional gas issues points out, 'but the potential is there to make the country into a hugely important source, particularly if gas is bought into southern Russia, which doesn't have its own gas supply.'[17]

It is not just America's European allies that would benefit from an accord with Iran. Another key potential beneficiary is Israel, which Iran's vast oil supplies could reach if they are in future channelled through Iraq's existing pipeline infrastructure. Such a possibility had already been raised in April 2003, when US and Israeli officials met to discuss the possible construction of a pipeline to siphon oil from Iraq to Israel, effectively bypassing both Saudi Arabia and Syria. This idea had originally been aired by Israel's Minister for National Infrastructures, Joseph Paritzky, who claimed that because Israel is currently dependent on expensive Russian exports, such a pipeline would cut his country's energy bill by more than a quarter. A former CIA officer also told one British newspaper in 2003 that this project had 'long been a dream of a powerful section of the people now driving this administration'.[18]

There is one other respect in which Iranian natural resources could potentially benefit the USA. In the wake of the 9/11 bombings, Bush and his officials had expressed their fear of 'failed states' whose dearth of material prospects disappointed their frustrated citizens and thereby fuelled resentment of the USA, its values and policies. Instead, Bush argued, 'a strong world economy enhances our national security by advancing prosperity and freedom in the rest of the world'.[19] Viewed in these terms, the exportation of Iranian oil via a planned 2,600-km overland pipeline to its eastern neighbours promises to bring just the sort of material benefits to the region – a cheaper supply of oil and gas as well as employment and transit fees to both India and Pakistan – that US policy-makers can only welcome. With a rapidly increasing population, India currently imports around 70 per cent of its energy requirements and is therefore rendered vulnerable to the same extortionate prices as Israel. 'Iran has gas,' as Prime Minister Vajpayee said in January 2003 after a meeting with the Iranian president, 'and we want it.'[20] The pipeline would also bring considerable benefits to Pakistan, hitherto one of the main breeding grounds for Islamist fanaticism, which under initial proposals is be allowed up to 40 per cent of the 30 billion cubic metres of gas moved by the pipeline as it is routed overland through Sindh province.

Developing such massive reserves could also mean more lucrative contracts for US companies, currently forbidden under American law from competing for them. In May 2003 Iran signed an accord with a consortium of Japanese, South Korean and Iranian businesses to build a liquefied gas-producing facility that will begin exporting in 2007, while another Japanese consortium, which comprised companies such as Inpex, the Japanese Petroleum Exploration Company and Tomen, negotiated a \$2.5 billion deal that would pump 300,000 barrels a day over two decades from the newly discovered Azadegan oilfield in south-west Iran. Another proposed pipeline that would pipe oil to India is in the meantime ready to be developed in part by Stroytransgaz, the construction arm of Russia's state-owned giant, Gazprom, while other international companies, notably Elf and Total SA, are already very well established in Iran's oil business.

There are a whole host of other problems that have created the 'many commonalities' between Iran and the West to which Foreign Minister Kamal Kharrazi has referred, and over which co-operation, not conflict, seems the obvious way forward. One is the huge and fast-growing number of those addicted to narcotics, which flow in vast quantities from Afghanistan into both Iran and Western Europe. Government sources in Tehran estimate that around two million Iranians, or 3 per cent of its population, take such substances on a regular basis and that more than half of this number have a strong addiction to opium and heroin, while another 800,000 or so others take drugs on a less regular basis. In a twelve-month period beginning in March 2002, around 70,000 addicts are reported to have been rehabilitated at various centres that the Iranian authorities have in recent years built in a desperate bid to solve a growing social menace that the efforts of its security forces, stationed along the long and porous border with Afghanistan, have so far failed to stem.[21]

If co-operation, not conflict, at first sight seems the obvious way forward for US–Iranian relations, how then does one account for American hostility?

Neo-conservatism

At one level, Washington's distinctive tone reflects the views of a particular mindset that since 9/11 has found considerable influence within the corridors of the US administration – the mindset of the 'neo-conservatives'. Although the term has come to be conflated with the hard-line 'hawkish' views held by Defense Secretary Donald Rumsfeld, Vice-President Dick Cheney and many others within the Bush administration, it really refers to a relatively small clique of advisers and decision-makers – notably Deputy Defense Secretary Paul Wolfowitz; the unofficial Pentagon adviser and former director of the Defense Advisory Board, Richard Perle; the writer and academic Irving Kristol; and Donald Kagan, a Yale historian who has called for sharp increases in defence spending – who had originally been affiliated to the Democratic Party but who had subsequently gravitated towards the Republican Party during the Reagan era.

The views of the neo-conservatives bear strong traits of the liberal, socialist and Marxist views that many of them held before moving into Republican circles. One such defining characteristic of neo-conservatism, for example, is a liberal idealism that argues that the 'democratization' of the outside world and the defence of human rights should play a prominent role in US foreign policy at the expense of a more 'realist' emphasis upon the national interest. A liberal-socialist commitment to social and economic engineering has also led to a neo-conservative conviction that armed intervention by the USA in the domestic affairs of other states can typically play a highly constructive role in bringing about these ethical changes. It is in this regard significant that one of the strongest critics of the Iran regime, Michael Ledeen, who articulates a near-revolutionary approach towards the Middle East from his desks at various Washington-based consultancies, was once affiliated to the political left, having 'campaigned for McGovern and [having] been a great admirer of the legendary Democratic Senator Henry M. "Scoop" Jackson'[22] before working in Ronald Reagan's administration and in the American Enterprise Institute, where he is regularly consulted as an international affairs analyst by Karl Rove, the closest adviser to George W. Bush.

Typical of this neo-conservative outlook is the justification for the war against Saddam Hussein that was pitched by Paul Wolfowitz, formerly a Pentagon official in the Carter administration, who has argued that a democracy in Iraq 'would cast a very large shadow, starting with Syria and Iran but across the whole Arab world'. Although such a highly theoretical perspective appears to have influenced President George

W. Bush, who later asserted that 'a new regime in Iraq would serve as a dramatic and inspiring example of freedom for other nations in the region'[23] and 'send forth the news, from Damascus to Tehran, that freedom can be the future of every nation',[24] such views have been regarded by their critics in the State Department and elsewhere as little more than a hubristic blueprint that ignored the much more common-sensical proposition that US intervention would in fact be 'much more likely to stir up a hornets' nest'.[25]

To comprehend the neo-conservative attitude to Iran, one important trait is the proximity of perceived US interests with those not so much of Israel, regarded in Washington as a key regional ally, but rather of the right-wing Likud Party. The aggressive approach to Iran that neo-conservatives advocate, it has been argued, is virtually indistinguishable from the policies propounded by the Israeli politicians who regard the Tehran regime, bearing a very deeply rooted hostility to Israel and al-legedly funding militant Palestinian terror groups, as just as much of an obstacle to a favourable Middle East peace as Saddam's Iraq. Prime Minister Ariel Sharon argued that the disarming of Iran straight after any assault on Saddam was of 'vital importance',[26] while his Defence Min-ister, Shaul Mofaz, speaking before the Conference of Major American Jewish Organizations, has also claimed that Israel and the USA 'have a great interest in shaping the Middle East the day after' regime change in Baghdad and that maximum 'political, economic, diplomatic pressure' on Tehran was central to that end. Similar calls for action had also been voiced by the Israeli ambassador to the United States, Daniel Ayalon, who called for 'regime change' in Iran through 'psychological pressure' soon after victory in Iraq,[27] and by John Bolton, the US Under-Secretary of State for Arms Control, who after talks with Sharon during a visit to Israel in February 2003 is reported to have argued that Iran was the clear favourite of the possible targets for America to 'deal with' after the then imminent war with Iraq was concluded.[28]

The Tel Aviv government and its neo-conservative sympathizers in Washington do not merely seek to 'expose the efforts of the Iranian regime to undermine progress towards Middle East peace', as the Washington-based pressure group, the Coalition for Democracy in Iran, publicly declares. A more aggressive strategy would be to manipulate the price of oil in a way that would indirectly undermine the regime's ability to fund terror or even cause a major crisis for the Iranian economy, heavily dependent upon oil exports, that would not only force its gov-ernment to support a compromising deal over the Arab–Israeli dispute but perhaps even bring the regime crashing down.

It is possible that this calculation formed an important part of the case for war against Saddam Hussein. For if a post-Saddam Iraq should in future privatize its oil reserves, some argued, then it would have no option but to leave OPEC, which requires each member country strictly to regulate output and export. And because Russia, rapidly moving up the league of oil-producing countries, is already a non-member of the organization, OPEC's ability to regulate oil prices would be seriously challenged, thereby causing a foreign-exchange crisis for Iran as well as other Middle Eastern regimes. This calculation explains why neo-conservatives such as Elliot Abrams, the director of Near East and North African affairs on the US National Security Council, argued that the USA, not the United Nations, should in future control Iraqi oilfields. Abrams has also favourably received proposals to privatize Iraq's oil that were put forward by, among other sources, the Heritage Foundation, whose authors, Ariel Cohen and Gerald O'Driscoll, argued for 'a massive, orderly and transparent privatization of state-owned enterprises, especially the restructuring and privatization of the oil sector'.[29]

This theory has also been reiterated by a former US Deputy Assistant Secretary of State, Edward L. Morse, who has argued that the neo-conservative aim of putting oil resources into private hands at the expense of OPEC would not just help bring down oil prices but also thereby undermine the economies of the Middle East governments that have greatly benefited by the high cost of oil. The USA had once sought to undermine the USSR in the same way, argues Morse, and in the mid-1980s senior Washington figures had met King Fahd and other senior Saudi officials to discuss a plan to reduce oil costs and thereby reduce access to the foreign exchange that was much needed by 'rogue' governments in Moscow, Tehran and Tripoli. In neo-conservative eyes this tactic had succeeded brilliantly and can now be repeated in the Middle East.[30]

Although the exact strength of the relationship between Tel Aviv and Washington is impossible to verify and has doubtless been exaggerated by some, it has none the less on occasion been made abundantly clear. When in August 2001 the Iran–Libya Sanctions Act (ILSA) required renewal, at the end of the five years for which they had been originally passed, hopes were soon dashed that the Bush administration might signal a change of approach. A spokesman for the US American–Iranian Council explained that 'we were advised by the State Department to refrain from lobbying against the extension of ILSA' and the reason for this, the spokesman added, was 'Iran's backing for the Palestinian *intifada*' and the fact that 'the mood in Washington has turned very much against Tehran since the Palestinian uprising'.[31]

The relationship has also become evident from the various appointments held by some of those who articulate the most aggressively anti-Iranian policies. Besides holding a post as a resident scholar in 'the Freedom Chair' at the American Enterprise Institute, Michael Ledeen is also a founder and board member of both the Jewish Institute of National Security Affairs (JINSA) and the Coalition for Democracy in Iran, which he jointly founded with Morris Amitay, a top lobbyist for the most powerful pro-Israel lobby in Washington, the American–Israel Public Affairs Committee; a senior adviser to John Bolton is David Wurmser, who has also been an adviser to Benjamin Netanyahu; Richard Perle also holds a directorship of the right-wing Tel Aviv paper, the *Jerusalem Post*, and in 1970 was overheard on a FBI wiretap discussing classified information with the Israeli embassy.

Perhaps the most concrete expression of the relationship, however, was a 1996 report – *A Clean Break: A New Strategy for Securing the Realm* – that was co-authored by Wurmser, Perle and Douglas Feith, who was later appointed as an Undersecretary of Policy at the Pentagon. The report argued for Israel to assert its control of the whole Middle East by 'containing and even rolling back Syria, removing Saddam Hussein from power' and to 're-establish the principle of pre-emption', and the following year Feith and others also urged Netanyahu to 'make a clean break' with the Oslo Accords, which they argued were in fact little more than a conspiracy to loosen America's ties with Israel. Ledeen later also denounced the same deal, arguing, 'I don't know of a case in history where peace has been accomplished in any way other than one side winning a war [and] imposing terms on the other side'.[32]

The American mind

It is, however, unfair to characterize US hostility to Iran as 'neo-conservative', 'hawkish' or even particularly 'Republican'. Many of those who hold such views are, like Donald Rumsfeld and the President, not strictly 'neo-conservative' because they are not former members of the Democratic Party. Others, like Dick Cheney, are not known to be of Jewish ancestry or to have strong affiliations with Jewish interest groups, despite their commitment to the cause of the Israeli right wing. Many of those advocating the harshest of hard lines to the Tehran regime in fact represent all shades of the American political spectrum and such views are strongly, if not typically, represented by members of the Democratic Party. As one US academic has written, 'Democrats have not been very effective critics of neo-conservative geopolitics ... they do not so much reject American "triumphalism" as offer a different variety of it [and] arguably the Clinton administration was no less "unipolar" than either Bush administration.'[33] The distinctively aggressive tone struck by the administration of George W. Bush towards Iran could therefore just as convincingly be viewed as an expression of much deeper traits within the American mind instead of as something particular to a much narrower interest group.

An example is provided by the Iran Democracy Act, introduced into Congress in May 2003, that advocates the allocation of $57 million to unspecified Iranian opposition movements in order to realize the ultimate goal of 'an internationally monitored referendum to allow the Iranian people to peacefully change their system of government'. The bill's chief sponsor has been a Republican Senator from Kansas, Sam Brownback, whose chief affiliation is not with any Jewish interest group but with the small but vociferous minority-interest groups that represent a southern 'Bible Belt' denominationalism and evangelicalism and whose own strong commitment to Israel is based on the shared perception of the country as the Biblical homeland of the Jews. Nor do these 'Christian Zionists' have staunchly Republican affiliations, although many of the followers of Jerry Falwell's Moral Majority and later Pat Robertson's Christian Coalition had begun to migrate towards the Republicans from the 1970s, a trend that accelerated during the Clinton years. Some have estimated that less than half of the 30 million or so evangelical Christians in the States nominally support the Republicans, despite various faith-based presidential initiatives that have included an interest in the sharing of government funds for welfare programmes with religious groups and a law allowing religion-based social service groups to receive federal funding even if they discriminate on religious grounds.[34]

Brownback's bill is also co-sponsored by two Democrats, Daniel Inouye of Hawaii and Charles Schumer of New York, while in the House of Representatives, a Californian Democrat, Brad Sherman, at the same time also put forward a new counterpart piece of legislation that proposes a blanket ban on all Iranian goods entering the States and the cessation of World Bank loans to Iran, which had during the previous year amounted to more than $180 million. One of the strongest-worded resolutions on Iran recently put forward in the House of Representatives was also sponsored by a Democrat, Tom Lantos, whose resolution[35] advocated undefined 'positive gestures' by Washington 'towards the people of Iran' at the expense of a regime that 'has actively and repeatedly sought to undermine the US war on terror'. And many of the congressmen and -women who gave strongest backing to a black-listed terror group dedicated to the overthrow of the Tehran regime, the MKO organization, were Democrats. These included Bob Filner (California), Edolphus Towns (New York), Sheila Jackson-Lee (Texas) and Lacy Clay, who in June 2003 wrote to President Jacques Chirac to protest against the French arrests of MKO members.

It is, then, misleading to view Washington's distinctive approach to the Tehran regime as essentially 'neo-conservative', 'hawkish' or even 'Republican'. Instead, something distinctive about the American mind lies at the heart of the issue.

National catharsis

In part, this attitude reflects the impact of the 9/11 bombings upon a country that had no collective memory of terrorist outrages like those that had scarred mainland Britain during the height of the Troubles in Northern Ireland, or of any invasion and occupation by a foreign power comparable to the traumatic experiences of France in both 1870 and 1940. From the time of the WTC bombings, most Americans suddenly feared for their future, fear that has become evident not just from the results of national opinion polls but also from the views of those who argue that US policy towards Iran should be driven exclusively by considerations of national security: a Democratic senator for Wisconsin, Russ Feingold, has for example argued powerfully that this policy should be driven by the need to stop future terrorism inside America, claiming that 'we knew that Iran [had the worse case of state-sponsored terrorism] long before the President and the administration became hell-bent on Iraq'.[36]

The World Trade Center bombings have also arguably created a need for national catharsis among ordinary Americans that transcends any party affiliation or political divide. A similarly therapeutic reaction had also followed the 'Irangate affair' some fifteen years before, when the USA was gripped by a public scandal that followed revelations of illicit arms supplies to Tehran in exchange for the release of American hostages in Lebanon. Some have argued[37] that Washington's subsequent intervention on behalf of Iraq during its eight-year war with Iran, made possible by broader rules of engagement that allowed the US fleet in the Gulf to assume the role of an undeclared belligerent in the conflict, was prompted by a need to purge the painful memory of Irangate from a traumatized American public, although it is also likely that most Americans were also still angered, and continue to be deeply affected, by the images of the 1979 Revolution and its aftermath. In the sixty years preceding the World Trade Center attacks, there can be little doubt that few images had haunted the general US public more than the carefully photographed footage of Iranian leaders, most notoriously Ayatollah Sadeq Khalkhali, gloating over the charred, dismembered remains of American servicemen killed during the disastrous bid to rescue the embassy hostages in April 1980.

The view that America continues to seek compensation for its losses in Iran is widely reiterated among Iranian conservatives. For the editor of the hard-line paper *Keyhan*, for example, the United States:

> has never recovered from losing its position in Iran. This was the jewel in the crown of its Middle Eastern empire, where at least 75,000 of its personnel were based and where our resources were fully at their disposal for them to maintain full hegemony over the region. The Americans still haven't got over this loss and are driven by vindictiveness against the regime that threw them out.[38]

But the real reasons for Washington's belligerence go much deeper and really reflect the origins of a country whose story is essentially one of settlement and expansionism.

Reliance on force, not diplomacy

The relevance of this early history is illustrated, for example, by the emphasis that many neo-conservatives place upon 'threats' and 'force' at the expense of diplomacy. Although such language echoes the vocabulary of the Likud Party, it also reveals much about America's early past and its formation of the American mind.

This emphasis has been forcefully made by Meyrav Wurmser, the director of the Center for Middle East Policy at the Hudson Institute and, bearing dual US-Israeli citizenship, widely talked of as a 'neo-conservative'. 'Rather than coming as victors who should be feared and respected rather than loved, we are still engaged in old diplomacy, in the kind of politics that led to the attacks of September 11,' complained Wurmser when Washington's envoy, Zalmay Khalilzad, was despatched to Geneva to negotiate with his Iranian counterparts in the summer of 2003.[39] For Senator Brownback 'standing firm' is of paramount importance, and for Donald Rumsfeld 'history teaches us that weakness is provocative', while Michael Ledeen argues that the need not 'to show weakness' is vital.[40] Another resident scholar at the American Enterprise Institute, former CIA officer Reuel Marc Gerecht, claims that 'the tougher Sharon becomes, the stronger our image will be in the Middle East'. And the same mindset reveals itself in the belligerent statements of commentators like Jonah Goldberg of the *National Review*, who has written that 'the United States needs to go to war with Iraq because it needs to go to war with someone in the region and Iraq makes the most sense'. All of the neo-conservative commentators agree that 'the perception of the United States as weak and on the run' had been fostered by 'the Clinton administration's tendency to scoot in difficult times',[41] and most also alleged that Israel's withdrawal from Lebanon in 2000 was a weak-minded climbdown to military pressure that had only encouraged its own enemies and those of the United States. Many also contrasted Ronald Reagan's uncompromising stance against the Soviet Union during the 1980s, claiming that the 'Evil Empire's' rapid demise validated the same approach to the War on Terror. In the case of Iran, the same mindset has argued that 'by turning the temperature up Washington will accelerate the internal debate about the morality and competence of Iran's leadership' because 'the Iranian people, at least most of them, are not going to rally long around the flag in defence of the people and institutions they detest most'. Instead there would be 'seething anger at the clerics who put Iran on a collision course with the United States'.[42] Such an approach closely resembles what Professor Andrew Bacevich of Boston University has neatly termed 'an unlikely collaboration between Woodrow Wilson and the elder Field Marshal von Moltke'.

But this emphasis is far from being distinctly 'hawkish' or 'neo-conservative' but is instead something distinctly American. For whereas the British had ruled their Empire with only highly limited resources and depended instead upon tactics not of confrontation but 'divide-and-rule', diplomacy and co-operation, America was built to a much greater extent by gunpowder. Bearing an overwhelming preponderance of firepower, the early settlers had pushed against the relatively helpless resistance put up first by the native American inhabitants and later, as subsequent generations looked further afield, by the Spanish, from whose grasp they easily seized Puerto Rico and the Philippines; by the Mexicans during the war of 1847–48; and by the inhabitants of large numbers of Pacific islands. These expansionary energies were also directed against the Far West, where the settlers seized all but two of the states in the thirteen years that followed the death of Abraham Lincoln in 1865.

The way in which, for these early Americans, 'influence' over neighbouring regions became synonymous with both 'military conquest' and 'control' emerges from the writings of one of the most enthusiastic expansionists, William H. Seward, a Secretary of State under both Abraham Lincoln and Andrew Johnson. Seward succeeded in purchasing Alaska from Russia but had grown frustrated in his inability to acquire many other regions, such as French Guyana and Western Hemisphere British Columbia: 'Give me fifty, forty, thirty more years of life,' he informed an audience in Boston in 1867, 'and I will engage to give you the *possession* of the American continent and *control* of the world' (italics supplied).

Viewed in these terms, the heavy-handed approach towards the Middle East advocated by some in Washington clearly emerges as a distinctly American trait. At the time of the Cuban missile crisis, for example, President Kennedy's initial interest in a surprise air attack had horrified European allies, who thought such a plan to be a 'slightly demented'[43] over-reaction to the arrival of Soviet missiles on Cuban soil, and which one American adviser, Robert Lovett, argued was like using 'a sledgehammer to kill a fly'.[44] In the early years of the Vietnam War, the US military in March 1965 also unleashed a major bombing assault, Operation Rolling Thunder, in a bid to deter the Hanoi regime from backing its sympathizers further south, an act that far from deterring such support merely escalated hostilities. US involvement was also justified in terms remarkably similar to those deployed by contemporary 'neo-cons' – as 'a test of American firmness', 'prestige' and 'credibility'.[45] More recently, in post-Saddam Iraq, the British General Sir Mike Jackson has criticized American heavy-handedness, reiterating earlier criticisms that had been levelled against US forces in Afghanistan by arguing that his own forces 'are not interested in gratuitous violence'.[46]

The same heavy-handed approach has emerged during recent debates on Iran. Some in the administration, it has been noted, have reportedly proposed the sponsorship of a terrorist organization in order to exert pressure on the Iranian government,[47] argued the case for a military strike on the Bushehr reactor or the imposition of UN economic sanctions before finding any clear-cut proof of any covert nuclear weapons programme that would justify them,[48] and advocated popular revolution instead of reaching out to reformist elements within the existing regime in order to effect a more gradual change. American threats of force or isolation against Iran on the grounds of its alleged pursuit of nuclear weapons have certainly struck a clear contrast with a more moderate British and EU approach. British Foreign Minister Jack Straw emphasized that 'the UK and EU have a policy of constructive engagement with Iran, but a policy that is open-eyed', while an EU counterpart pointed out that 'it's not clever to back people up against the wall to the point where they cannot acquiesce in what you're asking to do because it's become a trial of strength'.[49]

Rational blueprints

The tendency to deploy force at the expense of diplomacy and argument also partly reflects another American tendency: an inclination to think more in terms of blueprint plans at the expense of practicality. For just as the early settlers were able to map out their plans to expand into hostile terrain and enforce them by use of arms, so too have their latter-day descendants demonstrated a susceptibility to look at the wider world in the same terms.

Such an approach, however, has an obvious weakness in a world where many problems are insoluble and the outcome of every event unpredictable. Yet the tendency of every plan to err is something that US policy-makers are generally more reluctant to acknowledge than some of their European counterparts. When during the Korean War, for example, British diplomats had argued that communism was 'not a good fact of life but a fact of life',[50] their attitude stood in sharp contrast with what Robert McNamara later admitted was an American failure 'to recognize that in international affairs there may be problems for which there are no immediate solutions [and that] at times we may have to live with an imperfect untidy world'.[51]

Unfortunately, some US decision-makers appear to have adopted a similarly utopian perspective upon events not just in Iran but in the entire Middle East. Condoleezza Rice, the President's National Security Advisor, has argued that the USA must push for 'democratization, or the march of freedom, in the Muslim world', echoing Wolfowitz's views that a new Iraq would set 'a shining example for the Arab world', and that the toppling of Saddam was instrumental in realizing that end. The journalist William Kristol, writing in *The Weekly Standard*, has asserted that 'if Iran goes pro-Western and anti-terror, positive changes in Syria and Saudi Arabia will follow much more easily and the chances for an Israeli–Palestinian settlement will greatly improve [because] Iran is the tipping point in the effort to reshape the Middle East'.[52] And Ledeen, arguing that a strike on the Iranian regime should precede an attack on Saddam, has claimed that 'with a triumph in Iran, the democratic revolution would quickly gain allies in Syria and Iraq and transform our war against Saddam Hussein from a primarily military operation to a war of national liberation against a hated regime'. Meyrav Wurmser has also alleged that what the Bush administration 'has in mind is a broad vision which really involves changing the character of the Middle East'.[53] It was significant that although such views were certainly echoed by Benjamin Netanyahu, who testified to the US Congress in September 2002 that 'the choice of going after Iraq is like removing a brick that holds a lot of other bricks and might cause this structure to crumble', they 'failed to score in European capitals'.[54]

The susceptibility of some US decision-makers to think in terms of blueprint theory rather than mere practicality has become clear from the Bush doctrine of pre-emptive action against emergent aggressors, articulated in the presidential speech on national security in September 2002, and from the 'Wolfowitz doctrine', detailed in a 1992 Pentagon document that called on the USA to deter 'all potential competitors from even aspiring to a larger regional or global role' and thereby 'establish and protect a new order'. This reflects one of the most dangerous characteristics of American thinking: the sense of inevitability with which future threats have been viewed. The clearest example, and for Americans perhaps the most painful, is of course the domino theory that President Eisenhower had articulated in the 1950s and which later came to dominate administration thinking in the run-up to and course of the Vietnam War. Under-secretary of State Chester Bowles had also argued, for example, that 'we were going to have to fight the Chinese anyway in two, three, five or ten years and it was just a question of where, when and how', while Admiral Burke, briefing the National Security Council, claimed that 'unless the US prepared to intervene militarily in Laos, all Southeast Asia will be lost'.[55] Traits of the same viewpoint have emerged in the writings of US hawks on Iran. Michael Ledeen has claimed that the alternative to a hard-hitting approach to Iran is to 'wait until ... a new act of horror' is committed[56] and Gerecht that 'we may well be watching the clerics immerse themselves again in a wave of anti-American terrorism'.[57]

Moral superiority

Because there were few practical restraints upon the early settlers as they overran the vast regions that lay before them, another unfortunate legacy of this early record among latter-day Americans is an attitude of dismissiveness, perhaps even latent superiority, towards those who stand in their way. This was a trait that also showed itself most obviously in attitudes towards the native Americans, whose own behaviour towards the European conquerors was often far from exemplary but whose own territory was unquestionably seized by the new settlers with a brutal, even genocidal, ferocity. After the 1864 Sand Creek Massacre, during which more than 300 peaceful Cheyennes and Arapahoes in Colorado were unnecessarily slaughtered, the leader of the American army unit involved, a Colonel Chivington, was immediately hailed as a hero in Denver, where more than a hundred of the Indian corpses were paraded to great popular acclaim. A similar contempt for the native inhabitants was also often openly expressed elsewhere, including Kansas in 1867, where they were condemned as 'gut-eating skunks ... whose immediate and final extermination all men, except Indian agents and traders, should pray for', and the West Coast, where the popular cry 'let our motto be extermination, and death to all opposers' had been echoed. Two years before, in 1865, a General Phil Sheridan had coined what was to become a familiar phrase by claiming that 'the only good Indians I ever saw were dead'. In fact the extermination of perhaps as many as seven million native Americans over two centuries of colonisation unquestionably represents ethnic cleansing on a vast scale.[58]

Traits of the same dismissiveness can arguably be found in the rhetoric of contemporary Americans who have argued for their country's right to impose 'civilization' and 'liberty' upon other countries. When in 2003 Congressman Brad Sherman argued that 'the US needs to lead *civilized* nations in an organized effort against the clerical regime [of Iran], for the benefit of human rights'[59] (italics supplied), and Michael Ledeen spoke of the importance of 'the civilized world'[60] supporting democracy, their words eerily echoed those of nineteenth-century Americans who had justified acts of expansion and aggression in remarkably similar terms. 'The hunter or savage state requires a greater extent of territory to sustain it than is compatible with the progress and just claims of civilized life ... and must yield to it,' argued James Monroe, adding that 'a compulsory process seems to be necessary, to break their habits, and civilize them'. And William Henry Harrison also asked why 'one of the fairest portions of the globe [is] to remain in a state of nature, the haunt of a few wretched savages, when it seemed destined by the Creator to give support to a large population and to be the seat of civilization'.[61]

American self-righteousness

The mentality of the early settlers is interwoven with other themes that are central to America's history, especially the idealism of a Revolution that proclaimed the highest of high ideals, the validity of which appear axiomatic and of universal applicability. Few could contest these ideals, propounded since 1776 as 'truths' of life, liberty and the pursuit of happiness that were deemed to be 'self-evident' and which have since helped to give most Americans a sense of pursuing an entirely righteous cause. As President Wilson once declared, 'American principles are also the principles and policies of forward-looking men and women everywhere, of every modern nation, of every enlightened community ... [they are] the principles of mankind and they must prevail.'

These secular ideals also began to assume the status of religious truths, a status that reflected the strong influence of the immensely powerful and dynamic denominational beliefs that have held sway over much of the public mind since the arrival of the early settlers. The new republic was built with a strongly crusading spirit by intense and sometimes fanatical denominational groups for which the colonization of the old world, and the revolutionary subversion of an English rule that was charged with 'popish and arbitrary power', were God-given duties.

The result of this formative influence has been a wholly paradoxical mix of secular morality according to which 'freedom' and 'democracy' are elevated to the status of universal truths, with all the conviction and intensity of evangelicalism. The revolutionary cry of 'Equality', 'Free Election' and 'your Federal Band' has convincingly been termed 'a secular Trinity [that] replaced the Christian one' and the Founding Fathers of the Revolution 'the objects of a strange reverence' who had been 'canonized [by] the zealots who brought it about'. In particular, George Washington has been called 'the high priest of the Revolution', whose followers were convinced that he 'enjoyed divine grace'.[62] Bearing an overwhelming belief in its own self, it may be said that modern America continues to bear many of the traits of traditional Christianity, although its fanaticism is much better concealed by its secular language of 'freedom' and 'justice' and other seemingly self-evident values.

This moral confidence helps explain many of the characteristics of contemporary US foreign policy. The war on Iraq was unleashed by a President who was reportedly 'casting his mission and that of the country in the grand vision of God's master plan' and who 'really believes he was placed here to do this [his military policy] as part of a divine plan'.[63] Such a self-righteous conviction helps account for the apparent underestimation of the dangers such an invasion would pose.

Manichaeism

Another such characteristic, for example, is the tendency of many Americans to view the world from an overly black-and-white perspective that was most obviously manifested both by Ronald Reagan's condemnations of the Soviet Union's 'Evil Empire' as well as by George W. Bush's 2002 State of the Union address, in which he famously asserted the existence of an 'Axis of Evil'. The President has also divided the outside world into those who are 'with us' and those who are 'against us', neatly contrasted 'terrorism' and 'freedom' and, in statements made on 12 July and 2 August 2002, proclaimed a new Iranian policy 'based on moral clarity'. A similar frame of mind is also evident among senators such as Bill Bennett, who have argued that the USA is caught up in a 'struggle between good and evil';[64] among academics like Daniel Pipes, whose highly authoritative writings on Islam have none the less on occasion been described as showing 'all the way down, a Manichaean world, divided everywhere, as much among Muslims as among ourselves, between good and evil, perilously balanced';[65] from policy documents such as Condoleezza Rice's National Security Strategy, a paper published in August 2002 that argues for 'a single sustainable model for national success' – America's – that is 'right and true for every person, in every society';[66] and among ordinary Americans, three-quarters of whom, according to one national survey conducted for the Pew Global Attitudes Project in December 2002, felt that their own country typically takes the interests of other countries into account when it draws up its policies. This is a much higher figure than the 44 per cent of Britons who think the same of their own government.

This Manichaean viewpoint is unmistakeably evident in the particular case of contemporary Iran. After the presidential elections of 1997, in which the reformist candidate Muhammed Khatami was swept into power with a huge 70 per cent majority vote, 'a good-guy-Khatami-versus-bad-guy-Khamenei view took hold' in the State Department, and 'in the American business community and academe', as Gerecht has pointed out.[67] During and after 2002, for reasons that are currently not altogether clear, a similar divide was instead neatly drawn between 'Oppressors' and 'The People', as the US President declared that 'the people of Iran want the same freedoms, human rights and opportunities as people around the world' and that 'America affirms its commitment to helping those in captive nations achieve democracy'. This struck a clear contrast with President Clinton's earlier appeals to 'reformists' within the government.

Anyone who sees the outside world in these terms is of course at grave risk of hugely oversimplifying complex scenarios that demand a much more subtle approach if they are to be both understood and dealt with, a tendency that sometimes becomes clear only when it is too late to do so. Robert McNamara, writing years after the tragedy of Vietnam, admitted that 'we did not recognize that neither our people nor our leaders are omniscient', and that 'we do not have the God-given right to shape every nation in our own image or as we choose'.[68] The same dangers have of course been clear to onlookers who are alien to such a perspective, such as the French ambassador to the United States in 1918, who felt that Woodrow Wilson was 'a man who, had he lived a couple of centuries ago, would have been the greatest tyrant in the world, because he does not seem to have the slightest conception that he can ever be wrong', or even Wilson's own Secretary of State, Robert Lansing, who once complained of the President's 'semi-divine power to select the right'. The President's own rhetoric was certainly not full of humility: 'We had gone to war with Spain not for annexation', he insisted a few years after the 1898 war, 'but to provide the helpless colony with the opportunity of freedom.' And when, during his own presidency, he sent his soldiers to the Mexican border, he famously proclaimed: 'I am going to teach the South American Republics to elect good men!' But in both cases he was unable to acknowledge the material interests that had motivated these expeditions, interests that included both the protection of the Panama Canal on the one hand and the security of American financial investments on the other.

From the same Manichaean perspective, quite disparate entities can also easily be viewed as monolithic. Just as President Bush has spoken of an 'Axis' between two countries, Iran and Iraq, that fought an extremely bloody eight-year war and have since remained on bitter terms, so have other hawkish voices asserted the existence of alliances and relationships that have puzzled others highly familiar with the region. There is an 'alliance' between Syria and Iran, Michael Ledeen has written, 'in sending terror squads against Coalition forces in Iraq'[69] that 'seems counter-intuitive to those who believe it is next to impossible for Sunnis and Shiites to co-operate, and that Iran could never co-operate with the regime of Saddam Hussein'.[70] But such an assertion has been described by respected independent analysts as 'absurd'.[71]

Similar oversimplifications had been made by Washington decision-makers during earlier chapters in American history, notably the Cold War. McNamara, again writing years later, admitted to having made 'simplistic assumptions' about Vietnam, since 'like most Americans I saw communism as monolithic'. Chief among these false assumptions was the wholly erroneous proposition that China and the Soviet Union, because they were both communist countries, were jointly conspiring to push back American influence not just in South Vietnam but also in South-East Asia in general. 'China looms as a major power threatening ... to organize all of Asia against us,' he had once informed President Johnson[72] in a memorandum that he later admitted showed 'totally incorrect thinking [that] took no account of the centuries-old hostility between China and Vietnam' and instead revealed only 'a lack of expertise and historical knowledge [which] seriously undermined US policy'.[73] In fact, the existence of 'a monolithic and ruthless conspiracy' among communists the world over was one that few in Washington questioned: when in 1961 cracks started to appear in the 'Sino-Soviet bloc' that did not fit this preconceived idea, conservatives claimed that they were a hoax, designed to lull the free world into a false sense of security, with Dean Rusk referring to the 'alleged split between Beijing and Moscow' and liberals generally viewing them only as mere differences of opinion.

'Illusions'

Such misapprehensions were what John F. Kennedy, guarding his fellow compatriots from the facile hawkish assumption that 'every anti-American voice is the voice of Moscow', had in 1958 called 'illusions',[74] a term also later used by a senior White House official who retrospectively admitted that their mistakes had been partly caused by 'the stupidity of being wrapped in their own illusions'.[75] And however much every government and its people frequently misapprehend the motives of others, there can be no doubt that a Manichaean mind, tempted to force a complex picture into its two-dimensional framework, more easily falls prey to the self-deception or gross errors of judgement to which the President was referring.

Some of Washington's judgements on Iran have certainly revealed traits of such a mindset. The scale of the student protests in Tehran in November 2002, for example, was undoubtedly exaggerated by both President Bush, who hailed them as clear evidence of social change, and by hawkish American pundits: 'something like half a million Iranians had taken to the streets to protest', claimed Ledeen, although the real figure was judged to be around 5,000.[76] Such claims were in the spirit of his many other highly questionable assertions, including his argument that 'over the past year and a half as many as a million people have flooded the streets in open protest',[77] and that the late Shah's son, Reza Pahlavi, is 'widely admired inside Iran, despite his refreshing lack of avidity for power and wealth'.[78]

There have been several other issues upon which American accusations have approached the 'illusional'. The White House, for example, has on occasion asserted not the strong likelihood of a covert Iranian nuclear weapons programme but instead spoken in stronger terms, claiming emphatically that 'Iran is aggressively pursuing weapons of mass destruction, particularly nuclear weapons',[79] a claim that it has backed up only with the vague references to 'intelligence sources' that seem dubious in the wake of allegations of Iraqi weapons. Even more dubious assertions – again all unsupported – have been made about the scale and extent of Iranian intervention in Iraq by senior administration officials, notably Donald Rumsfeld, as well as by pundits. Ledeen has claimed that 'inside Iraq there are thousands of Iranian agents at work' who had been 'committed' by Tehran to sabotage peace in post-Saddam

Iraq in a 'brilliantly managed campaign to mobilize the Iraqi Shiites'.[80] Such claims become more unconvincing when the author switches, within just a few sentences, from saying there are 'more than a hundred highly trained Arab militants' that the Iranians have smuggled into Iraq, to claiming that 'thousands of Iranian-backed terrorists have been sent',[81] and adds that these terrorists are 'next to impossible to identify'. These claims have also been doubted by respected observers on the ground, such as the British commander in charge of the Persian Gulf who, despite these American claims to the contrary, has said that he has seen no sign of Iranian meddling,[82] and by Ahmed Chalabi, leader of the Iraqi National Congress, who has said that such allegations are 'basically unfounded'.[83]

These accusations are not the first that Washington has pitched against Iran for no apparent reason. When on 25 June 1996 a 2,000-kg bomb rocked a vast complex used by American troops at Dhahran airbase in Saudi Arabia, killing nineteen and injuring 400, US spokesmen asserted that its perpetrators were all trained inside Iran and that the CIA had even identified the location of eleven of the camps where they had been trained. Such allegations seemed questionable, however, when US officials working on the ground with the Saudis admitted that they had found no evidence of any Iranian involvement and seemed even more unlikely when the following year Riyadh officially admitted that 'Saudi nationals alone were responsible'. Only a few weeks after Dhahran, however, the Clinton administration still alleged Iranian complicity in the crash of a TWA airliner near Long Island, even though its exact cause has never been precisely determined.

These illusions follow a long American tradition that well pre-dates the Cold War. America took up arms with Britain in 1812 convinced that London's agents were orchestrating trouble for them amongst the native Americans, even though it was their own heavy-handedness, not a British conspiracy, that was then causing such restlessness. And in 1898 America declared war with Spain against a background of vehement accusations – voiced by politicians and in the popular press – of a fiendish Spanish plot to keep the Americans out of Spain's colonial lands in Puerto Rico, Guam and the Philippines. There never was any such conspiracy, however, and the massive explosion that had downed the US battleship *Maine* in Havana harbour that year, thereby sparking the conflict, was almost certainly an accident. This uncomfortable truth scarcely suited the purpose of the American papers and politicians, who in preceding years had virtually concocted many horror stories of Spanish atrocity in the New World to justify a covert expansionist agenda against its colonies.

It is possible that the particular vulnerability of the Americans to fallacy and illusion has some origins not just in its Manichaeism but also in the highly formative experiences of the century that began after peace with Britain in 1814 and ended with a declaration of war with Germany in 1917. Regarding themselves as detached from any 'entangling alliances', the American people, geographically remote from the rest of the world in any case, became particularly susceptible to misapprehending the motives of those elsewhere. And having either avoided international war altogether, or steamrollered the few enemies with which it did cross swords, its populace became unused to the tragedies faced by its European counterparts and as a result still remains highly susceptible to an element of hysteria in which fallacy and invention thrive. It is also significant that American independence was declared amid highly charged fears – wholly unfounded – of 'a transatlantic conspiracy' that was allegedly being hatched in London against the liberties of the colonies.[84]

Viewed from this perspective, Ledeen's own assertions of an international conspiracy against the United States seem a distinctly American affair. As an 'anti-terrorism' adviser to Ronald Reagan's Secretary of State, Alexander Haig, Ledeen alleged an anti-American conspiracy headquartered in the Kremlin and saw the fingerprints of the KGB on nearly all terrorist atrocities. In particular, Ledeen strongly asserted the involvement of Soviet intelligence in the attempted assassination of Pope John Paul II by the Turkish extremist Mehmet Ali Agca, even though such an association has certainly never been proved.[85]

'Popular support'

One false assumption to which US policy-makers are particularly susceptible, however, is that 'enemy regimes' are not merely oppressive of 'the people' but of a populace distinctly sympathetic to the United States and its values. From this premise follows a preference for dealing directly with 'the people' instead of a government and of erroneously assuming that the imposition of regime change is likely to be widely welcomed inside that country.

In the wake of mass riots in Tehran in July 1999, November 2002 and again in June 2003, it has been easy for some Washington voices to argue for just such a populist approach. Michael Ledeen has claimed that Iran 'offers Americans the possibility of a memorable victory, because the Iranian people openly loathe the regime and will enthusiastically combat it if only the United States supports them in their just struggle'.[86] For Gerecht, anti-government demonstrations in Iran were a sign not of despair but of 'pro-American emotions',[87] emotions that would soon soar and then be 'beyond the scope of regime-loyal specialized riot-control units' to control.[88] 'Popular discontent in Iran tends to heat up when US soldiers get close to the Islamic Republic,' he added, arguing that 'an American invasion could possibly provoke riots in Iran'.[89]

In October 2001, as the War on Terror began in earnest, Ledeen stepped up his attack, arguing that 'Iran is ready to blow sky high' and that 'the Iranian people need only a bright spark of courage from the US to ignite the flames of democratic revolution'. One of the declared goals of the Washington pressure group, the Coalition for Democracy in Iran, is also to support the 'sizeable pro-democratic and predominantly pro-American Iranian society, which considers the American democracy as its ultimate model'.

The American assumption is dangerous for the obvious reason that the whole edifice of plans and operations can quickly crumble if they are mistaken.[90] In 1958, a CIA-backed rebellion against President Sukarno of Indonesia collapsed without any sign at all of the anticipated popular support, while in April 1961 the invasion of Cuba at the Bay of Pigs went disastrously wrong for the same reason. The CIA had envisaged disaffected civilians rushing towards the beachhead to pick up arms and supplies, and reckoned that a hard-core dissident population of around 3,000 would be joined by an uprising made up of around a quarter of the population, a judgement that immediately proved a huge miscalculation. During the Iraq invasion, the mass popular uprising that the Americans had hoped for failed to materialize, and although this hardly imperilled the progress of an overwhelming preponderance of firepower, the false assumptions of finding popular support have probably blinded Washington to the longer-term task of enforcing a post-Saddam peace. There could scarcely be any more striking contrast with the radically different calculations made by other would-be invaders of the region: in 1838, for instance, the British Prime Minister Lord Palmerston noted that 'the presence of an invading British army in Persia would create such agitation and so much insurrection amongst the Persians that the shah would afterwards become still more dependent, if possible, on the Russians, and that is not what we want'.[91]

Using questionable means

Anyone who holds absolute faith in the righteousness of his or her cause may of course often demand very high ethical standards in the means deployed to pursue it. But at other times the self-righteous will be prepared to sanction highly questionable means on the grounds that a short-term measure will be offset by the long-term establishment of genuine values and institutions. There are also other occasions when the Manichaean-minded will be wholly unaware of any such moral dubiousness, since such a limited perspective is always at grave risk of being wholly blind towards the failings of those seen in a positive light.

In an Iranian context, this latter tendency has shown itself in the reported willingness of some Pentagon officials to sanction a blacklisted terrorist group, the MKO, to pressurize the Tehran regime, or to overlook the shortcomings of the Southern Azerbaijan National Awareness Movement (SANAM). The MKO's track record could greatly appeal to some quarters in Washington, where other guerrilla groups have previously found allies precisely and only because of their ability to inflict immediate casualties on a perceived enemy, and where other considerations have been regarded immaterial. During the Cold War, for example, organizations like Unita in Angola, the Contras in Nicaragua and the more extreme Islamist groups that fought the Soviet army in Afghanistan all had dubious track records on human rights that were conveniently overlooked by their Washington sponsors. And although raison d'état can often create highly questionable alliances, the strong sense of American self-righteousness renders Washington particularly susceptible to making them.

Moreover, by declaring their strong support for 'the people' instead of mainstream reformist politicians, US officials at times appear to sanction a popular revolution, an obvious recipe for mass bloodshed in a country ruled in part by an extremely determined hard-line elite that controls a strong security apparatus. And when in November 2002 and June the following year President Bush spoke out strongly in favour of protesters who took to the streets in Tehran and other cities, many also argued that his message unnecessarily risked complicating an already complex situation in a way that might result in a great deal of blood being spilled. In any case, the perceived dichotomy between 'oppressors' and 'people' certainly overlooks the highly disparate motives of millions of different individuals who have hitherto been united only by a few general slogans but certainly not by any coherent political programme, and ignores the fine line that lies between protest and a lawlessness that Washington would readily condemn elsewhere.[92]

Similar traits can arguably be found in the tendency to 'skew' intelligence material instead of weighing up evidence in a more balanced, open-minded way. This particular danger has already been evident as allied forces in Iraq have tried to find the weapons of mass destruction that had been trumpeted on both sides of the Atlantic as the main justification for war against Saddam, a failure prompting allegations that one particular department within the Pentagon, the Office of Special Plans, had manipulated intelligence to suit an ulterior purpose. In the summer of 2003, moreover, a Defense Department spokesman announced that a four-man team within the OSP had already begun to deal with Iranian issues and, according to respected intelligence sources within the administration, were pushing hard for regime change in Tehran.[93]

Ethical intervention

All these various dangers, born of the United States' unique historical condition, have undoubtedly also been augmented by their confluence with a contemporaneous idea, one not narrowly American but which commands a much more internationalist following. This is the modern-day preoccupation with human rights and the alleged legality of intervention by 'an international community' in the domestic affairs of sovereign states in order to protect those rights. For while the long-established rule, laid down in the Treaty of Westphalia in 1648 and subsequently enshrined in the United Nations Charter, that one state does not have any inherent right 'to intervene in matters which are essentially within the domestic jurisdiction of any state' has certainly not been rendered obsolete, it has no longer been considered an axiom ever since NATO justified its military attack on Serbia in the spring of 1999 on overtly humanitarian grounds. As some have recently argued, 'We have passed from an era in which ideals were always flatly opposed to self-interests into an era in which tension remains between the two, but the stark juxtaposition of the past has largely subsided.'[94]

However laudable the aims of some humanitarian interventionists may be, such an approach merely aggravates the dangers to which US foreign policy is already prone. Speaking before the American–Iranian Council, Zalmay Khalilzad adopted a familiar black-and-white approach towards Iran but also mixed American axioms of liberty with those of contemporary humanitarianism, arguing:

> Freedom and human rights are universal values, enshrined in the Universal Declaration of Human Rights, to which Iran is a signatory, that declares that all people everywhere are entitled to basic freedoms of religion, expression and equal protection under the law. These values transcend differences of culture and religion. Iranian civilization and Islam own them just as fully as Western civilization ... [but] the will of the Iranian people is repeatedly undercut by the unelected but powerful forces.[95]

This more 'universal' perspective upon the outside world still bears all the same traits as the more narrowly American viewpoint, since both are characterized by the same self-righteousness of approach that creates all the same dangers to which US foreign policy is prone.

Viewed in these terms, the pending state of crisis in Iran is not just a reflection of events and developments within that country, but instead also partly manifests certain traits within the American mind that have been expressed with particular force during the administration of George W. Bush. But what can be said, however, of the perceived provocations that have inflamed American anger? The subsequent chapters consider the substance of Washington's accusations that Iran is complicit in sponsoring international terror, pursuing nuclear arms, undermining peace in Iraq and Afghanistan and brutally suppressing the search of the Iranian people to find democratic freedom.

Notes

1. *The Times*, 31 October 2003.

2. Below, Chapter 8.

3. *Washington Post*, 25 May 2003.

4. Senator Sam Brownback's Iran Democracy Act 2003 is similar in approach to the Iraq Liberation Act passed by Congress in 1988; below, Chapter 7.

5. Bernard Lewis, *Iran in History*, published at <www.dayan.org>, 2001.

6. Baqer Moin, *Khomeini: Life of the Ayatollah* (London: I.B. Tauris, 1999); see also Mehdi Bararan, *Inqilab-e Iran dar Dow Harakat* (Tehran, 1984), p. 84.

7. Below, Chapter 5.

8. Author's interview with former Western ambassador to Iran, 20 September 2003.

9. Author's interview with an editor of a reformist newspaper, Tehran, 17 November 2003.

10. Reuters, 2 December 2002.

11. Associated Press, 2 August 2002.

12. Interview with *Der Spiegel*, 8 November 2003.

13. Human Rights Watch, 5 March 2003.

14. <www.freedomhouse.org>.

15. Speech in Tehran, 1 December 1996 (IRNA).

16. *Financial Times*, 21 October 2002.

17. Author's interview with Jonathan Stern, Director of Gas Research at the Oxford Institute for Energy Studies, 22 September 2003.

18. *Guardian*, 20 April 2003.

19. Speech on National Security, 20 September 2002.

20. BBC News, 27 January 2003.

21. IRNA, 29 June 2003.

22. Michael Ledeen's communication with the author, 15 June 2003.

23. Speech to the AEI, 26 February 2003.

24. Speech to the National Endowment for Democracy, 6 November 2003.

25. A leaked State Department report, highly critical of the Wolfowitz doctrine, was leaked to the press in March 2003. See *Guardian*, 15 March 2003.

26. Address to US congressmen, Washington DC, 23 February 2003.

27. Reuters, 29 April 2003.

28. *Guardian*, 29 March 2003.

29. See generally 'Over a Barrel', *The New Republic Online*, 9 January 2003.

30. *Oxford Energy Forum*, vol. XLVI, 18 August 2003.

31. Quoted in *Middle East International*, 14 August 2001.

32. See generally Jim Lobe's reports for the Inter-Press Service, 27 May and 24 June 2003.

33. David P. Calleo's essay 'Power, Wealth and Wisdom' in *The National Interest*, Summer 2003.

34. Michael Lind, 'The Texas Nexus', *Prospect*, April 2003; see also 'The Christian Zionists', *Prospect*, July 2003.

35. H. Res. 140, of 18 March 2003.

36. *The Hill*, 11 June 2003.

37. See, for example, John Bulloch and Harvey Morris, *The Gulf War* (London: Methuen), p. 9.

38. Interview with the author, Tehran, 11 November 2003.

39. 'The Future of Iran', AEI, 6 May 2003.

40. *National Review Online*, 30 April 2003.

41. 'On to Iran (Part 2)', *Weekly Standard*, 9 February 2003.

42. See the chapter 'Iran: Fundamentalism and Reform' in Robert Kagan and William Kristol (eds), *Present Dangers: Crisis and Opportunity in American Foreign and Defense Policy* (San Francisco: Encounter Books), 2002.

43. Ernest R. May and Philip S. Zelikow, *The Kennedy Tapes: Inside the White house During the Cuban Missile Crisis* (Cambridge, MA: Harvard University Press, 1997), p. 134.

44. J. F. Kennedy Library Oral History, interview with Robert Lovett, 19 November 1964.

45. Robert S. McNamara, *In Retrospect* (New York: Random House, 1995), pp. 107, 124, 131.

46. *Guardian*, 1 April 2003.

47. See below, Chapter 8.

48. *Daily Telegraph*, 19 July 2003.

49. *Guardian*, 17 June 2003.

50. Max Hastings, *The Korean War* (London: Pan Books, 2000), p. 71.

51. McNarama, *In Retrospect*, p. 323.

52. *Weekly Standard*, 2 May 2003.

53. Quoted on *Asia Times Online*, 28 September 2002.

54. Reuters, 31 January 2003.

55. Quoted in Lawrence Freedman, *Kennedy's Wars* (Oxford and New York: OUP), p. 301.

56. *New York Post*, 11 March 2003.

57. *Weekly Standard*, 18 February 2002.

58. See generally Hugh Brogan, *The Longman History of the United States of America* (London and New York: Longman, 1999), pp. 62–9.

59. Press statement from Congressman Sherman's office, 4 April 2003.

60. *National Review Online*, 9 July 2003.

61. Bob Woodward, *Bush at War* (New York: Simon and Schuster, 2002), p. 67.

62. See generally Jonathan Clark, *The Language of Liberty* (Cambridge: CUP, 1994), pp. 387 et seq.

63. Woodward, *Bush at War*, pp. 67, 205, 256.

64. CNN, 12 September 2001.

65. *New York Review of Books*, 3 July 2003.

66. *New Yorker*, 14 and 21 October 2002.

67. *Weekly Standard*, 18 February 2002.

68. McNamara, *In Retrospect*, p. 323.

69. *National Post*, 8 April 2003.

70. *The Spectator*, 12 April 2003.

71. Author's correspondence with Alan George, author of *Syria: Neither Bread nor Freedom* (London: Zed Books, 2003).

72. Memo to the President, 7 November 1965.

73. McNamara, *In Retrospect*, pp. 30–5, 219.

74. Arthur Schlesinger, *A Thousand Days* (New York: Fawcett, 1965), p. 181.

75. The words of McGeorge Bundy, formerly President Kennedy's assistant for national security affairs, are quoted in Ewan Thomas, *The Very Best Men: Four Men Who Dared: The Early Years of the CIA* (New York: Simon and Schuster, 1995).

76. *National Review Online*, 25 November 2002; *The Economist*, 16 January 2003.

77. 'The Moment of Truth', AEI, 30 May 2003.

78. 'The End of the Beginning', *The Spectator*, 12 April 2003.

79. Zalmay Khalilzad, speech to the American–Iranian Council, 23 February 2002.

80. 'Timing is Everything', NRO, 22 April 2003.

81. Ibid.

82. Associated Press, 28 April 2003.

83. *Financial Times*, 10 June 2003.

84. Clark, *The Language of Liberty*, p. 277.

85. Inter Press Service, 24 June 2003.

86. *National Post*, 8 April 2003.

87. *Weekly Standard*, 9 February 2002.

88. *Weekly Standard*, 5 August 2002.

89. *Weekly Standard*, 21 May 2003.

90. *New Statesman*, 16 September 2002.

91. Letter to Hobhouse, 27 August 1838.

92. Below, Chapter 7.

93. *Forward*, 6 June 2003.

94. Leslie H. Gelb and Justine A. Rosenthal, 'The Rise of Ethics in Foreign Policy', *Foreign Policy*, May/June 2003.

95. Zalmay Khalilzad, speech to the American–Iranian Council, 13 March 2002.

2 | Iran and international terror

Of all the various accusations that have in recent years been levelled against Iran by US officials, the most long-standing is its involvement with international terrorism. Since the 1979 Revolution, the Tehran regime has without question pursued and assassinated many of its exiled opponents, helped to build an armed militia group in Lebanon, the Hezbollah movement, that has long been blacklisted by the US State Department, and also allegedly sponsored suicide bombing attacks in Israel and the Occupied Territories. Such a track record has prompted the annual US State Department report *Patterns of Global Terrorism* to describe Iran as the world's 'most active sponsor of state terrorism' and argue that its elite corps, the Revolutionary Guard,[1] and the Ministry of Intelligence and Security (MOIS) have been 'involved in the planning of and support for terrorist acts and continued to exhort a variety of groups that use terrorism to pursue their goals'. For Donald Rumsfeld, Iran has been guilty, like Syria, of 'inspiring and financing a culture of political murder and suicide bombings' and for senior adviser Richard Perle it is a state that is 'up to its eyeballs in terror'.[2]

Since the onset of the War on Terror in September 2001 such charges have been raised with particular vehemence. Some of these have been allegations of unwarranted interference inside neighbouring Iraq and Afghanistan – issues considered separately in the next chapter – while others have asserted the regime's association with Al Qaeda, a relationship that came under particular scrutiny in the wake of terrorist bombings in Saudi Arabia on 12 May 2003 that killed thirty-four.

On this particular count, however, the American case against Iran has a number of important weaknesses. At a general level, Washington has never made any effort to define what constitutes 'terrorism': it is of course far from clear whether the use of arms for legitimate self-defence can ever constitute 'terror', and how and why the United States is uniquely able to judge into which category a particular faction or campaign falls. Washington has also failed to substantiate many of its claims with convincing evidence, and is also open to charges of double standards by condemning Tehran for carrying out the same actions that it overlooks, or encourages, when perpetrated by its allies.

'Elements within the regime'

Since the election of the reformist President Muhammed Khatami in 1997, most of the allegations of Iranian involvement in international terror have focused upon the activities of a small but determined number of unelected conservative hard-liners whose freedom from parliamentary scrutiny has allowed them considerable freedom to pursue agendas that reflect not the official policies of the elected government but those of the Supreme Leader, Ali Khamenei, who has authority under the Iranian constitution to appoint or dismiss them. Since Khatami started to bring the Ministry of Intelligence and Security (MOIS) under greater parliamentary scrutiny from 1999,[3] the hard-line elements that are able to pursue their own private foreign-policy agenda are believed to be located to some extent within the Ministry of Foreign Affairs but to a much greater degree within the ranks of the Iranian Revolutionary Guard Corps (IRGC). Some of these influences are also believed to be independent advisers, not officially affiliated to any ministry but enjoying close access to and influence upon the Supreme Leader, whose 600-strong staff includes a considerable number of such advisers. 'There is still scope for parallel structures of government to exist within particular ministries,' one former Western ambassador to Iran has said, 'but the main problem is with the Supreme Leader's office.'[4]

While the links between these hard-liners are informal, particularly close associations are believed to have been forged between the IRGC's current deputy leader, Brigadier-General Mohammed Baqer Zolqadr, and two senior clerics, Ayatollahs Rasti Kashani and Haeri Shirazi, who are based in the holy city of Qom where one particular seminary, the Madrasse-ye Haqqani, has acquired a reputation for being especially close to the Supreme Leader's office. Other important links have been forged between the head of the Assembly of Experts, Ayatollah Ali Meshkini, the secretary of the Guardian Council, Ayatollah Ahmad Jannati, and maverick elements of the intelligence services.[5]

The semi-autonomous role enacted by such unelected elites has enabled a multi-tiered Iranian foreign policy to emerge. While at one level official policy is put forward by the elected government of President Khatami, in practice very different agendas are on occasion pursued not just by the IRGC and Foreign Ministry but also by individual officials or departments within them. This has allowed for the pursuit of often contradictory policies, including the support of Kurdish nationalism in Iraq and Turkey by some military units at the same time as others have sought to curb it in Iran, the toleration of narcotics production by one political ally despite the efforts of the civil authorities to curb a major and growing drugs menace,[6] or an alleged effort to disrupt the peace process in Afghanistan while the Tehran government has tried hard to support it.[7]

Most of the allegations pitched against Iran by Washington and Tel Aviv have focused upon the activities of these 'hard-line, unaccountable elements within the regime'[8] that have in recent years operated against exiled dissidents, allegedly sponsored Middle Eastern violence and allegedly co-operated with elements of the Al Qaeda organization.

Operations against exiled dissidents

Iran's reputation as a sponsor of international terror has been forged partly by its willingness to pursue and execute its exiled dissidents. Although since the election of Muhammed Khatami as President in 1997 such operations have been brought to a virtual standstill inside Western Europe and are currently carried out mainly in the regions of Iraqi Kurdistan where they pass relatively unnoticed by the outside world, there is a convincing reason why this track record remains an important one: these killings were perpetrated by a ruling body, the Supreme National Security Council (SNSC), whose membership has barely changed since the early 1990s, when some of the most ruthless attacks were carried out. Contemporary Iran is therefore still governed by essentially the same mindset that for many years has regarded assassination as an important instrument of foreign policy.

Many of the operations that took place in the early–mid-1990s were carried out at the instigation of Ali Fallahian, appointed as the Intelligence Minister in September 1989 by President Rafsanjani. Under Fallahian's directorship Iranian agents carried out what Amnesty International spokesmen called a 'growing pattern of killings' and 'a bloody trail leading back to Tehran'[9] that included several high-profile murders. Foremost among these was the killing of the Shah's last serving Prime Minister, Dr Shapour Bakhtiar, who was stabbed to death inside his Paris home on 8 August 1991 while policemen patrolled outside;[10] the following year, Iranian agents bombed two cars belonging to a dissident activist, Ali Akbar Ghorbani, hours before he was kidnapped from his home in the Shishli district of Istanbul;[11] on 16 March 1993 Mohammed Hossein Naghdi, a former Foreign Ministry employee who had claimed political asylum in Italy in 1981, was shot dead outside his home in Rome's Monte Sacro district by the automatic fire of an assassin passing by on a scooter;[12] and on 20 February 1996 two dissidents were shot at point-blank range at their homes in Istanbul.[13]

By far the best-known single incident, however, took place in Berlin in September 1992, less than three weeks after Fallahian had issued a warning that the Islamic Republic would track down and kill its expatriate opponents.[14] The target that Fallahian and his gunmen had in mind was Dr Sadiq Sharafkandi, the leader of a dissident movement, the Iranian Kurdish People's Organization (KDPI), that was deemed to pose a threat both to the Islamic regime and to the integrity of Iran.[15] The leader of the Kurdish Democratic Party of Iran, Dr Abdul Rahamn Ghassemlou, had already been murdered in July 1989 by Iranian envoys who had supposedly met him in Vienna to negotiate peace but instead lured him to his death. While visiting Berlin on 18 September to attend the Socialist International Conference, Sharafkandi had arranged a meeting with several Iranian exiles at the Mykonos Restaurant in the city's Wilmersdorf suburb, where he was shot dead, together with three other KDPI officials, by two masked gunmen who had burst in shortly before midnight and opened fire with automatic weapons. Despite an elaborate escape plan, several men were arrested including the leader of the assassination team, thirty-three-year-old Kazem Darabi, a former member of the Revolutionary Guard who had lived quietly in Germany under the cover of being a fruit and vegetable dealer while waiting for instructions from Tehran to carry out active operations. Warrants for the arrest of Ali Fallahian were issued some years later.

Many of these Iranian intelligence operations were planned and executed from what has been called the 'nerve centre' of Iranian intelligence in the West: the Iranian embassy at Godesberger Alle 133–7 in Bonn. Six offices and a radio room were put aside on the building's specially secured third floor for around twenty full-time intelligence officers, who monitored the activities of Iranian dissident and diaspora groups, as well as co-ordinating efforts to acquire the materials needed for Tehran's weapons programme. Other intelligence centres are said to be at the consulates in Frankfurt and Hamburg and the vast 'Imam-Ali' mosque complex in Hamburg.[16]

In 1997 one dissident organization published a list of the regime's intelligence sources in France that probably gives some indication of how its operations have worked. The Iranian Intelligence Ministry had an espionage network in France on a 'considerable scale', claimed the Organization of the People's Fedayeen Guerrillas, that was comprised of full-time members and of others 'who carry out their missions under commercial cover and sometimes pose as opponents of the regime, in order to infiltrate cultural and artistic groups'. In this category, the source named one Ali Ashgar Salehi, head of the French branch of a company called Behnam, who was 'responsible for transmitting information to Tehran on opposition organizations' and who reported directly to a senior intelligence official named Jafar Jalali; a lawyer named Mohsen Assadollahi, who was allegedly paid to supply Tehran with the details of the Iranian refugees whose claims for political asylum in the West he accessed; and a Ms Laleh Moein, who had once infiltrated the MKO, even infiltrating its leader Massoud Rajavi's compound at Camp Ashraf, and who later helped to run a Paris-based company, Limo SARL, that was used by the Iranians for the clandestine procurement of military equipment, particularly aircraft spare parts.[17]

An exposé of how the assassination operations of political opponents of the regime were planned and organized took place after the killing of two dissidents, Zahra Rajabi and her colleague, Abdul Ali Moradi, in Istanbul on 20 February 1996.[18] According to a report later compiled by the Turkish Prosecutor's office, two Iranian intelligence officials, Morteza Mohsen Zadeh (whose real name is Sa'eed Chub-Tarash) and Sa'eed Karamatian (or Rahim Afshar), had left Tehran for Istanbul using standard civilian passports and headed straight to the Berr Hotel. At the same time, the commander of the assassination operation, one Nasser Sarmadi-Nia (or Haj Ghassem Zargari-Panah), also flew into the Turkish capital on a separate flight and booked in at the Buyuk Sehzad Hotel. Using plans that had been prepared in part by Mohsen Kargar-Azad, a Consular-Secretary at the Iranian embassy, the three killers met up only at the last moment before taking up positions close to their target, using a getaway car driven by a local contact. All three then left the country, again on different flights, within hours of the killing.

In more recent years, however, the main focus of Iranian terrorist operations has instead been the Middle East, where the regime has allegedly sponsored suicide bombings and remains strongly linked to a blacklisted 'terrorist' organization, Hezbollah, that it helped to create in the early 1980s. Iran's role in the region, US envoy Zalmay Khalilzad argued, 'has contributed to the downward spiral of the [Middle East] conflict',[19] while President Bush has claimed that the Iranian support of terror presents 'the greatest obstacle to the creation of a Palestinian state' and its 'supporting and harbouring [of] terrorists undermines prospects for peace in the Middle East and betrays the true interests' of the Palestinians.[20] Donald Rumsfeld has also alleged that 'terrorists have declared war on civilization, and states like Iran, Iraq and Syria are inspiring and financing a culture of political murder and suicide bombing'.[21]

The intense hostility that such terrorist actions would manifest is not just the hatred of the Jewish state typically found in nearly all Muslim countries. Instead, its roots lie in the way anti-Israeli sentiment became merged both with the radical message that Khomeini voiced as he incited the Islamic Revolution as well as a more profound suspicion of foreign intervention that is deeply rooted within the Iranian national mind.

Iranian hostility to Israel

Hostility to the 'Zionist', 'racist' and 'imperialist' state of Israel has undoubtedly been one of the few things that has hitherto united Iranian political factions that otherwise remain deeply divided. Members of all political affiliations frequently put aside their differences to condemn Israeli policies and assert 'the inalienable national rights' of the Palestinians, a unity that became clear at a two-day conference held in Tehran on 24–25 April 2003 by the Iranian Majles to show solidarity with the *Intifada* and which was addressed by President Khatami; every year, on the last Friday in the fasting month of Ramadan, hundreds of thousands of Iranian citizens demonstrate in the streets to mark Qods (Jerusalem) Day, a commemoration of the 'occupation' of holy Islamic territory by the Jews that was marked by as many as 120,000 protesters in Tehran on 29 November 2002 and a comparable number on 21 November 2003; and on 15 April 2002, President Khatami won wide political support by writing to the Emir of Qatar, then head of the Islamic Conference Organization, and the leaders of Saudi Arabia, Kuwait and the United Arab Emirates to urge them to impose a one-month ban on the sale of oil by Muslim countries to Israel's 'main supporters' in protest at the incursion by the Israeli Defence Force (IDF) into Jenin and other areas of the Palestinian-controlled West Bank.

Such hostility is directed not only towards Israeli policies but, in many cases, towards the right of the Jewish state to exist at all. Foreign Minister Kamal Kharazzi, for example, has previously stated: 'We do not think that Israel is a legitimate government. It's not a country to us. Israel has occupied the territories of people in that region and it should be recognized as an occupying entity.'[22] The only way to solve the Middle East crisis, Khamenei has asserted, is to 'destroy the Zionist regime'[23] that is merely 'a cancerous tumour'[24] that 'harps upon the holocaust to justify its expansionist policies in the Middle East'.[25] In the seminary town of Qom, where highly influential clerics pull many of the strings of political power, Islamic decrees (*fatwa*) in support of suicide bombings against Israeli targets have been decreed by hard-liners such as Ayatollah Nouri Hamadani and Ayatollah Fazel Lankarani. In 2002 the Israeli government also compiled a dossier of public statements by Iranian officials that lists no fewer than 150 threats against Israel's very existence, including a speech by the ex-premier, Ali Rafsanjani, that contrasted the 'devastation' of Israel by a nuclear bomb with the mere 'damage' to the far greater population of the Islamic world.[26]

Among many of Iran's leaders such an uncompromising stance has been moderated, not least in reaction to US pressure, which increased sharply as the War on Terror got underway. Signs of this moderation emerged in the autumn of 2002 when statements by both Khatami and Kharrazi, who claimed that the region's future was a matter only for the Palestinian, Jewish and Christian populations to decide among themselves and that Iran 'would not hamper' any deal that subsequently emerged, drew sharp criticism from the militant movement Hamas.[27] Hints of a new open-mindedness have also since been signalled by Sadeq Zibakalam, a Tehran University professor with close links to the government, who has spoken of 'signs of changes' in attitude,[28] and by Hojjatoleslam Sayed Safavi, a cleric now in exile and the brother of the IRGC commander who in a letter to the *Daily Telegraph* on 30 June 2003 described suicide bombings as a 'crime' and who has since implicitly accepted the existence of Israel by reiterating the Khatami/Kharrazi note of compromise.[29] And in 2002, Iranian willingness to pass information on the fate of a missing Israeli Air Force (IAF) pilot, Captain Ron Arad, who had been shot down over Lebanon on a training mission in 1986, perhaps also signalled signs of a rethink. This deal was arranged with the mediation of the authorities of Kazakhstan, whose leader was on friendly terms with Khatami and whose intervention also played a part in the early release of three Iranian Jews who had been jailed in July 2000, ostensibly for espionage, but who were pardoned by Ayatollah Khamenei in October 2002, perhaps to help placate a US administration then sharply turning up the heat against Saddam's Iraq.

Above all, the regime's preoccupation with the Palestinian issue is questioned by the large number of young Iranians too young to remember the events of 1979. Although there are many Iranians under the age of thirty who attend the annual Qods Day parades, they are present in proportionately far fewer numbers than in the street, while on university campuses many students claim in private that the Arab–Israeli dispute is 'nothing to do with us'.[30] In mid-June 2003, students held a series of large rallies at Tehran University that called not only for more democracy in Iran but for the government to 'forget about Palestine [and] think of us!'[31] There is probably no better illustration of the importance of demographic change in Iran than the widely differing attitudes to the Arab–Israeli dispute generally embraced among different age groups.

There is certainly no reason to suppose that any rethink on the Palestinian issue by the Supreme Leader and his followers is likely. While in

April 2002 some Iranian reformists voiced support for Yasser Arafat's diplomatic overtures to Tel Aviv, Khamenei derided the Palestinian leader as 'capitulationist', and when on 11 April officials of Khatami's administration were meeting Arafat's Foreign Minister, Faruq Qaddumi, a senior figure in the conservative establishment and adviser to Ayatollah Khamenei, Ali-Akbar Nateq Nuri, was also holding a series of meetings with the Tehran representative of Hamas, Abu Osama Abdul-Mo'ti, as well as spokesmen for Hezbollah and Islamic Jihad, which also have offices in the Iranian capital.

The origins of this highly aggressive attitude to the state of Israel lie in the informal alliance that the Shah had struck up from the 1950s with an Israeli government that sought regional allies against the perceived threat posed by Iraq. As Israel began to supply training and advisers to the royal security service SAVAK, and the Shah in return adopted an overtly dismissive approach to the plight of the Palestinians, Ayatollah Khomeini began to make accusations against Israeli interference that were motivated partly by conviction and partly by political opportunism. Many of the Shah's actions, he and his followers argued, were inspired by 'Israel and its agents', while the country's problems were alleged to have been 'caused by America and Israel [which] derives from America'.[32]

This early association forged between Israel and the Shah's regime allowed a hatred of the Jewish state to take its place at the heart of revolutionary dogma. After the Shah was toppled, the new Iranian constitution, introduced some months after the revolution, was justified on the grounds that 'the roots of imperialism and Zionism have not yet been severed', and the Shah's former ministers and henchmen were executed and imprisoned not just on the grounds of 'undermining Islam and the clergy' but also of 'friendship with Israel'. And nearly a quarter of a century on, similar rhetoric and chants of 'Death to Israel' continue to form part of Friday prayers throughout the country.

But Khomeini's message had been given a particularly sharp edge because it merged with deeply rooted Iranian fears of foreign intervention and domination that had already been inflamed by the American- and British-inspired coup against the Shah's Prime Minister, Mohammed Mossadeq, in 1953.[33] More generally, Khomeini's sentiments also reflected a growing sense of victimhood that was felt by many Muslims in many different parts of the world, as the Ayatollah was aware: 'Who would have dreamt it possible for a bunch of Jewish thieves to take Palestine while the Islamic countries slept? How could the [British] have reached India to take our beloved Kashmir?[34]

This ideology has not prevented the Islamic Republic from accepting Israeli assistance when it suits, just as similarly pragmatic considerations have at times also prompted Tel Aviv to offer it. During the 1980–88 war between Iran and Iraq, for example, the Israelis sought to play off either side by bolstering Iranian military capabilities at a time when Saddam's armed forces looked capable of winning the battlefield initiative.

This prompted the Israelis to devise and manufacture huge, lightweight polystyrene blocks that allowed the Iranian assault forces to build instant makeshift causeways across the shallow Iraqi water defences that lay in front of Basra, to service Iranian warplanes, and to deploy hundreds of military advisers at a secret camp just north of Tehran to train its infantry officers. During 1983 alone, Tel Aviv sold at least $300 million of military hardware to Tehran, and the full extent of their shared interests unmistakeably became clear in 1981 when Tehran granted Israeli warplanes permission to cross its airspace to approach Iraq's Osirak nuclear reactor and deliver a knock-out blow.

Hezbollah

But at the same time as accepting some Israeli assistance in its war with Iraq, Tehran was also helping to build a movement in Lebanon that has long been deemed by Washington and Tel Aviv a 'terrorist' organization: Hezbollah ('The Party of God'). Iran's relationship with this movement, an organization that has not just perpetrated attacks on Israeli targets but which in October 1983 also orchestrated the suicide bombings of a US barracks in Beirut that left 243 servicemen dead, is one that is frequently cited by those who argue that it is a 'state sponsor' of international terror. Although the organization now claims to have transformed itself from a purely military force into a much wider political movement that commands respect within the mainstream of Lebanese society, such claims do not diminish the hostility of both the United States and Israel towards it. As one of President Bush's most senior envoys has pointed out: 'The Iranian regime also supports Hezbollah, a terrorist group with global reach. Its support includes training, financial support and weapons for use not only in the Middle East but more broadly. The Iranian regime's support for Hezbollah's terrorist activities, which have killed innocent civilians, is inconsistent with Iranians' desire to fully join the community of nations.'[35]

The origins of this relationship went back to the early 1970s, when an Iranian dissident association, the Coalition of Islamic Societies, assisted various armed guerrilla organizations committed to the overthrow of the Shah's rule by sending them to training camps in Lebanon to receive military instruction. Among those who made contact with the

Lebanese Shias at this time was Mustafa Chamran, an Islamic activist who had received military training with the Shiite Amal ('Hope') Party in Lebanon and who was appointed by Khomeini as one of the founders of the new Revolutionary Guard in 1979.

These initially tentative associations between the Iranians and Lebanon's 1.5 million Shia population were forged much more closely soon after the Israeli invasion of Lebanon in May 1982, when Khomeini ordered the deployment of several hundred hand-picked IRGC soldiers to resist the incursion of the Israeli Defence Force (IDF) more effectively and to make effective a wider ambition of 'exporting the Revolution'. Initially headquartered at Zabdani in Syria, the Iranians soon moved to Baalbek in Lebanon, quickly turning it into a miniature version of their own republic that was visibly policed by uniformed IRGC militia and where pictures of Iranian mullahs were openly displayed. The IRGC's unmistakeable presence meant that many Lebanese Shias soon came to regard Iran, rather than their own shattered state, as their natural protector, a perception that reinforced the admiration most already felt for the Islamic Revolution that had so dramatically swept away the Shah's rule only three years previously.

It was into this political climate that Hezbollah was born in 1982 as a small circle of young Shi'ite activists who wanted to thwart the Israeli invasion and occupation of Lebanon turned to a charismatic cleric of the al-Da'wa Party, Sheikh Mohammed Hussein Fadlallah, as their spiritual guide. The Iranian connection with the movement they founded also emerged through his involvement because Fadlallah had been a one-time associate of Khomeini at Najaf in Iraq, where his own period of study had coincided with Khomeini's own exile from the Shah's Iran. The informal relationship between them meant that, under Fadlallah's guidance, the Lebanese Hezbollah movement started off with very strong links to Iran, a relationship encouraged by a Tehran regime that sent envoys such as Ali Akbar Muhtashemi-Pur, a former ambassador to Syria and currently a leading figure in Iranian politics, to help form the new organization.

The strength of the association between Iran and Hezbollah was soon expressed in unmistakeable terms by the party's political manifesto and slogans. In 1985 its spokesmen declared Iran 'the vanguard and new nucleus' of the Islamic world, and its leader, Ayatollah Khomeini, as 'the one single wise and just leadership [by whom] we abide'.[36] But the link became most obvious during the 1986 Irangate scandal, when Oliver North sought to engineer the release of US captives held by gunmen thought to be linked to Hezbollah in Lebanon by effectively bribing the Iranian government to use their influence over the hostage-takers. More recent evidence of the association at this time was also cited in the US law courts when a US Federal judge, hearing a lawsuit in 2003 for compensation on behalf of the relatives of those killed by the Beirut bombings twenty years before, used CIA reports to argue that it was 'beyond question' that the Hezbollah agents who had perpetrated the attack had all 'received massive material and technical support from the Iranian government'.[37]

Although the strength of the relationship is officially denied, Tehran certainly makes no secret of its admiration for the movement. The organization, Foreign Minister Kharrazi has claimed, is 'a legitimate party in the Lebanese political system that has been resisting occupation',[38] one that 'has been able to liberate Lebanese territories and is fully respected in the whole region',[39] and which the Iranians 'consider liberating forces, not terrorists'.[40] At the International Conference in Support of the Palestinian *Intifada*, held in Tehran in April 2001, Khamenei called on Hezbollah members 'to assist the Palestinian resistance', while Khatami has also praised the organization as 'a liberation movement' that defends 'the freedom, Islamic and Arabic dignity of the occupied land'.[41]

Nor has Tehran ever denied providing the movement with financial support for ostensibly humanitarian and educational purposes, particularly by means of trust funds. Some of these trusts have been run with great success in the West, where they have drawn upon voluntary donations made by the Lebanese diaspora. In September 2002, for example, the New York Police Department (NYPD) charged the Al Alavi Foundation, a large Iranian charity with US assets worth around $100 million, with funding four Islamic educational centres in New York, Maryland, Texas and California 'that support Hezbollah and Hamas' and claimed that though 'ostensibly run by an independent board of directors' the foundation was in fact 'controlled by the government of Iran'.[42] Whether such contributions were intended or used for military ends, rather than just humanitarian assistance either 'to the families of the Hezbollah martyrs, wounded and handicapped' or to the large educational network it runs in Lebanon, as some Arab sources have claimed, remains unclear.[43]

But there is also considerable evidence that Tehran's support goes well beyond this and has included the movement of considerable quantities of military supplies. In January 1996 three Iranian trucks, all loaded with arms, were intercepted en route to Lebanon via Syria by the Turkish authorities, and a large number of Iranian cargo planes, bearing supplies for the movement, have also apparently been flown into airports at both Damascus and Beirut. Although these supplies have reportedly tapered off since the US invasion of Iraq, they continue to include considerable quantities of military equipment, notably the Fajr-3 and Fajr-5 land-to-land missiles that potentially put parts of northern Israel within the group's striking distance.[44] Hezbollah, argues one senior Western diplomat in the Middle East who has monitored the organization closely, is 'largely dependent upon Iranian funding'.[45]

The strength of the association has also become clear since the onset of America's war in Iraq, where at least ninety Hezbollah militia are believed to have established a presence since the end of major combat operations in May 2003. Although their exact motives have not as yet been determined, US officials claim that the militia has been reined in from attacking American forces by the influence of Tehran.[46]

Although Hezbollah has allegedly staged attacks on Israeli targets since the IDF's withdrawal from Lebanon in May 2000, the chief threat to Israeli security has since emerged elsewhere, including from the use of suicide bombings by Palestinians against both military and civilian targets in Israel and the West Bank. Here too the Iranian regime has probably had a hand, although the full extent of this involvement remains highly uncertain.

Israeli targets

While nearly all of these attacks have taken place in the Middle East, undoubtedly the most spectacular such terrorist operation masterminded by the Iranians in recent years was the bombing on 18 July 1994 of a Jewish community centre at Pasteur Street in the Argentinian capital, Buenos Aires, when a suicide bomber detonated a bomb-packed lorry outside the Israeli Argentine Mutual Association, killing eighty-five and injuring more than 200.

Despite a huge and very costly effort by the Iranians to hide their role in the attack – Tehran allegedly paid a $10 million fee to bribe Argentinian officials into keeping quiet – some details of their involvement have been put forward by a former intelligence agent, Abulghassem Mesbahi, who defected to the West in 1996 and who has since given evidence in several terrorism investigations in Europe. According to his testimony, the attack was allegedly planned at the highest level on the mistaken assumption that the centre was used as an operations base by the Israeli intelligence service Mossad. These plans were finalized in August 1993 at a meeting of the Supreme Council for National Security, whose thirteen permanent members at that time included President Rafsanjani, the Intelligence Minister Ali Fallahian, Muhammed Hijazi, commander of the IRGS's auxiliay forces, and the foreign minister Ali Velayati.

The operation was carried out under the orders of Mohsan Rabbani, a cultural attaché at the Iranian embassy in the Argentinian capital who, Israeli intelligence has since claimed, had close contact with the Overseas Operations Unit of the Lebanese Hezbollah movement.[47] Some of the others involved in the attack have since been named as the embassy's Third Secretary, Ahmad Reza Asghari, whose background as a member of the IRGC's Seventh Corps, which specializes in intelligence operations, qualified him to join the Foreign Ministry in 1986; a consular affairs and financial officer called Abdullah Nowrouzi, another former officer of the Revolutionary Guard; and the Economic Attaché, known as Zaanganeh, who is also reported to have had extensive contacts with Hezbollah.[48] Over several months the joint efforts of these embassy members planned the execution of the attack, co-ordinating the movements of the suicide bomber, a Hezbollah member named Hasin Baro, and helping to arrange for the rental of a Renault Trafic commercial van that was later packed with explosives before being driven into its target.

The attack proved to have long-lasting repercussions when, nine years later, in August 2003, the indictment by an Argentinian judge, Juan Jose Galeano, of four Iranian officials led to the arrest in Britain of Iran's former ambassador to Argentina, forty-seven-year-old Hadi Suleiman-pour, and a sudden upsurge in Anglo-Iranian tension that for a time threatened to lead to the expulsion of Britain's ambassador, Richard Dalton, from Tehran.

Nearly all Iranian-inspired attacks against Israeli targets, however, have allegedly taken place in the Middle East, where in recent years Tehran is said to have taken a prominent role in the sponsorship of suicide bombings and thereby become, in the words of Lieutenant General Shaul Mofaz, a former IDF Chief of Staff, 'one of the chief architects of the homicide bombing spree in Israel'. Israeli officials say Iran offers $50,000 to the families of bombers, double the figure ever offered by Saddam Hussein, and has strong links not just with Hezbollah but also with Hamas, Palestinian Islamic Jihad (PIJ) and cells of the Fatah movement situated in Gaza and the West Bank. Such claims have also been reiterated by CIA officials, who have confirmed claims that since September 2000 Tehran has employed an incentive system, paying the PIJ millions of dollars in cash bonuses for successful attacks. Such financial backing has allegedly been channelled by the efforts of a key middleman, Majid al-Masri, the head of the military wing of Fatah in the northern West Bank before his arrest in Nablus in December 2002,[49] and intermediary bodies such as the Al-Wali Al-Faqih office and Liberation Organizations Bureau of the Revolutionary Guards, formerly headed by General Beg Yazdi, who defected to the West in 2001.

Although there is no real doubt about Iranian complicity with some of those who orchestrate suicide attacks, it is impossible to verify the amount of financial backing that Tehran provides. A report in the London-based Saudi paper *Al-Sharq Al-Awsat* on 13 June 2002 claimed that Supreme Leader Khamenei stood at the centre of such efforts to fund the PIJ directly and to increase the available resources by as much as 70 per cent in a bid, as one CIA official put it, 'to make the West Bank another Lebanon'. The Israelis also claim that captured Palestinian intelligence reports provide evidence of Iranian money transfers equalling $400,000 to the Hamas representative Iz Al-Din Al-Qassam, and a further transfer of $700,000 was designated to 'support the Hamas military arms "inside" and to encourage suicide attacks'.[50] But such reports have been described by Western diplomats in Tehran as simply 'impossible to verify'.[51]

Any such resources would not emanate from the democratically elected members of the Iranian parliament or their sympathizers but from the unelected hard-liners whose implacable hostility to the state of Israel has already been noted. Among those who follow the example of their Supreme Leader are the directors of several state-owned monopolies, Al-Shahid, Imdad al-Imam and Al-Mustaz'afin, who take pride in sending money to Palestinian causes,[52] humanitarian or otherwise, and who make detailed arrangements for this sponsorship during discussions with visiting representatives of the various militant bodies such as Ramadhan Saleh and Ahmad Jibril, the leaders of Islamic Jihad and the Popular Front for the Liberation of Palestine General Command (PFLPGC), who are known to have made one such visit to Tehran in June 2002.

What is certain, however, is that the importance of any such financial backing for the *Intifada*, even if it exists at all, is easily exaggerated. Palestinian violence possesses its own dynamic and would therefore be no different in form even without foreign 'sponsorship' designed to incite it. The same should also be said of the Iranian military supplies and training for which more convincing evidence is available.

Military supplies and training

The issue of Iranian military supplies to Palestinian militia seized international headlines on 3 January 2002, when the Israeli authorities intercepted the *Karine A* as it moved through international waters 300 miles off Israel's Red Sea coast. The vessel was laden with fifty tons of arms, including Katyusha rockets and anti-tank missiles, that had allegedly been loaded at an Iranian port before being sent on their way to the areas of the Gaza Strip controlled by the Palestinian Authority. The cargo's seizure, said the Israelis, therefore provided 'incontrovertible evidence' that Iran was supplying military equipment to the radical Palestinian cause. 'The connection between the Palestinian Authority and the smuggling operation is unequivocal, clear and undeniable,' said Chief of Staff Shaul Mofaz at a press conference in Tel Aviv on 4 January 2002 as Prime Minister Sharon, inspecting the cargo at Eilat, argued that it proved the existence of a 'network of international terrorism spearheaded by Iran'.

The Iranians, of course, denied any involvement in such an operation, claiming not just that the seizure had never been independently verified but that there was no evidence that any such shipment had been loaded at an Iranian port. It was, therefore, Foreign Minister Kharrazi argued, just 'a plot of Israel'[53] designed to discredit Iran just as President Bush prepared his State of the Union speech. Most independent observers now accept the Israeli claims, however, not least because a large part of the weapons and ammunition found on board – including PG-7 anti-tank rockets, YM3 anti-tank mines and YM1 anti-personnel mines – had recently been manufactured in Iran. 'We had a rock-solid belief that the Iranians had been caught red-handed,' one Western diplomat has claimed recently.[54]

Respected independent observers feel equally sure that Palestinian and Lebanese militants receive military training inside Iran from members of the Revolutionary Guard, although the precise numbers remain unverifiable. 'It's a military equivalent of Western government inviting foreign nationals to study at our own universities,' as one former ambassador to Iran has put the point, 'since it helps create a bond of loyalty between the host country and those who accept its hospitality.'[55] Much of this training is said to be 'carried out by troops from the Revolutionary Guards' unit at Tehran's Imam Ali garrison' where 'fifty recruits, in groups of ten, have been receiving courses in ambushes, bomb-making, counter-surveillance and hand-to-hand combat', while at another camp, at Bahonar garrison north of Tehran, a small group of invitees are said to have taken courses 'in urban guerrilla warfare and ideological studies'. Overall, 'scores of Muslim militants from across the Middle East' are said to be receiving terrorist training at camps in Iran'.[56] Some of these are trained at other bases run by the Qods force, a semi-autonomous organization within the IRGC that is discussed in the following chapter.

Somewhat less certain are claims that the IRGC has in recent years continued to maintain a significant presence outside Iran, notably in Lebanon. Western diplomats cite one 'very well-placed source' within the Iranian regime who has claimed that 'hundreds' of Revolutionary Guard officers are still based in Lebanon having been instrumental in bringing about the Israeli withdrawal. This reiterates the claims of Western journals, which have named a General Ali Reza Tamzar as the corps' regional commander with responsibility for training militants in the Bekaa Valley,[57] as well as those of IDF officers. 'A few weeks ago we had Iranian patrols, you know like supervisors or experts that came with Hezbollah and patrolled the entire area from the mountain to the ocean, along the border,' as Major General Benny Gantz, head of Israel's Northern Command, claimed in September 2002.[58] But although such claims seem plausible, even after years of IDF military operations in Palestinian and Lebanese-controlled areas, no such officer has ever been captured and no convincing evidence of their presence ever been put forward. In particular there has to date been no verification of 'captured documents', allegedly seized during raids on Palestinian offices, that the Israelis claim prove the full extent of this involvement.[59] Moreover any small-scale Iranian presence in the region could in any case be no different in kind from the presence that every intelligence service seeks to maintain in troubled parts of the world.

Equally uncertain are Iran's exact links with the other terrorist network that has dominated the American agenda since September 2001: Al Qaeda.

Iran and Al Qaeda

Since the World Trade Center bombings, Washington has not only alleged that the Iranian regime has sponsored Middle Eastern terror, but has also asserted the existence of a relationship with the Al Qaeda movement. *Patterns of Global Terrorism* argues that some of Al Qaeda's members have allegedly found 'virtual safehaven and may even be receiving protection from elements of the Iranian government', a claim that was openly made by the head of the CIA, George Tenet, who told the Senate Committee on 11 February 2003, without citing any evidence for his claims, that 'we see disturbing signs that Al Qaeda has established a presence in Iran'. Donald Rumsfeld has also argued that the Iranians 'have permitted senior Al Qaeda to operate in their country and that is something that creates a danger for the world'.

Once again, however, it is the same 'elements' within the regime that are suspected of this involvement, and for this reason *Patterns of*

Global Terrorism speaks of the 'mixed' record of a country that has also detained or deported many suspected members of the organization. The efforts of the Iranian authorities to clamp down on any Al Qaeda presence began straight after the 11 September bombings when, according to a source close to Iran's Intelligence Ministry, the Supreme National Security Council issued a secret communiqué to officials warning that 'any member of the intelligence or security forces providing assistance of any kind to Al Qaeda members will receive swift punishment as a traitor'. Spokesmen for the Iranian government also vociferously denounced Bin Laden's organization and strongly forswore any association with it: 'Iran's policy is not to shelter Al Qaeda members and to prevent such people from entering the country,' as Hamid Reza Asefi, a Foreign Ministry spokesman, emphasized.

Over the months that followed, the Iranian government continued to demonstrate its commitment to fighting Al Qaeda. At the beginning of 2002, the state-run Iranian Republic News Agency (IRNA) quoted anonymous officials as saying that Tehran had arrested 150 people suspected of having links to the movement, and on the eve of Khatami's official visit to Kabul on 13 August 2002, Tehran authorized the extradition of sixteen suspected Al Qaeda members to Saudi Arabia and gave a nod of approval to Riyadh's reported willingness to provide Washington with information obtained during the interrogations that followed. Two months later, a very senior Iranian intelligence figure is reported to have visited Western Europe to provide his counterparts with good-quality information on Al Qaeda activities,[60] while in December the Iranians astonished US diplomats by deporting around fifty further suspected members to Pakistan and Saudi Arabia.

But the 'official' Iranian bid to clamp down on the organization, although its sincerity was not in question, has always faced two main obstacles. One is that the borders with Afghanistan, Pakistan and Iraq, as the success of the narcotics trade amply testifies, are all extremely difficult to control because of their length and porosity. 'Some of Al Qaeda's members might easily have crossed into Iran over Pakistan's Baluchistan border, which is obviously a very difficult terrain to monitor,' as one senior Western diplomat has recently reiterated.[61] Despite a statement in February 2002 by the Minister of Intelligence and Security, Ali Yunesi, that no Al Qaeda members had entered Iran, no one pretended that some had not slipped across the border. 'We have solid proof that Al Qaeda has been able to move in and out of Iran,' said Hilal Udain, Afghanistan's deputy Interior Minister.[62] Such movement was particularly noticeable in the chaotic aftermath of the defeat of the Taliban. While the local Afghan warlord Ismail Khan had initially shut down the main routes leading into Iran, most Taliban fugitives had found other, much lesser-known, ways out of the country. One such Taliban soldier, a Mullah Nadar, claimed that he had been summoned by his commander on 1 December 2001 to escort an Al Qaeda group from Kandahar to Iran because he was uniquely familiar with the back roads. As he drove along the dust tracks that are almost entirely used by drug smugglers, he eventually reached Rabat, where an Arab called Abu Zudir radioed comrades across the Iranian border who led them on the last stage of the journey to Zahedan.[63]

The other chief obstacle to the efforts of the Iranian government is the possible complicity between Al Qaeda and the hard-line elements of the regime, particularly the Revolutionary Guard. Despite an obvious major difference between the Sunni terrorist organization and the Shiite regime, it is plausible that a shared anti-Americanism might have prompted Iranian sympathizers to allow various high-ranking Al Qaeda members to take up residence inside Iran. On 28 July 2002 the *Washington Post*, quoting Arab sources, named some senior lieutenants of Osama Bin Laden said to be in Iran, including Mohammed al Masri, one of the group's trainers and guides; Mahfouz Ould Walid, who had reportedly been killed in Afghanistan the previous autumn but allegedly living in Mashhad; and Abu al Khayr. Another senior member, Abu Hafs, known simply as 'the Mauritanian', has also reportedly been living in a guesthouse in the same place.[64] Such claims were reiterated in February 2003 by a former Iranian intelligence officer, Hamid Reza Zakeri, who told *Al-Sharq al-Awsat* that Al Qaeda had considerable contacts with the Revolutionary Guard.[65] Zakeri, a former official in both the IRGC and the Ministry of Intelligence who before defecting had been close to the IRGC deputy commander Brigadier-General Mohammed Baqer Zolqadr and a senior Qods commander, Hussein Mosleh, claimed that these ties had been built by IRGC officers who were present in the Sudan during the mid-1990s, when Bin Laden had also been based there.

Proving the Iranian–Al Qaeda connection

But such assertions quickly run into the same difficulties as the much-criticized US efforts to demonstrate a link between Saddam Hussein and Al Qaeda. Many of the allegiances of those who have been identified as key players in the relationship between 'rogue states' such as Iran and Al Qaeda are both fickle and very difficult to prove, and have made movements that are extremely hard to track.

Such difficulties are aptly illustrated by the American bid to identify

Abu Mussab Al Zarqawi, a Jordanian terrorist, as a 'key player' in the terrorist network that has allegedly been constructed between Tehran and Al Qaeda. No one has disputed that Zarqawi was the leader of a radical group, Al Tawhid, dedicated to the overthrow of the Jordan regime, or that he had at one time run training camps in western Afghanistan. It also seems likely that after the US campaign against the Taliban Zarqawi had relocated to Iran before suddenly and mysteriously leaving for Iraq in May 2002. The source of this information, an ex-bodyguard of Bin Laden known as Shadi Abdallah, also told a German court in 2002 that Al Tawhid ran a small cell in Germany that forwarded as much as $40,000 a month to Zarqawi in Iran.[66]

The real bone of contention has been Zarqawi's supposed affiliation to Al Qaeda. In a Cincinnati speech on 7 October 2002, just before a congressional vote authorizing the use of force against Saddam, Bush had made a clear reference to Zarqawi as 'one very senior Al Qaeda leader', while on 5 February 2003, during his presentation to the United Nations, Secretary of State Colin Powell had described Zarqawi as 'an associate and collaborator of Osama Bin Laden and his Al Qaeda lieutenants'. Yet as the trial of Shadi Abdallah progressed before a Dusseldorf court, it emerged that Al Tawhid, far from being an affiliate of Al Qaeda, was in fact not only a wholly independent entity but sometimes acted 'in opposition' to Bin Laden's movement, competing with it for funds and members.[67]

The immense difficulty of tracking Al Qaeda members, or proving the true loyalties of those alleged to be its affiliates, has allowed some highly questionable, occasionally incredible, assertions to be made. Some of Iran's neo-conservative enemies in Washington have claimed, for example, without any evidence to back their claims, that Bin Laden's deputy, the Egyptian al-Zawahiri, 'has long been admired in Tehran, where he has visited on occasion',[68] an assertion that echoed another claim that 'throughout the 1990s, Zawahiri travelled repeatedly to Iran as the guest of Minister of Intelligence and Security Ali Fallahian'. Yet such claims not only remain unproven but also seem most unlikely at a time when Al Qaeda was strongly associated with a Taliban movement that was fast becoming a threat to Iran's national interests.[69]

Similar unproven assertions concerning the movements of key players in the Al Qaeda network have also been made about Imad Mughniyeh, one of the FBI's twenty-two most wanted terrorists, who is sometimes said to act as Hezbollah's main liaison with both Al Qaeda as well as Iran. Claims have been made not only that 'Bin Laden met with Hezbollah leader Imad Mughniyeh in the 1990s' but also that 'fugitive Lebanese terrorist Imad Mughniyeh met in Masshad with a senior Iranian intelligence officer'.[70] Yet in fact very little is known about Mughniyeh and even his alleged links with Hezbollah have been labelled 'a red herring'. 'We have seen no evidence whatever that [Mughniyeh] takes orders from or even co-operates with Hezbollah's leadership,' one Western intelligence officer has told a respected defence journal.[71]

The same uncertainty emerges from the contradictory assertions that have been made about twenty-four-year-old Saad Bin Laden, one of Osama's sons and undoubtedly an important figure in Al Qaeda. In the summer of 2003, Western officials confirmed Tehran's claims to be detaining Saad Bin Laden as well as several of the movement's top people including Sulaiman Abu Ghaith, a well-known spokesman for the group, and above all Saif al-Adel, a deputy commander of its military operations. Some reports also emerged that an even bigger prize, the movement's number-two figure, al-Zawahiri, had also been detained.[72] Holding such captives gave Tehran an immensely powerful bargaining chip with Washington, one that it sought to put to good use by seeking to trade its own prisoners with senior leaders of the exiled dissident group, the MKO.[73]

But a few weeks later a completely different story emerged. Saad Bin Laden, US officials claimed, was not only actively running the Al Qaeda organization from inside Iran, but doing so with the full protection of an elite Iranian military force, the Qods unit, which had provided him with a series of bases along the border with Afghanistan. Such claims became even more questionable when Saad was variously described by different US analysts as a 'leader' of Al Qaeda while others claimed only that he is 'more of a player than most of the offspring, but not that significant'.[74]

Nor is Iranian complicity with Al Qaeda demonstrated by the involvement of elements of its security forces with the Kurdish guerrilla group Ansar al-Islam ('Helpers of Islam'), an organization previously regarded by US officials as 'an affiliate'[75] of Bin Laden's movement. This is partly because Washington's assertions of such an 'affiliation' have been based partly upon reports that remnants of both the Taliban and Al Qaeda had fled to the remote corner of Iraqi Kurdistan, along the border with Iran, where they had been offered sanctuary by the Ansar movement. But the members of the Qods force who did help to create and sponsor the Ansar movement in the late 1980s had no real reason to regard it as an anti-Western organization and instead only sought to build a proxy force on behalf of Tehran that could curb any possible resurgence of Kurdish nationalism. 'The Iranians have tried to use the

Ansar to put pressure on us to adopt the policies they want,' a representative of a leading Kurdish party has said, claiming that the group had been trained and supplied by members of both the Qods force and the Intelligence Ministry from the main military base at Ramezan, near Kermanshah.[76]

In any event the support for the movement by just a small number of Iranian hard-liners has been much overshadowed by the efforts of others in the regime to curtail it. In 2002 such efforts led to the immediate deportation from Iran of the group's leader, Najmeddin Faraj Ahmad, known by his *nom de guerre* 'Mullah Krekar', who was flown straight out of the country on arrival. And as the US offensive against Saddam Hussein got underway in March 2003, the Iranian authorities turned back wounded Ansar militia who had been bloodied during their war with rival Kurdish gangs. 'They went inside one kilometre but then Iranians made them go back,' said Mohammed Hagi Mahmud, a leader of the Kurdistan Socialist Democratic Party who, like many other Kurdish leaders, had previously bitterly complained about Iranian support.[77]

Allegations of double standards

There are many other unanswered questions prompted by the association, both factual and alleged, between Iran and international terror. Most obviously, because it remains far from clear what constitutes 'terrorism', critics of the USA and Israel have been able to ask an obvious question that strikes an immensely powerful note in the Muslim world: why is it wrong for Iran to sponsor violence that might allow Palestinians to defend their own land but right for Israel to use its own violence to enforce its own policies that are regarded throughout the Muslim world as aggressively expansionist? If no one has ever disputed that Israel has always pursued a policy of assassination of political opponents, killing enemies such as Dr Fathi Abdul Aziz Shikaki, head of Islamic Jihad, in Malta in October 1995, Gerald Bull, a maverick rocket engineer, in Brussels in 1990 and hundreds of Palestinian militants throughout the Middle East, why did not the White House or any Western government ever seriously propose castigating Israel as a terrorist state?

The question has become much more important since the onset of the Palestinian *Intifada* in September 2000, which has prompted a significant increase in what the IDF terms 'targeted killings', including particularly controversial pre-emptive assassinations. According to the Israeli human-rights organization B'tselem, Israel conducted eighty-five such assassinations in the following two years, often carried out by helicopter-borne missiles that also claimed the lives of many innocent bystanders.

Although voices from within the US State Department have sometimes expressed 'concern' about such attacks, claiming that 'we're against this practice of targeted killings',[78] such views have hitherto been drowned out by the more influential views of leading figures such as US Vice-President Dick Cheney, who supported an Israeli attack on 31 July 2001 in which two young boys were killed by arguing that there is 'some justification' for Israel's policy of assassinating suspected terrorists 'by pre-empting'. Moreover, reliable reports have emerged that Washington, far from merely justifying such acts, has also been encouraging and supporting them. On 15 January 2003, a UPI correspondent, Richard Sale, quoted several US and Israeli officials as saying that Tel Aviv had been authorized by Washington to carry out assassinations in the territory of 'friendly countries, including the United States'. The following month, the New York-based Jewish weekly *Forward* reported that US and Israeli legal experts had met to discuss ways of justifying the legality of assassination, a topic that had become particularly important in the wake of the killings in Yemen on 3 November of Al Qaeda suspects, detected by a Predator drone, with remotely fired Hellfire missiles.[79] The matter became most glaringly obvious on 14 September 2003, when Israeli Deputy Prime Minister Ehud Olmert told Israel Radio that for the Tel Aviv government the assassination of the Palestinian leader, Yasser Arafat, 'is definitely one of the options'.

Without attempting to answer this question, the USA remains extremely vulnerable to the allegations of hypocrisy and double standards frequently made both in Iran and the wider Muslim world. At its conference in Tehran in November 1997, for example, the Islamic Conference Organization (ICO) felt free to condemn all terrorist acts by 'distinguishing terrorism from the struggle of peoples against colonial or alien domination or foreign occupation', an unmistakeable reference to the Arab–Israeli dispute, while Supreme Leader Khamenei has never shied from declaring that Israel is 'the world's biggest terrorist'.[80] But just as alarming for the USA and Israel are the condemnations of the IDF's assassination policies by figures such as UN Secretary-General Kofi Annan, who has admitted to being 'deeply disturbed' by its 'targeted killings' and who has openly deplored them.[81]

There are other questions that US critics of Iran have failed to answer. Washington hawks have argued that regime change in Iran is a sensible response to the regime's sponsorship of international terrorist groups 'whose most potent protection', as President Bush argued in a key speech on national security on 20 September 2002, 'is statelessness'. But Bush's assertion appears to undermine the case for regime change inside Iran and instead support the case for supra-national action targeted at such stateless organizations. A case in point is the Ansar al-Islam movement, which has been in part created by Iranian military officers but which had by 2002 become an autonomous entity. Why, in this situation, is terror combated more effectively by action against Tehran rather than an intelligence and military response directed at the Ansar organization?

Despite such unanswered questions, US officials have not previously shied away from accusing Tehran of sponsoring terror in two recent theatres of the war on terror: Afghanistan and Iraq. These accusations, and the substance of truth they hold, merit specific attention in the following chapter.

Notes

1. Also referred to as the IRGC or Sepah-e Pasdaran.

2. AP, 6 November 2003.

3. Below, Chapter 5.

4. Interview with the author, 18 September 2003.

5. Information based on author's interivews with dissident sources, Tehran, November 2003.

6. Below, Chapter 3.

7. Ibid.

8. Zalmay Khalilzad, speech to the American–Iranian Council, 13 March 2002.

9. James Dea, Washington director of Amnesty International, *International Herald Tribune*, 22 November 1993.

10. *Independent*, 9 August 1991.

11. *Hurriyet*, 23 February 1996.

12. *New York Times*, 18 March 1993.

13. *Sunday Telegraph*, 25 February 1996.

14. *Observer*, 30 September 1992.

15. See Chapter 8.

16. The Federation of American Scientists, <www. fas.org/irp/world/iran>.

17. The Middle East Data Project, 2 May 1997.

18. *Sunday Telegraph*, 25 February 1996.

19. Khalilzad speech, 13 March 2002.

20. White House statement, 21 July 2003.

21. AP, 1 April 2002.

22. *Newsweek*, 14 February 2000.

23. Speech, 20 October 2000.

24. Quoted in US State Department, *Patterns of Global Terrorism*, 2002.

25. Speech at a conference held in Tehran, 24–25 April 2001, to show solidarity with the Palestinian Al Aqsa *intifada*.

26. Below, Chapter 4.

27. Reuters, 16 October 2002.

28. Interview with the author, Tehran, 18 November 2003.

29. Interview with the author, London, 10 September 2003.

30. Author's observations and interviews in Tehran, November 2003.

31. *New Republic*, 3 November 2003.

32. Ruhollah Khomeini, *Sahifeh-ye Nur*, vol. 1, pp. 109–11.

33. See Chapter 5.

34. Khomeini, *Sahifeh-ye Nur*, vol. 1, p. 99.

35. Khalilzad speech, 13 March 2002.

36. Excerpt from Hezbollah's political platform, February 1985.

37. BBC News, 31 May 2003.

38. *Washington Post*, 21 September 2002.

39. *USA Today*, 18 September 2002.

40. Kamal Kharrazi, *Newsweek*, 14 February 2000.

41. Yossef Bodansky, *The High Cost of Peace: How Washington's Middle East Policy Left America Vulnerable to Terrorism* (Roseville, CA: Forum), 2002, p. 250.

42. *New York Sun*, 5 December 2002.

43. This claim of the Al-Shahid Social Association in Lebanon is made at <www.shahid.org.lb>.

44. See the report 'Hezbollah', published by the Intelligence and Terrorism Information Centre for Special Studies, Tel Aviv, June 2003, pp. 130 et seq.

45. Interview with the author, Tehran, 4 November 2003.

46. *International Herald Tribune*, 25 November 2003.

47. 'How Iran planned the Buenos Aires Blast', *Ha'aretz*, 17 March 2003.

48. *New York Post*, 28 August 1994.

49. *Ha'aretz*, 18 June 2003.

50. Palestinian intelligence reports on 10 December 2000; IDF report TR6-548-02, 'Iran and Syria as Strategic Support for Palestinian Terrorism', September 2002, p. 15.

51. Interviews with the author, Tehran, November 2003.

52. *Al-Sharq Al-Awsat*, 8 and 13 June 2002.

53. Foreign Minister Kharrazi quoted in *USA Today*, 18 September 2002.

54. Interview with the author, Tehran, 9 November 2003.

55. Interview with the author, 18 September 2003.

56. *Sunday Times*, 14 April 2002.

57. Middle East Newsline, 8 August 2002.

58. See CBS TV, '60 Minutes', 29 September 2002.

59. Ibid.

60. <www.crosswalk.com>.

61. Interview with the author, Tehran, 18 November 2003.

62. *Daily Telegraph*, 7 September 2002.

63. *Newsweek*, 19 August 2002.

64. *Daily Telegraph*, 7 September 2002.

65. 18 February 2003.

66. *Newsweek*, 5 February 2003.

67. *Newsweek*, 25 June 2003.

68. Marc Reul Gerecht, *Weekly Standard*, 18 February 2003.

69. See subsequent chapter.

70. <http://66.34.243.131./Iran/html/article5.html>.

71. *Jane's Intelligence Review*, March 2003.

72. *Christian Science Monitor*, 28 July 2003.

73. Below, Chapter 8.

74. *Washington Post*, 14 October 2003.

75. White House document, 'Results in Iraq: 100 Days towards Security and Freedom', 8 August 2003.

76. Interview with the author, 7 September 2003.

77. *Washington Post*, 24 March 2003.

78. US State Department, Richard Boucher, press statement, 3 August 2001.

79. *Foward*, 7 February 2003.

80. Friday prayers, 27 September 2003.

81. CNN, 5 July 2001.

3 | The other domino effect

In the summer of 2003 the toppling of Saddam's regime in Iraq seemed likely to unleash a domino effect upon the neighbouring countries of the Middle East. But this domino effect threatened to be very different from the one envisaged by the Washington hawks who had wanted a new regime in Baghdad to be 'a watershed event in the global democratic revolution' by acting as a 'beacon' of American values that would inspire the entire region.[1] It was, on the contrary, a recipe for further destabilization and conflict as the US administration looked beyond Iraq's borders and accused its regional neighbours of inciting civil unrest among Iraqis that it was unable to contain.

The relative ease with which one war could in this way lead to further disorder became clear almost as soon as President Bush had, on 1 May, formally and prematurely declared hostilities in Iraq to be over. While preparing legislation to sponsor democracy in Iran, Kansas senator Sam Brownback argued that the USA would never be able to establish a 'free and secure' Iraq 'as long as the clerical regime remains in power next door'.[2] And as casualties began to mount over the weeks and months that followed, so too did US allegations of Iranian involvement in Iraqi affairs become ever more aggressive. Paul Bremer, the chief US administrator in Iraq, claimed that there was 'incontrovertible' evidence of 'meddling and interference' by Iran, whose leaders 'know they are doing it, they know we are unhappy about it and they ought to stop it',[3] while President Bush spoke of a general threat to Iraq's stability posed by 'foreign terrorists'. In Washington, hawkish influences like Michael Ledeen also claimed that action against Iran was essential as 'a prerequisite for limiting further fighting and safeguarding the lives of our soldiers now exposed to Iranian terrorism in Iraq',[4] and to avoid the realization of a 'second Lebanon' scenario in which the USA would have to suffer the humiliation of pulling out of a lawless Iraq in the same way that the Israeli Defence Force had been driven out of Lebanon in May 2000.

The tension between Washington and Tehran was not helped by the occasional boasts of some Iranian figures that could easily be taken as proof of bad intent: Major-General Yahya Rahim-Safavi, for example, the commander of the Revolutionary Guard Corps, had publicly stated on 4 November 2002 that 'given their political, economic and military capabilities, the Muslim and Middle Eastern nations have the ability to obstruct and create problems for the Americans' warmongering policies in the region. Just as the resistance of the Palestinian nation has obstructed American and Zionist strong-arm policies, resistance by the regional nations can create problems for inflammatory US strategies.' Although his basic observations were of course quite sound, such remarks could easily confirm the views of those who already suspected Iran of inciting Iraq's anarchy and disorder.

But signs of this new, inadvertent domino effect in the War on Terror had in fact emerged some months before, as the USA sought to entrench the new regime of Hamid Karzai in Afghanistan and angrily alleged that Tehran was trying to undermine it. In the spring of 2002 Zalmay Khalilzad made this accusation against the same unelected hardline elites that are alleged to sponsor international terror: 'Elements in the Iranian government have been hard at work to destabilize Afghanistan,' he claimed, because they 'feel threatened by the emergence of a moderate and Western-orientated Afghanistan that might encourage the Iranian people to demand the same for their country'.[5] These allegations had begun to disappear by the summer of 2002 either because US intelligence was instead focused more on the monitoring of Saddam's Iraq or because the Iranians, anxious not to provoke the Americans, had reined in such activities. Even as tension between the capitals reached a new height, in the summer of 2003, US officials made no mention of any unwarranted Iranian interference in Afghanistan and instead concentrated more on the nuclear programme and involvement in Iraq. But Afghanistan nevertheless currently remains an extremely volatile region that can easily generate further tension between Iran and the USA.

The US administration certainly has good reason to suspect some unwarranted Iranian involvement in both Iraq and Afghanistan, regions to which Iran's strategic, cultural and commercial interests have historically been closely tied. But there are also grounds for supposing that Washington's accusations and policies, perhaps revealing something about the American mind, have also exacerbated the tension with Iran.

Iran and Afghanistan

Viewed from a historical perspective, much Iranian influence in the affairs of its eastern neighbour has been born only of the peaceful intercourse of people who moved across a highly porous border and who shared both the Farsi language and Shiite Islam. The rulers of both lands vied constantly for political influence in the region, however, and war sometimes broke out as either side asserted often tenuous claims to each other's territory. Until the end of the nineteenth century, for example, the Persians claimed to be the rightful owners of Herat, the capital of western Afghanistan that lies only 80 km from Iranian territory, and of its surrounding regions. In 1838 the Persian army laid siege to the city, withdrawing only when British forces, sent into action by a London government alarmed about the security of British India, occupied Kharg Island in the Gulf and threatened an invasion of the Persian mainland.

When, in 1856, the Persians did finally succeed in capturing Herat, the British government declared war, ordering its forces to storm the Persian city of Khorramshahr in retaliation and forcing the Shah to withdraw. Using words that echo strongly those used 150 years later by the world's strongest power, the British Foreign Secretary, the Earl of Clarendon, told his Tehran envoy in 1854 to watch out for unwarranted Persian involvement in the affairs of its neighbour: 'It is essential that the Persian government should be clearly informed of the determination of the British government not to tolerate any attempt by Persia to extend her influence over the Afghan races in such a way as to interfere with their independence.'[6]

But although there is of course a long tradition of Iranian involvement in Afghanistan, Washington's suspicions about more recent efforts to destabilize the regime of Hamid Karzai seem unconvincing at first sight because such interference would risk destabilizing the US-backed Karzai regime and thereby risk a return of Sunni Pushtun militants, perhaps hostile to the Tehran regime, or even of Taliban remnants and sympathizers with whom the Iranians had long been on deeply hostile terms. For since 1998, when the Taliban had become very closely linked with Bin Laden and Al Qaeda, Iran had been effectively working in America's national interest, acting as the very military force against the Taliban that an increasing number of voices in Washington were urging the White House to sponsor.[7] The Iranians never sought to take Washington's side, of course, but only sought to advance their own interests in Afghanistan at the expense of a radical force whose own interests seemed implacably opposed to their own.

Although the Taliban were of course Islamist to a degree that gave them worldwide notoriety, they were also Sunni Muslims who had no ethnic or religious ties either with Iran or the Farsi-speaking Shias of Herat. The Iranians therefore had no reason to sympathize with the dramatic rise of the Taliban militia that eventuated after the defeat and capture of the Herati warlord Ismail Khan in August 1995 and took immediate measures to counter Taliban power by setting up a military force, comprised of several thousand exiles, based in a handful of camps outside Masshad and later led by Ismail, who escaped from Taliban captivity in March 2000. After the capture of the Afghan capital Kabul by the Taliban militia in September 1996, the level of Iranian support increased dramatically with the establishment of an air bridge between Masshad and the Afghan bases at Bagram and Kulyab that ferried a huge quantity of arms and supplies to the Northern Alliance: Pakistani observers reported in 1997 that on one particularly busy day alone thirteen such flights had arrived at Bagram. Other supplies were taken by road or rail, and one train that was stopped in the Kyrgyz city of Osh en route to Tajikistan was found to be carrying 700 tons of arms.[8]

Besides supplying the Taliban's enemies with arms, the Iranians also proactively attempted to instigate popular uprisings. In May 1999, for example, a Taliban official, Mullah Amir Khan Muttaqi, claimed that Tehran had unsuccessfully tried to stir up an uprising in Herat by providing arms and munitions to a group of Shia villagers as they visited Iran. Discovering the plot and raiding their homes, he continued, the Taliban police had arrested more than 100 and killed eight of the ringleaders, whose bodies were put on display to the public. Some unconfirmed reports suggested that the scale of the revolt had in fact been much bigger than he admitted and had been quickly downplayed by a regime that exerted only a tenuous hold on the Farsi-speaking areas surrounding Herat. These independent sources claimed that twenty-nine had been killed and 400 arrested during disturbances that had lasted several days.[9]

In the summer of 1999, reports also emerged that Iranian personnel were stationed inside Afghanistan to give military training to the soldiers of the Northern Alliance, a role that had been energized by Tehran's fury at the Taliban's slaughter of thirteen captured Iranian diplomats in May 1998. Each comprised of six or seven members, these small groups of military instructors were flown in secretly from Tajikistan to offer instruction in infantry tactics and the use of specialized weapons.[10] *Jane's Defence Weekly* also reported on 21 July that Iranian engineers were providing technical assistance and helping to construct a new bridge in the Dasht-i-Qala region that greatly facilitated the movement of arms from Tajikistan over the Amu Darya River. To a degree that currently remains far from clear, further military training was also covertly provided in Masshad.

This put Tehran in a good position to assist the US-led war on the Taliban regime in the fall of 2001. Iranian special forces are reported to have assisted the Northern Alliance on the ground, and Tehran gave

Washington assurances that any American pilot downed over Iranian territory would be immediately and extensively searched for by their rescue teams. The Iranian government was also instrumental in helping to forge a new coalition government following the Taliban's defeat. It did this partly by exerting immense pressure on its key Afghan ally, Ismail Khan, who was renowned for his spirit of independence, to co-operate: 'It was the Iranians who put a reluctant Ismail Khan on their plane and flew him to Kabul to attend Karzai's swearing-in ceremony on December 22,' one diplomat told *Middle East International*.[11] Iranian pressure also helped to persuade another ally, the Tajik leader Berhanuddin Rabbani, to renounce his ambition to become President and thereby allow Hamid Karzai, whose nomination would have been acceptable to his fellow Pushtuns of Afghanistan's southern tribes, to take over instead.

The Iranians have also since been busily rebuilding a shattered country and at the Tokyo Conference in December 2001 pledged $567 million over five years to this end. In particular, Afghanistan's transport links have been much enhanced by the $38 million construction of a 76-mile road that connects Herat with Iran's Khorassan province. Financed, designed and built by the Iranian government with the help of Afghan labour, this road has cut the journey time from Herat to the Iranian border from eight hours to two. From the summer of 2002, Iran also began to supply electricity to Herat's streets, government offices and hospitals, spending $15 million on the creation of a 150-km circuit to the city from power stations at Torbat-e Jaam in Khorassan, and sending Afghan personnel to Masshad to undertake training courses in the use and maintenance of the new power grid. A more ambitious project to build a longer line, supplying a more powerful voltage, also began a year later, while Tehran has also committed itself both to improving Afghanistan's state television network and extending a new cross-border rail link. Having visited Tehran in March 2003, Ismail Khan proclaimed Iran's considerable interest in the redevelopment of Afghanistan: 'they really did take an interest', he told Herat TV, and were ready 'to continue the support' they had already provided against the Taliban.[12]

Viewed from this perspective, US allegations that 'elements' within the Iranian regime were undermining such efforts are clearly paradoxical in the same way as other contradictions already noted (Chapter 1). Yet during the spring of 2002, the US government still made claims that these 'elements' – to use Khalilzad's term – were involved in 'negative' activities that ran in parallel with the 'constructive' efforts made by others.

Iran and Afghanistan: US allegations

Washington was certainly on strong ground in claiming that there were some important unanswered questions about Iran's activities, notably its relationship with a maverick Afghan warlord, Gulbuddin Hekmatyar. An Islamist leader of rabidly anti-American views, Hekmatyar had openly sided with the Taliban as soon as US hostilities began in October 2001 and was later strongly suspected of masterminding a number of devastating attacks on the Karzai regime, which he accuses of being a US puppet government. Most of these attacks – such as a simultaneous assassination attempt on Karzai in Kandahar and a massive bomb blast in Kabul that killed thirty on 5 September 2002, a few days after Hekmatyar had backed a call for *jihad* against foreign powers in the country – have been carried out with a ruthlessness and efficiency that have been his personal trademark ever since he began his involvement in Afghan politics in the mid-1970s.

Iranian relations with Hekmatyar went right back to at least the winter of 1995, when Tehran had urgently sought to broker an accord between Rabbani and Hekmatyar to build a more effective anti-Taliban alliance that would be based in Kabul. To do this, Iranian envoys had enlisted the support of Qazi Hussain Ahmed, the leader of the Jama'at-i Islami movement in Lahore that has always unofficially acted as an effective political wing of Hekmatyar's armed party, the Hezb-i Islami ('Party of Islam'). But the real relationship between them had begun in 1996 when Hekmatyar, driven out of Afghanistan by a resurgent Taliban army, had fled to Iran and set up home in north Tehran, establishing political offices across the country and basing a series of tented military camps along the Afghan border for the remnants of his once sizeable militia.

Washington became seriously concerned that Hekmatyar could be working with Iranian hard-liners to destabilize the Karzai regime when in February 2002 the Afghan warlord, just identified by the US government as a wanted international terrorist, suddenly left Iran for either Pakistan or Afghanistan. No one took seriously the Iranian claim to have somehow 'lost sight' of the warlord, an excuse clearly designed to deflect pressure from a US administration that had just condemned Iran as a member of the 'Axis of Evil'. The real question was why the Iranians had allowed him to leave the country, knowing that he would attempt to undermine the Karzai regime, instead of detaining him in the same way that the imprisonment of Al Qaeda members was later not only to undermine the US case against Iran as a sponsor of terror but also acted as a powerful bargaining chip (Chapter 2).

The circumstances of Hekmatyar's mysterious disappearance quickly generated rumours of collusion between Iranian hard-liners seeking ways of challenging a newly founded US hegemony that had emerged since the fall of the Taliban, and rogue elements of the Pakistani Inter-Services Intelligence (ISI) that had backed Hekmatyar against the Soviet army of occupation in the 1980s and who now regarded him, being a Sunni Pushtun, as a relatively pro-Pakistan influence in the region. US officials currently claim that he still travels to and from the border and receives aid from his associates within Iran's religious establishment and security forces.

The main allegation levelled by Washington, however, was that elements of the IRGC were setting up a subversive fifth column active inside Afghanistan. Khalilzad claimed, for example, that:

> The Iranian regime has sent some Qods forces associated with its Revolutionary Guards to parts of Afghanistan. It has also sent Sepah-e Mohammed, an Afghan militia created by the Iranian Revolutionary Guards, to various parts of Afghanistan ... Iran should [therefore] dismantle its Qods force network in Afghanistan and Iranian-supported splinter groups because they destabilize Afghanistan and could again make the country a base for international terrorism.[13]

This was not the first time that Khalilzad had referred to this particular 'network'. In January 2002, he had also claimed that the presence of Qods officers inside Afghanistan posed a threat to the regime's stability, while in April 2003 Pentagon officials also spoke of the work inside Iraq of 'irregular members of a special unit'.[14]

Khalilzad's allegations are widely believed to have been based on some sound facts. A force of around a hundred operatives is thought to have been trained and despatched into Afghanistan at this time before being disbanded and absorbed into the Afghan national army in May 2002. It is also almost certain that members of the Qods force, as the US envoy argued, were the military force behind this operation. The exact purpose of this deployment, however, has remained wholly unclear and there is no evidence that the Iranian commanders who planned this operation ever intended actively to disrupt the Afghan government.[15]

Because the Qods force would have a central role in any Iranian interference in both Afghanistan and Iraq, it is an organization that merits further scrutiny.

The role of the Revolutionary Guards' Qods force

Responsible for the planning and execution of special military operations outside Iran, the Revolutionary Guards' Qods ('Jerusalem') force is well qualified to wage a low-intensity war in these two theatres. Its 2,500 members are a hand-picked elite who are chosen from the IRGC on the grounds of ideological commitment to the regime as well as for their military prowess, and since the end of the Iran–Iraq War in 1988 they have acquired considerable experience and expertise in operations similar to those that Washington has accused them of undertaking.

This specialist force within the Revolutionary Guard was founded in the winter of 1985 as part of a drive by the Tehran government to regain the initiative in its protracted conflict – 'the first Gulf War' – with Saddam Hussein. Iranian strategists were particularly keen to take control of Fao, a heavily defended industrial town set in the marshlands of southern Iraq whose capture was seen to be dependent upon highly specialized seaborne commando operations that could penetrate its superb natural defences. A new unit of around 500 men, all volunteers from the ranks of the Pasdaran, was subsequently raised and despatched to North Korea for specialized training that included, according to the leading defector from the force, Hamid Reza Zakeri, combat drills, counter-intelligence, psychological operations and flying skills. This preparation paid off in spectacular style on the night of 8 February 1986, when Fao fell in a swift and brilliantly executed assault by Qods units that used specially modified dinghies to approach the city by stealth and capture it with unexpectedly light casualties.

The present-day Qods force is stationed at four main bases inside Iran: at its central command in Tehran, situated in a northern district of the city where its offices are located next to several other defence and intelligence departments, including the general headquarters of Iranian forces; at Sanandai, in Iranian Kurdistan; at Masshad, capital of Khorassan province; and at Zahedan in Baluchistan, close to the border with Pakistan. Other much smaller detachments are located on Iranian-controlled islands in the Persian Gulf, and in the north of the country, near the Azerbaijani border. Each of these smaller bases has been reported to harbour around fifty armed Qods members and at least five of its intelligence officers.

In addition, the force also operates a number of training camps, the most important of which are at Manzariyah near Qom, and at Sa'dabad in northern Tehran. While basic training of its recruits takes place at these two camps, more advanced courses in the use of more specialized weaponry, including rocket-propelled grenades (RPGs), Katyusha rockets and explosives, are carried out at other bases near Esfahan and Shiraz. The main base camp near Masshad is also believed to have provided more specialized courses in airborne operations. Altogether these camps train between 200 and 500 recruits every year, all volunteers who must have served a minimum of two years within the ranks of the Revolutionary Guards. Although their loyalty to the Iranian regime is judged to be beyond question when chosen, they are believed to undergo further ideological training once accepted into the force.

In extreme circumstances the members of the Qods force could be briefed to intervene in domestic situations: during the July 1999 student uprising, for example, President Khatami is reported to have warned the protest leaders that he would instruct the Qods force to take action against them unless they took immediate action to bring the violent disorder under control. But nearly all of its active operations take place overseas and, being broadly defined, range from the assassination of the regime's political opponents abroad to the execution of specialized military operations behind enemy lines.

There are six corps within the force to which these volunteers can then be assigned, three of which have infantry roles, each with a different specialization, while the others are responsible for external operations, intelligence and logistical support. In 2002 the overall head of all these departments, including the intelligence department, was Brigadier-General Qasim Suleimani, then in his late forties, while since 2000 the wing responsible for the gathering of intelligence upon particular individuals, organizations and governments has been headed by forty-five-year-old General Ahmed Vahedi, who had been one of the original founders of the Qods force in 1986. The Qods Intelligence Unit, which accounts for about 10 per cent of the unit's personnel, shares the same task as other Iranian organizations responsible for military intelligence, although it works wholly independently from them. These other departments are the IRGC's own intelligence unit – headed by General Morteza Rezai, a much bigger department than its Qods counterpart and one that is briefed to watch over a much wider range of activities, including student protests; regular Army Intelligence; and the Central Intelligence Unit of the Iranian Armed Forces, led by the Head of the Chief of Staff of the Armed Forces, General Hassan Firuzabadi.

Because Qods is in theory an integral part of the Revolutionary Guards, it is accountable only to the Supreme Leader. But because loyalty is a key ingredient in the making of any member, the unit has in recent years become particularly close to hard-line elements within the Tehran regime and it is the private agendas held by such elements, rather than any monolithic higher command, with which the force has in recent years become strongly associated. The force was particularly active during the 1992–95 Bosnian civil war, when its officers worked alongside other military and paramilitary organizations to help the cause of Bosnian Muslims. In particular, a senior officer in the Iranian paramilitary Hezbollah organization, General Hussein Haram, was heavily backed by Qods to establish and fund a travel agency in central Tehran that arranged to fly Iranian volunteers directly to Bosnia to fight for the Muslim cause. Other operations were the product of co-ordination between the IRGC and Qods, such as the airlifting of military supplies from the north-western Orumiyeh airbase directly into former Yugoslavia and the running of a specially commissioned intelligence unit inside Bosnia, headed by General Hussein Ali, a senior commander within the Pasdaran.

The unit was also indirectly implicated in an alleged plot against the government of Bahrain. On 5 June 1996, the Bahraini Interior Ministry announced that a terrorist organization called Hezbollah-Bahraini had been discovered and was allegedly trying to establish a network of around 3,000 supporters that could incite a mass revolt against the rule of the royal family. Although it remains unclear exactly how much truth lay in these allegations, there is no doubt that the organization's leader, one Ali Kazim al-Mutaqawwi, had forged connections with hard-line elements in the Iranian regime when he was resident at Qom in the early–mid-1990s and had by 1996 become acquainted with senior officers of the Qods force, including Ahmad Sharifi, a corps commander, and its overall director, Ahmed Vahedi.

The force was also heavily involved in the 1993 Buenos Aires bombings: Kamal Za're and Karim-Zadeh of its logistics section visited Argentina for three months before the attack, often using private rather than diplomatic passports to visit the country and very rarely making contact with the embassy. But since the end of the war with Iraq in 1988 the main operative area for both the Qods force and the IRGC has been the Kurdish districts of Iran and Iraq, where its units have often sought, in very different ways, to suppress any resurgence of Kurdish nationalist sentiment that the Tehran regime, like its predecessors, has always deemed to be a threat to the integrity of Iran.

Military operations in Kurdistan

During the mid-1990s, this concern prompted Tehran to sponsor one of the two main political movements in Iraqi Kurdistan, the Patriotic Union of Kurdistan (PUK), led by Jalal Talebani. When in 1994 an accord finally broke down between the PUK and its rival organization, Massoud Barzani's Kurdistan Democratic Party (KDP), both parties looked further afield for support in the vicious feuding for territory and resources that followed. Mainly because of the location of their main bases, the KDP turned more easily to Saddam's Iraq while the PUK, based in the south east of the Kurdish enclave, looked for backing to the Tehran regime which at this point undoubtedly gave strong backing to its militia forces. An accord between the PUK, the exiled Shia group the Supreme Council of Islamic Revolution in Iraq (SCIRI) and Tehran was subsequently signed.

Defeated by the Iraqi-backed KDP at Arbil and Sulaimaniyah on 31 August 1996, many PUK militia took refuge inside Iran, where they were refreshed before returning to Iraq, recapturing Sulaimaniyah on 12 October. Operating from a distance of around 35–50 km behind the frontlines, Iranian artillery provided cross-border support that was particularly strong as the PUK militia fought along the Rawanduz and Piranshahr fronts that straddle the border. Around 700–800 members of the Badr Brigade, the armed wing of the exiled Iraqi Shia force SCIRI, who were based at Salaam Camp 75 km south of Sulaimaniyah, also acted as a proxy force for the Iranians and took an active part in the fighting.[16] Their support, and perhaps the covert presence of IRGC officers in their midst, help account for the PUK's success in pushing home their newly founded initiative, driving the KDP back some 60 miles to the town of Koi-Sanjak.

Central to the calculations of Iranian commanders was their ability to strike at the forces of a militant separatist group, the Kurdistan Democratic Party of Iran (KDPI), that had in recent years waged a low-level but costly guerrilla war against the Iranian military from the relative safety of its bases on both sides of the Iran–Iraq border. Although the PUK had long been on peaceful, if hardly co-operative, terms with the KDPI, Iranian support for its war with the KDP was made conditional upon taking up an overtly hostile stance towards the organization. When, on 26 July, around 2,000 IRGC soldiers pushed into northern Iraq at Marivan-Penjuin to strike the bases of both the KDPI at Koi-Sanjak and the Komala-e Jian-e Kurdistan (Association of Revival of Kurdistan) near Sulaimaniyah, they were escorted by guides of the PUK. It is also possible that PUK insiders gave the IRGC information on the whereabouts of the KDPI's sources of support, such as the refugee camps of Taqtaq, near Koi-Sanjak, that eyewitnesses claim were targeted by Iranian warplanes during August.[17] Throughout the mid–late 1990s, the PUK also allowed elements of the IRGC to use their territory as a staging post for military operations – mainly assassinations – against KDPI militia who migrated into the KDP zone of control after 1994. Spokesmen for the KDP today claim that at least eighty-three such KDPI activists were killed by the Tehran regime in this way between 1993 and 1996.[18]

Since 1996 the Iranian military has continued to interfere heavily in the affairs of Iraqi Kurdistan, although different agendas have on occasion led to contradictions similar to those discussed above. Talebani's movement has been backed more strongly by the Revolutionary Guard, which has provided 200–300 PUK militia with sanctuary at an IRGC base near the border town of Orumiyeh and run liaison offices at the PUK's main headquarters at Irbil and Sulaimaniyah. But from the autumn of 1999 the Kurdish political parties provided compelling evidence – notably intercepted radio communications – that the Qods force was backing a newly emerged group, Ansar al-Islam. Because Ansar was waging a brutal low-intensity war against the PUK and other Kurdish groups, it was probably regarded by its Iranian sponsors as an effective means of exerting political leverage over them. 'The purpose of this strong support for Ansar', one senior Kurdish official has claimed, was in large part 'to pressurize the Kurdish political parties into adopting certain policies'.[19]

The efforts of the Qods force to limit the threat of Kurdish separatism have also contradicted the backing given by the IRGC to another militant organization, the Kurdistan Workers' Party, Partiya Karkeren Kurdistan (PKK, currently known as Kadek), which between 1984 and 1999 fought bitter battles with the Ankara government for the rights of Turkey's Kurds. There are highly credible reports that the IRGC, perhaps regarding the PKK as a possible future ally against any possible Turkish attempt to find influence inside northern Iran or in the Central Asian republics, has hitherto provided the PKK with new bases, all disguised as medical facilities, near Orumiyeh. Since 1984 Ankara has also regularly levelled accusations of such support and alleged the regular movement of resources from the main PKK camp at Makhmour, south of Arbil, across the border into Iran.

Tension between Tehran and Ankara climaxed in the summer of 1999 when on 18 July Ankara ordered its warplanes to bomb suspected PKK camps in Iran, killing five Kurds as well as a senior IRGC officer, while its ground forces also launched a small-scale land offensive in the border region of Qottur. Although the Turks have never produced convincing evidence of any military training provided by the IRGC, there is no doubt that PKK militia have been given shelter and humanitarian aid, reflecting a basic strategic truism that 'it would be very useful in Iran to give degrees of sustenance to people and organizations that pose threats to neighbours'.[20] Moreover the IRGC has also supported the PKK in a more negative way, by merely failing to stop its activities on Iranian soil: a main PKK base at Kandil mountain, where as many as

3,000 of its militia have been sheltered, lies exactly on the Iranian–Iraqi border but has none the less been supported logistically only because resources have been moved through Iranian territory.

But any support given to the PKK would be directly at odds with a wider concern to forestall a Kurdish nationalism within Iran's own borders that the PKK, unashamedly pan-Kurdish in aspiration, would doubtless instigate. It was for this reason that protests mounted by Iranian Kurds in February 1999 at Turkey's arrest of the PKK leader, Abdullah Ocalan, were repressed on the orders of the Tehran authorities. And because the PKK is regarded by many as responsible for smuggling narcotics into Iran on a vast scale, any support provided by the IRGC would clearly run counter to the desperate efforts of the Iranian authorities to contain Iran's growing scourge of drug abuse.

US allegations of Iranian interference in Iraq

It is clear, then, that in the decade preceding the war on Saddam Hussein in 2003, Iranian involvement in Iraqi affairs had at times been both busy and protracted, a track record that at first sight makes US allegations of covert Iranian interference in post-Saddam Iraq highly plausible. Some of this interference was just media influence, such as the broadcasting of an Iranian television channel, Al-Alam, into Iraq that prompted Colin Powell to protest that the USA 'would not like to see Iran try to get undue influence and essentially start inserting its own agenda on to Iraq'.[21] But the substance of Washington's allegations was that, in the words of Defense Secretary Donald Rumsfeld, 'organized elements' had been despatched by Iran into Iraqi territory that were trying to 'hijack' democracy.[22] 'Iran continues to meddle in various ways in Iraq's internal affairs,' argued the chief American administrator, Paul Bremer, six months after hostilities against Iraq had begun, and had 'provided support for various people, some of whom have taken both violent action against both Iraqis and against the Coalition'.[23]

Said to have been central in this regard is an armed organization of Iraqi Shias, the Badr Corps. On 28 February 2003, before the US offensive began, Rumsfeld warned its militia to keep out of Iraq and said that they would be treated as 'combatants' if caught, while a spokesman for the State Department, Richard Boucher, pointed out that the USA 'would oppose any Iranian-supported presence' in Iraq and that a Badr deployment 'would be a very serious and destabilizing development'. While Washington later regarded its leader as an ally in the quest to stabilize Iraq, any alleged or actual Iranian influence inside Iraq is always likely to be exerted through Tehran's contacts and influence with this organization.

Iran and SCIRI

The Badr Brigade acts as the effective armed wing of the Supreme Council of Islamic Revolution in Iraq (SCIRI) which, since its formation in Iran on 17 November 1982, has represented the interests of much of Iraq's huge Shia population, concentrated mainly in the south of the country. On the outbreak of war between the two countries in 1980, tens of thousands of these Iraqis had fled to Iran, facing persecution by Saddam Hussein, the leader of an essentially secular regime who was highly suspicious of where their loyalty would lie during the conflict. As they fled, these Iraqi Shias turned to a highly charismatic cleric, Ayatollah Mohammed Baqir al-Hakim, as their leader.

From the moment he arrived in Tehran in 1980, Hakim had good reason to want to take up arms with Baghdad. He had by this time already lost six of his brothers, all murdered, to Saddam's regime and more were to follow in the wake of the 1991 Shia uprising, whose bloody repression also led to the disappearance of another brother and to the arrest of twenty-two family members. The particular interest of the Iraqi authorities in the family reflected the prominent role it had long played in the religious and political life of Iraqi Shias ever since his father, the late Grand Ayatollah Muhsin al-Hakim, had stood as the spiritual leader of the Shia community in Iraq, and indeed of those throughout the world.

The close relationship between Iran and SCIRI can in part be explained on grounds of mere convenience. No one seriously denied the strength of its association with the Revolutionary Guard, which initially provided the Badr Corps with two camps on the outskirts of Tehran and later with a whole series of tented bases, usually in the vicinity of the Iraqi border. Badr commanders also had to seek permission from Tehran authorities to conduct any active operations, or even just to move military equipment from one site to another, and liaised closely with a specially appointed Iranian representative, usually a member of the IRGC, to obtain this permission.

This did not mean that either SCIRI or its armed wing was just an Iranian puppet. The Badr Brigade's militia and officers were almost all Iraqi exiles and their training was often provided by sometimes high-ranking defectors from Saddam's army, who instructed the militia on using equipment that was on occasion captured from the frontlines. This degree of autonomy was also reflected in the movement's workings, since its twelve-man central committee – currently made up of religious scholars such as Sayyed Mohammed al-Hayderi, the head of its political bureau; Sheikh Brahim Hamoudi, a political adviser; and

Bayan Jabr, responsible for Arab affairs – has always exercised control over the day-to-day running of the organization.

With the support of the Revolutionary Guard, the Iranians were able to utilize Badr against the Iraqis as an effective fighting force whose ranks had by 1988 grown in number to perhaps as many as 10,000 soldiers, although estimates of its full strength have varied widely. The corps had individual units for a wide range of operations, including the artillery of the al Hassan Mohammed Battalion and the anti-aircraft teams of the al Abbas Battalion, but most of its operations against Iraq involved intelligence gathering and infiltration behind enemy lines, tasks to which its personnel, most of whom were originally natives of southern Iraq, were ideally suited. The familiarity of some militia members with the vast Howeiza marshlands of southern Iraq also made the brigade particularly proficient at carrying out many hit-and-run attacks against the Iraqis, a proficiency that in 1991 prompted Saddam to order the draining of much of the marshland.

After the end of the Iran–Iraq War in 1988, SCIRI continued to mount similar attacks, although on a much smaller scale. Classic Badr attacks took place on 10–11 February 1995, during a large-scale offensive throughout the marshland region, when around fifty operatives travelled through the swamps in motorboats to hit an Iraqi outpost, killing five and capturing twenty, and on 19 April 1999, when a remote-controlled detonation of a car packed with explosives led to the wounding of former Iraqi minister Mohammed Hamza al Zubeidi as he was driven along the Najaf–Baghdad highway. But the strength of the relationship between Badr and the Iranian authorities has become clear from the way in which many of these attacks have targeted the Iranian dissident movement, the Mujahideen-e Khalq (MKO), which has mounted its own raids on Iranian targets from its bases inside Iraq (see Chapter 8). On 10 July 1995, the day after the Iranian army had struck an MKO base at Ashraf with long-range rockets, three Khalq members were mown down along the Mohammed Qasim highway in Baghdad by attackers using Uzi machine-guns; on 7 March 1996 an MKO commander, Hamed Reza Rahmani, was shot dead as he walked along Sa'dun Street in Baghdad, and a bomb exploded outside MKO's main office in the Iraqi capital on 22 December 1997. Some of these attacks have on occasion clearly been acts of reprisal. On 22 March 2000, a mortar attack on Baladiyat killed four and injured thirty-eight in a clear act of retaliation for an MKO missile attack nine days earlier; huge explosions that rocked the Baladiyat district of Baghdad, wounding eight, on the night of 1 May 2000 took place the same night as an MKO attack in Tehran killed six;

and on 13 May 2000 eight missiles were fired on the residential al-Karkh district of Baghdad, ostensibly targeting one of Saddam's palaces, a few days after further attacks inside Tehran. Although some of these attacks may have been perpetrated by Iranian agents, rather than SCIRI militia, there is no real doubt that they were carried out using a well-established network of safehouses, escape routes and weaponry that has been built up inside Iraq by al-Hakim's movement.

While such timing demonstrates the proximity between Tehran and SCIRI, the Iraqi government and its protégés have also made many efforts to prove such a link further. At a press conference in Baghdad on 15 May 1995, for example, the National Council of Resistance, the political wing of the MKO, displayed various weapons that it had claimed had been seized from a foiled operation jointly mounted by Badr and Iranian intelligence. Assisted by Badr militia, an Iranian hit squad had been moved across the border into Iraq with a specially designed 320-mm calibre mortar, 163 cm in length, whose individual shells each contained 25 kg of explosives. The mortar was of such a size, claimed the NCRI, that it had to be dismantled into three pieces to be transported over the border towards Baghdad, and its opera-tion required special training that had been provided at the Gayoor Asli Garrison and the Nawab Safavi Centre in Ahvaz, at a camp near Baharestan Square in Tehran and a test-firing range a few miles outside the city of Qom.

The close relationship between SCIRI and Tehran has reflected not just military dependency but also some strong common political ground that has prompted many onlookers to believe that the vision of an Iraqi Shiite theocracy drawn up by the late al-Hakim would not differ widely from the Iranian model. Exactly how close their views are is difficult to judge from the statements made both by the late al-Hakim and his older brother, the sixty-three-year-old Ayatollah Mohammed Baqir al-Hakim. Both have always officially denied wanting to create Iraq in the image of the revolutionary regime in Iran, arguing instead for more democracy, and although al-Hakim has written tracts on human rights and 'the freedom of the individual within the rules of the Islamic Sharia' that, superficially at least, would seem out of place inside Iran, most of his remarks are too vague to be meaningful: 'There is no separation between politics and religion because religion guides politics for the benefit of the people,' he told one British newspaper in March 2003, five months before his assassination,[24] 'but we must distinguish between extremist elements that would seek to impose religion. We want to concentrate on the spirit of religion, on its morals.' SCIRI representatives also make superficially appealing but ultimately meaningless statements of their commitment to 'democracy' and 'freedom'.[25]

The particular episode that really confirmed all of America's worst fears about the extent of Iranian influence over the movement, however, came in the spring of 1991 as the Badr Brigade moved into southern Iraq to take advantage of the political chaos that ruled the country during the Shia uprising. Soon after the uprising broke out, in Nasiriyah on 2 March, SCIRI's leaders appeared to renege on a deal struck the previous December with a coalition of thirty-two political groups that were committed to the overthrow of the Iraqi regime. For although SCIRI's representatives had promised only to remove Saddam Hussein and not to replace his rule with a theocracy, Badr's armed intervention into Iraq was not only accompanied by the green flag of Islam and pictures of Ayatollah Khomeini but also revealed a degree of organization that indicated a strong Iranian influence.[26]

By the spring of 2003 the US clearly had good reason to suspect that any Badr deployment would help extend Iran's influence into Iraq and was therefore deeply alarmed by reports that forward units of the brigade were moving into Kurdish northern Iraq before the USA had even commenced its military campaign. At the village of Banibi, forty miles south of Sulaimaniyah, one journalist approached a SCIRI camp[27] and found a very impressive array of firepower, including Katyuska rockets, mortars and field guns, in the process of being moved into the country. At another village, Meydan, at the base of Zimnako mountain, a former army camp left over from the Iran–Iraq War that was positioned about eleven miles from the border, a Reuters correspondent reported seeing at least 200 Badr militia wearing camouflage uniforms and carrying assault rifles. The base had around 120 tents, he added, but was being prepared to accept far more personnel. Although al-Hakim's local representative in Sulaimaniyah, Abu Mohammed Kharsani, claimed that the brigade's only presence in northern Iraq was a small outpost in Maydan Saray, three miles from Banibi,[28] it soon became common knowledge that the Badr Brigade was utilizing the open border to position itself to maximum effect as soon as US forces commenced their attack against Saddam.

As the war with Iraq got underway, relations between Washington and SCIRI deteriorated sharply as the USA decided that the movement could not be trusted after all. A furious al-Hakim, outraged at being sidelined, castigated the invasion and issued a joint condemnation with Iraq's radical Shia group, the Islamic Call Party (Hezb al Dawaa al-Islamiya). Disagreements continued throughout the spring as SCIRI boycotted the US-sponsored gathering of former opposition leaders in Al Nasariya, claiming that such a conference simply 'wasn't necessary', and declared their own preference for a national conference made up of hundreds of representatives, each eligible to cast a vote for a provisional government, and criticized the US plan for a twenty-five–thirty-five-member council to act as an Iraqi administration. Suspicions of Iranian influence were confirmed in the wake of military victory. On 10 May, al-Hakim made a triumphant return to Iraq after twenty-three years of exile and was greeted by a huge 100,000-strong crowd that lined his route into the holy city of Najaf. Speaking in Basra, his message hardly seemed threatening as he promised his fellow Shias a 'modern Islamic government' that would be 'freely elected' and 'tolerant'. But independent eyewitnesses to the Ayatollah's return were adamant that 'you only had to watch Hakim's return to see that it had been stage-managed by Iran', being a procession that bore symbols, rituals and slogans that were 'all Khamenei trademarks'.[29] But by later changing tack and pragmatically agreeing to co-operate with the allies by allowing his brother, Abdul Aziz, to join the US-appointed Iraqi governing council, al-Hakim had, by the time of his assassination on 29 August 2003, become a central part of US strategy to create a new Iraqi order acceptable both to the large Shia population and to the Iranian government.

Unanswered questions about the US approach

In the light of the events of recent years, it is clear that Washington has good reason to suspect a high degree of Iranian influence in both Iraq and Afghanistan. Yet there are some respects in which America's own policies have arguably exacerbated the tension with Tehran over this issue.

This is most obviously true because US condemnations of Iranian interference in the affairs of its neighbours are easily perceived to be as unfair as allegations of its support for international terror, consciously overlooking the positive contributions made by the elected government and instead emphasizing only the negative actions of what Washington admits is merely 'a minority' within its ranks. Just as Iran was condemned as 'evil' just weeks after it had contributed to the US War on Terror and had pledged millions to the reconstruction of Afghanistan, in similar vein the US government has sometimes also given the impression of being interested only in seeking to identify the malign influence of Iranian hard-liners inside Iraq. Yet during the allied campaign Tehran had overlooked violations of Iranian airspace by US aircraft and missiles and even one reported incident, on 23 March, of American warplanes mistakenly opening fire on Iranian targets. Such co-operation even fuelled speculation that there might be a secret deal between the two capitals that went far further than either side was publicly willing to admit.

Washington's approach has appeared all the more questionable while its allegations have remained unproven but such incidents of Iranian co-operation have never been in dispute. While the Americans have generally had little difficulty in asserting the presence of Iranians or their protégés inside Iraq or Afghanistan, for example, they have never produced any evidence of, or even made any detailed allegations about, their activities inside those countries. Although the Qods 'network' inside Afghanistan really did exist, why were its operatives a disruptive force rather than merely an intelligence-gathering body similar in type to those that most regional governments could be expected to deploy? 'The Iranians undoubtedly deployed Sepah-e Mohammed into Afghanistan as the Americans claimed,' as one Western diplomat has since pointed out, 'but it was probably meant as a form of insurance policy, to give them influence in the region if things should break down either in Afghanistan or with the Americans.'[30]

Similarly, Washington also claims to have tracked the movements of around a dozen Revolutionary Guard intelligence officers who, in the early summer of 2003, travelled from Tehran into Iraq, prompting one CIA officer to claim, 'We are absolutely 100 percent positive that there are Iranian operatives in town.'[31] But if such intelligence lay behind the charges of interference in Iraqi affairs levelled by Rumsfeld and other senior administration figures, then it was unclear why the mere 'presence' of Tehran's agents had become synonymous with their 'interference'. 'Iran has no interest in creating, or being linked to any kind of problems the Americans are facing in Iraq,' a Western diplomat told the *Christian Science Monitor*, echoing the views of most analysts, who are dismissive of US claims that Iran has been trying to undermine the new Iraqi order.[32] It is likely that Iranian influence in Iraq is based on the same calculation as its 'interference' in Afghanistan: to safeguard its interests should a worst-case scenario eventuate.

The paucity of firm information about both Iraq and Afghanistan means that US allegations echoed the many other questionable 'intelligence reports' that emerged from both countries, where rumours and speculation are always rife, only to disappear again. In Afghanistan's Nimruz province, for example, security chief Mohammed Naim Khan told the *Daily Telegraph* in September 2002 that he had passed intelligence to US forces that several key Al Qaeda players were attempting to buy weapons from local arms dealers and planning to carry out unspecified terrorist operations in Afghanistan from bases inside Iran,[33] although this 'intelligence' has never since been cited. And in Washington, Michael Ledeen argued that 'Hassan Rassouli, a former Iranian army officer and governor of Khorassan, travels to and from Iran in great secrecy, handling money and weapons',[34] although his claim does not appear to have been echoed by the CIA or anyone within the administration.

There have also been occasions when US policies have given the Iranian authorities good reason to fear for their security, thereby prompting them to take some of the measures of which Washington has accused them. The establishment of a big American military presence at Zaranj, on the Afghan–Iranian border, soon after the defeat of the Taliban, for example, outraged Iranian commanders, who responded by redeploying elements of their 110th Brigade and Revolutionary Guard and constructing new defences against a perceived risk of US incursions.[35] A similar reaction probably explains the activity of the Qods forces inside Afghanistan that were perhaps briefed with finding ways of counter-attacking US forces if Washington should ever launch any such assault on Iran. It is probably not coincidental that these activities took place soon after the presidential 'Axis of Evil' speech that fuelled Iranian fears that their own country, after Iraq, was next on the hawks' hit-list.

Besides malign interference inside Iraq and Afghanistan, the other main American charge against the Tehran regime is its pursuit of a nuclear warhead. This is looked at in more detail in the following chapter.

Notes

1. George W. Bush, speech to the National Endowment for Democracy, Washington, 6 November 2003.

2. *Financial Times*, 7 May 2003.

3. *Financial Times*, 10 June 2003.

4. 'The Moment of Truth?', AEI, 30 May 2003.

5. Speech to the American–Iranian Council, 13 March 2002.

6. India Office Board's Drafts, Sec. Despatch to India, vol. 21, 23 November 1854.

7. *Time*, 4 August 2002.

8. AFP, 12 October 1998.

9. BBC News, 21 May 1999.

10. Author's correspondence with Anthony Davis, *Jane's Defence Weekly* correspondent, June 2003.

11. *Middle East International*, 28 June 2002.

12. *New York Times*, 17 June 2003,

13. Khalilzad, speech to the American–Iranian Council, 13 March 2002.

14. *New York Times*, 23 April 2003,

15. Information to the author from a Western diplomat, Tehran, 12 November 2003.

16. Information supplied to the author by Kurdish eyewitness, London, October 2003.

17. Author's interview with Kurdish eyewitness, London, 15 August 2003.

18. Author's interview with KDP representative, London, 20 October 2003.

19. Author's interview with senior Kurdish official, September 2003.

20. Author's interview with former Western ambassador to Iran, 18 September 2003.

21. Interview on Free Iraq TV, 24 April 2003.

22. *Washington Times*, 27 April 2003.

23. *Daily Telegraph*, 19 September 2002.

24. *Guardian*, 29 March 2003.

25. Author's interview with SCIRI representative, London, 3 July 2003.

26. See generally Anthony Cordesman and Ahmed S. Hashim, *Iraq: Sanctions and Beyond* (Boulder, CO and Oxford: Westview Press, 1997), pp. 101–2.

27. *Daily Telegraph*, 5 March 2003.

28. *Washington Post*, 7 March 2003.

29. Author's correspondence with independent Western observer, June 2003.

30. Interview with the author, Tehran, 12 November 2003.

31. *Newsweek*, 28 April 2003.

32. *Christian Science Monitor*, 25 September 2003; this view was reiterated to the author by Western diplomats in Tehran.

33. *Daily Telegraph*, 20 September 2002.

34. *National Review Online*, 9 September 2002.

35. *Daily Telegraph*, 20 September 2002.

4 | An Iranian bomb?

For all the differences over Iran that lie between them, there is one
nightmare vision that has united America and the member-states of the
European Union: the prospect of a nuclear warhead being held firmly
in the hands of an Islamist regime linked with Middle Eastern terror
groups and also well positioned to target Tel Aviv and even some capitals of Western Europe. But as the Iranians have continued to actively
develop an ostensibly peaceful nuclear programme that may perhaps
hide a covert military agenda, just such a scenario has in recent years
become far from remote.

Western concerns have been temporarily alleviated by the Iranian
decision of 21 October 2003 to 'engage in full co-operation' with the
International Atomic Energy Agency (IAEA) and thereby reassure the
outside world that its peaceful energy programme, which the deal does
allow, is not used as a cover for any such military agenda. Although Iran
has always been a signatory of the 1968 Nuclear Non-Proliferation Treaty
(NNPT), the October deal obliges it to respect an additional protocol,
to which all of the treaty's other members have been signatory since
1997, that gives international inspectors much more sweeping powers.
Iran is now obliged, for example, to disclose a 'general description and
information specifying the location of nuclear research and development
activities not involving nuclear material', and to 'provide the Agency
with access to any location specified by the Agency [and] to carry out
location-specific environmental sampling'. Moreover the Iranians have
also agreed to suspend their existing programme for the processing of
heavily enriched uranium (HEU), a main ingredient for any warhead,
and instead accept deliveries of enriched uranium, from some other
approved source, that would later be sent back to its country of origin
to prevent its misuse. The IAEA has also professed itself satisfied by
documentation supplied by the Iranians intended to account for all its
past nuclear activities.

But in the foreseeable future there are a number of reasons why
this agreement nevertheless seems most unlikely to conclusively ban-
ish Western fears about Iran's weapons programme.[1] The agreement
includes no firm definition of what constitutes a 'suspension' of Iran's
enrichment programme, and while Tehran's negotiators have wanted

to continue with research and experimentation of its production, their Western counterparts have sought an outright ban on all such activities. Disagreement over such interpretations much increases the chances of the Iranians officially revoking such a suspension, which is in any case officially declared to be only a 'temporary' measure. 'It could last,' in the words of the chief Iranian negotiator, Hassan Rouhani, 'for one day or one year – it all depends on us.'

Even if the Tehran authorities ostensibly agree to respect the agreement, they could still conceivably force a hidden arms programme further underground, confirming Western fears that the agreement is 'a clever device, a way to divide Europe and America while giving the Iranians a public relations coup'.[2] This could involve efforts either covertly to enrich its own uranium or, alternatively, a bid secretly to divert used uranium – 'spent fuel' – from the reactor at Bushehr to develop the weapons-grade plutonium that can also be used to make a nuclear warhead.

It is also possible that disagreements will emerge over which sites IAEA personnel should have the right of immediate, unconditional access to inspect. Just as, during the 1990s, UN weapons inspectors in Iraq fought long-running battles with the Iraqi authorities over their right to visit the self-declared 'presidential palaces' of Saddam Hussein, so too have the Iranian authorities warned that the IAEA's inspections should not be allowed to compromise their 'sovereignty, national dignity or national security'. Some Iranian conservative clerics have gone further, adding that there should be no compromise, not just of 'national security', but of 'national dignity and pride'.

Any such dispute will undoubtedly spark a major international crisis with the USA and its allies, who have good reasons to fear the development of an Iranian nuclear bomb. Washington has long been concerned that any newly acquired nuclear status would embolden Iran's policies towards other states in the Middle East, not least by using the bomb, as Gerecht has claimed, 'as leverage to enhance their security and sphere of influence throughout the Middle East',[3] but also by encouraging militants in the region to adopt a yet more aggressive approach against the Israeli Defence Force. Moreover, because Iran would be the first self-declared enemy of the Jewish state and the first US-declared state sponsor of terrorism to acquire nuclear arms, Washington clearly has some reason to fear that the regime could transfer warheads into the hands of terrorist networks that, as President Bush has pointed out, 'are hungry for these weapons and would use them without a hint of conscience'. An Iranian bomb would also be at risk of inadvertently falling into the hands of third parties, just as the weapons programmes of all developing countries, rife with corruption and bedevilled by poor security arrangements, are similarly vulnerable.

Some of these points were detailed in a report of the US Department of Defense issued in 1997:

> Tehran strives to be a leader in the Islamic world and seeks to be the dominant power in the Gulf. The latter goal brings it into conflict with the United States. Tehran would like to diminish Washington's political and military influence in the region. Iran also remains hostile to the ongoing Middle East peace process and supports the use of terrorism as an element of policy.

America and its allies have several options in trying to prevent their nightmare scenario from becoming a dangerous reality. The most extreme is the use or threat of military force against known Iranian facilities, an option that some Washington hawks have urged the White House strongly to consider if the Iranian nuclear project ever approaches completion. Reports have also emerged that Israel's National Security Council, in weighing up its options in dealing with the rapid development of Iran's main nuclear reactor at Bushehr, have considered 'using force to prevent Tehran from achieving nuclear weapons capabilities' that constitute 'a huge concern' for the Jewish state.[4] Tel Aviv had already deployed the same tactics to brilliant effect against the emergent Iraqi nuclear programme in 1981, when during Operation Babylon its warplanes had struck and destroyed the Iraqi Osirak nuclear reactor, an act that paid stark testimony to the warnings of premier Menachem Begin, who asserted that no enemy of Israel would be allowed to have nuclear weapons, and of Agriculture Minister Ariel Sharon, who argued for a policy under which the development of nuclear weapons by a hostile regional power would constitute grounds for war. While few voices in Washington or Tel Aviv have openly argued for such a strike except as a very last resort, such an attack has not been ruled out by a US President who has said that 'all options' are open and by Israeli officials who 'will not take the Osirak option off the table'.[5] Its effectiveness would be highly questionable, however, without extremely accurate intelligence about the exact whereabouts of any key facility, and it is far from clear that information of such a quality is available to Western governments.

Washington could also use military means to try and hold Tehran to ransom by sponsoring armed Iranian dissident groups that could conceivably mount low-level guerrilla-style wars against the regime. This option is believed to have been aired in the Pentagon from the summer of 2003, when some senior officials proposed backing the militants of the MKO organization either to topple the regime from within or to make US support for such a campaign conditional upon an Iranian compromise over its nuclear programme (Chapter 8). 'There are some who see the overthrow of the regime as the only way to deal with the danger of Iran possessing a nuclear weapon,' as one government official, closely linked to the White House, told the British *Sunday Telegraph*.[6]

If, on the other hand, the USA should choose to deploy only peaceful means in its bid to negate the Iranian programme, then several other options are open. Washington could, for example, flex its financial and economic muscle upon the programme's foreign sources of support, notably the Russian government, by applying what John Bolton, US Under-Secretary of State for Arms Control, called in congressional testimony 'the logic of adverse consequences'. Because this would be in contravention of the October deal, however, which allows Iran the right to import approved foreign sources of uranium, the USA could instead offer the Iranian government powerful incentives to freeze or renounce its programme, incentives that range from the ending of ex-ecutive and legislative trade sanctions, the return of financial assets held since the 1979 Revolution and the provision of economic assistance in areas such as the development of energy resources that would be of mutual benefit. This option has, for example, been strongly favoured by some senior figures in US politics, such as the former Democratic Party Congressman Lee Hamilton, who has argued that 'while we have to keep uppermost the nuclear-weapon component of our policy, at the same time we ought to try to engage Iran'.[7] Finally, Washington can simply continue to threaten severe financial penalties against Iran should it appear to renege on its obligations, reporting any possible violations to the United Nations and thereby paving the way for the imposition of devastating economic sanctions against an already stricken economy.

What, then, has helped to create this state of tension between Iran and much of the outside world? And has it in any respect been aggra-vated by the behaviour and policies of the US government?

The West's nightmare scenario

The Tehran regime has never disputed that it is pursuing its own nuclear programme but has always claimed, in the words of President Khatami, that this project is only 'focused on civilian applications and nothing else'. The possession of any warhead, its senior ministers claim, is an act of *haram* – something strictly forbidden by Islamic law – and 'inhuman, immoral, illegal and against our basic principles'.[8] The US government has from time to time claimed to have heard guarded references to such a weapons programme but these are far too imprecise to constitute any declaration of policy: in February 2003, for example, Washington hawks pointed to an interview with the conservative Iranian daily *Siasat-e Rouz* by Defence Minister Ali Shamkhani, who had argued that 'Iran's defence structure and future are based on a foundation of "strategic deterrent defence"', and that the country's 'defence and national security must be reflected in manufacturing new armaments so as to achieve deterrence'. But such remarks are, of course, far too vague to constitute any admission.

The Iranians have also long asserted that their ostensibly peaceful nuclear programme cannot realistically act as a cover for any military agenda because of the safeguards imposed by their long-standing membership of the Nuclear Non-Proliferation Treaty (NNPT), to which Iran has been a signatory since it was first drawn up in 1968. Even before its powers were extended by the later Additional Protocol, which in 2003 Iran agreed to respect, the 1968 treaty has always allowed international inspectors of the IAEA considerable powers to examine its nuclear facilities to prevent 'the diversion of nuclear energy from peaceful uses to nuclear weapons'. In the typical words of one spokesman for the Atomic Energy Association of Iran (AEAI), such powers have meant 'no nuclear activity or study without the knowledge of the IAEA: all our nuclear sites are for peaceful purposes and open to IAEA inspection'.

Tehran also points to the official and unofficial visits to suspected sites that inspectors have in the past been allowed to make. Two such random inspections were made in 1992 and 1993, for example, and although they were denied permission to carry out the full range of tests they wanted, the inspectors had subsequently concluded that the sites were intended only for peaceful ends. Some prearranged visits have also not yet yielded anything suspicious: in February 1992, the IAEA found one alleged nuclear research centre to be little more than a lecture hall and a Chinese-supplied reactor so small that it could barely produce isotopes for medical research. None of the IAEA's inspections, the Iranians continue, has as yet revealed any substantial breach of Iran's obligations. As the head of Iran's nuclear programme, Reza Aghazadeh, pointed out after an inspectors' report was announced in June 2003: 'There is no mention of the word "violation". The report only mentions "failure", which is still a debate between us. And these are normal differences.'

Even before the October 2003 deal, then, the Iranian authorities strongly argued that there was almost no chance that their nuclear programme could be abused. But such claims have never reassured much of the outside world, and these fears remain in spite of the additional safeguards. As detailed above, the Iranians could conceivably still covertly obtain either of the two fissile materials – plutonium or heavily enriched uranium – that lie at the heart of every nuclear weapons programme, either by constructing their own hidden enrichment plants or by diverting spent fuel from Bushehr to develop weapons-grade plutonium. No matter exactly how the Tehran government might succeed in obtaining these key fissile materials, it could then conceivably realize Washington's greatest fears by withdrawing from the 1968 treaty, giving the ninety-day notice period the agreement requires on the grounds that 'extraordinary events have jeopardized the supreme interests of its country'. At this point it could hide its fissile materials from the outside world as a safeguard against a pre-emptive attack before declaring itself, quite legally, to be a new nuclear power.

How Iran has built its nuclear programme

The mere possibility of such a 'break-out' scenario explains why the US government has tried to thwart any peaceful Iranian nuclear development ever since 1979, when the Shah bequeathed Khomeini an ambitious $20 billion programme to build twelve nuclear plants. Initial fears that this would provide the new regime with a quick route to a bomb were certainly unfounded, however, partly because the main reactor at Bushehr, begun in 1974, was at least three years off completion as the main contractors, the German firm Siemens and its subsidiary Kraftwerke Union, made a very swift departure from a country embroiled in political chaos. Any subsequent hopes that Tehran may have entertained of quickly resurrecting what the Germans had left behind were dashed when war broke out with Saddam Hussein the following year and Iraqi jets blasted the Bushehr reactor in six separate attacks launched on 24 March 1984, 12 February 1985, 5 March 1985, 12 July 1986 and on two separate occasions in November 1987. But although these raids devastated the reactors, the West German authorities noted that because none of the core equipment had been installed and vital components had been moved elsewhere, the Iranian nuclear project was certainly not written off.[9]

The issue of Iran's nuclear reactor emerged again at the end of both the eight-year Iran–Iraq conflict and the Cold War. In a deal that marked a major geopolitical shift for a country that had strongly backed Saddam Hussein during his war with the mullahs, the Russians signed a new trading agreement with Tehran after a landmark visit to Moscow by

President Rafsanjani in June 1989, and several defence agreements for the sale of warplanes, notably MiG-29s and Su-24s and three Kilo-class submarines, followed soon after. Three years later, in an agreement that deeply alarmed Washington, the Russians also agreed to start rebuilding the remnants of the Bushehr reactor for 'the peaceful uses of atomic energy' and also to provide some nuclear research units to enrich the uranium that Moscow would also be willing to supply.

It was not just Russian support that Tehran enlisted at this time for its newly emergent nuclear programme. The Chinese government secretly agreed in principle to supply Iran with two nuclear power reactors and in 1991 approved the export of around two tons of uranium hexafluoride, a crucial ingredient for the complex process by which uranium is enriched to make fissile material. Tehran also approached potential sympathizers inside the Pakistani government, then busily constructing their own bomb, and as one independent watchdog has since written, 'Pakistan's assistance may have been crucial to the Iranian effort to develop a centrifuge programme'.[10] The CIA later claimed that the Pakistani nuclear genius, Abdul Qadeer Khan, who had long masterminded Islamabad's own programme, had made at least one trip to Tehran, travelling in disguise in a secret bid to assist the Iranians in enriching a large quantity of uranium concentrate. It is likely that the assistance of Abdul Qadeer, who was being carefully watched by the Americans because of his earlier trips to North Korea, was purchased by Iranian agents who had offered a Pakistani general, Aslam Beg, significant sums in return for his support.[11] It has also subsequently emerged that the design pattern of Iran's centrifuges suggests that Pakistan may also have continued to support the Iranian programme some years later, after Islamabad first tested a nuclear device in May 1998, for reasons that currently remain unclear.[12]

Iranian agents were active wherever a possible source of nuclear materials was detected, allegedly acquiring uranium from South Africa in the late 1980s – although this claim has been much disputed – and soon afterwards making approaches to the authorities of Tajikistan, which had facilities not to enrich uranium but to convert the raw 'yellowcake' material to uranium oxide. Iran at this time also struck illicit deals with the Ulba Metallurgical Plant in Kazakhstan, a vast complex that produced reactor fuel and where considerable quantities of highly enriched uranium had just been – as the CIA later put it – simply 'left behind' when the USSR fell apart.[13] Tehran's plan to buy large amounts of its HEU was discovered almost by chance by a US team that happened to be visiting the plant and saw packages, all ready for export, clearly labelled for Iran.[14]

The US authorities, watching many of these developments with alarm, lobbied hard to forestall all international assistance to the re-emergent nuclear programme, even though it was being pursued under IAEA safeguards. In 1994 the Clinton administration persuaded Beijing to terminate its nuclear assistance to Iran, an agreement that three years later formed part of an official US–Chinese deal to implement peaceful nuclear co-operation. With Moscow, however, Washington had a much more difficult task and could not prevent the Russian Atomic Energy Minister, Viktor Mikhailov, from signing a new $800 million contract in January 1995 to rebuild two 1,000-megawatt light-water generators at Bushehr where vast complexes and workshops were also to be constructed. Moreover, despite immense US pressure to call off the deal, notably at the Moscow summit[15] four months later, the Russians secretly added to this deal by agreeing to supply the Iranians with key fuel cycle facilities, including light-water research reactors, fuel fabrication facilities and an uranium-enrichment centrifuge plant.

Moscow claimed, quite convincingly, that its own reactors could not be used to make weapons-grade plutonium any more easily than many other reactors to which the USA was turning a blind eye or whose development it was even supporting: 'We are only talking about peaceful economic co-operation to the military – we can offer no help to Iran in making nuclear weapons,' as government spokesman Alexei Gorshkov later argued. But the real reasons for the Kremlin's obstinacy towards US pressure went much deeper. There was at times perhaps at least a streak of old Cold War rivalry, coupled with resentment at the subsequent loss of Russian status, discernible in the attitude of a former Soviet *apparatchik*, Yevgeny Adamov, who was appointed as the new Minister of Atomic Energy ('Minatom') in March 1998 and who nodded approval to a new 'upswing of co-operation' with the Iranian nuclear programme.[16] The main reason, however, was the simple financial desperation of a government that urgently needed foreign exchange. Moreover, the Russian government's chronic shortage of cash meant that thousands of Minatom's highly skilled scientists were going unpaid and were therefore vulnerable to the direct approaches of foreign governments or to the headhunting skills of Russian mobsters who wanted to upgrade old military equipment before selling it on to international buyers. Moscow often simply lacked the resources to prevent this illicit trade, just as the then Georgian President, Eduard Shevardnadze, was later forced to admit that a number of his republic's scientists, including nuclear physicists and aircraft engineers, had been working in Iran on private contracts that his government had not authorized but which they had been unable to stop.[17]

Russian support has since proved instrumental to the continuing development of Iran's ostensibly peaceful nuclear programme. Taking over as President from Boris Yeltsin in 2000, Vladimir Putin strongly defended Russia's right to provide Iran with nuclear power reactors, partly because of the obvious financial benefits – Russia stood to gain as much as $1 billion by continuing to develop the Bushehr project – but also in reaction to the existence of what the new President called a 'unipolar world' dominated by 'US hegemony'. But whether motivated more by financial or geo-strategic considerations, Iran and Russia had self-proclaimedly opened a 'new chapter' in their military relations following a visit to Tehran in December 2000 by the Russian Defence Minister, Igor Sergeyev, who made an announcement, alongside his Iranian counterpart, Admiral Ali Shamkhani, of further military and defence co-operation between the two capitals. The previous month Moscow had also renounced a 1995 agreement with the USA to bring an end to the sale of conventional weapons to Iran,[18] a renunciation that has since allowed Iran, taking 10 per cent of the Russian defence market, to become the Kremlin's biggest arms customer after China and India.

In the course of 2002, it had become clear that these promises had borne some fruit, as details of a new light-water reactor, built with Russian help, came to light in the spring and when in July Moscow casually announced the construction of five nuclear reactors in Iran, dismissing Western security concerns as 'groundless fears' that ignored the 'peaceful, economic co-operation with no connection to the military'. This project, which formed part of a much broader ten-year economic co-operation plan, involved the building of three more light-water reactors at the Bushehr site and another two at a new power station at Ahvaz, 65 miles from the Iraqi border.

Unanswered questions about Iran's nuclear programme

American concern about the Iranian nuclear programme is not just based upon the way in which the resources for any peaceful nuclear programme could potentially be diverted to a military programme. There are instead more specific reasons why it has long raised eyebrows in Washington.

Part of this mistrust focuses on the essential premise upon which the Iranians claim their nuclear programme is based. Washington has long argued that Iran has no need for nuclear energy because the country is superbly endowed with natural resources of oil and gas that are significantly cheaper to develop. As the White House spokesman, Ari Fleischer, has argued:

Such facilities are simply not justified by the needs that Iran has for their civilian nuclear programme. Our assessment when we look at Iran is that there is no economic gain for a country rich in oil and gas like Iran to build costly indigenous nuclear fuel cycle facilities. Iran flares ('burns') off more gas every year than the equivalent power that it hopes to produce with these reactors.

While the Americans claim that this clearly points to a hidden, darker agenda, the Iranians retort that a nuclear energy programme would release up to 190 million barrels of crude oil, worth $5 billion, for export every year and back their argument up by pointing to statements made by some EU spokesmen that acknowledge these claims[19] and by alleging that Iran is not the only oil-producing country that has sought to develop nuclear energy. Tehran also points out that its own viewpoint was once taken by US administrations, which in the 1960s and 1970s had encouraged the Shah to develop his own nuclear programme on exactly the same grounds, and to prove their point highlight one study by Stanford University in 1972 that recommended 'the building of nuclear plants capable of generating a 20,000 MW nuclear-energy programme'. This support led the Shah to give the go-ahead for the construction of twenty-two power reactors that were intended to be operational within twenty years. Expert opinion is still divided, however, on whether such considerations would justify spending the billions of dollars needed to build reactors and the much higher costs of producing nuclear energy rather than using natural gas.

Another aspect of the Iranian programme that has deeply alarmed Washington is the highly furtive manner in which it has sometimes been pursued, a furtiveness that seems barely consistent with its obligations under the 1968 treaty. This tendency became clear in December 2002 when Tehran disclosed the existence of two secret nuclear plants that had been detected the previous summer by US satellites and then subsequently raised as a matter of concern by the IAEA. What the international inspectors found on their visits of 21–22 February 2003 caught both the agency and the outside world by surprise. For at the main site, near Natanz, 40 km south east of Kashan, was a huge and 'extremely advanced' facility to house gas centrifuges that enrich uranium, 160 of which were already in operating order, ready to test and process the uranium hexafluoride gas that constitutes the raw materials of the enrichment process. The site had the capacity for perhaps 50,000 more centrifuges, held in at least 1,000 specially designed machines, that could potentially feed a 1,000-MW reactor.

The existence of the sites, which were not expected to become operational until at least the summer of 2003, did not technically violate the terms of either the 1968 treaty or of its 1976 subsidiary arrangements. These agreements, to which Tehran was signatory, obliged the Iranians to inform the inspectors 'of design information on a new facility no later than 180 days before the introduction of nuclear material into the facility', a much less stringent requirement than the later Additional Protocol, which it had not as yet signed, that would have obliged it to inform the IAEA of the plant's design information as soon as its construction was first authorized. Moreover, the Iranians had a plausible answer to allegations that the plants were rendered unnecessary by the Russian agreement to supply the Bushehr reactor with fuel: their planned expansion of nuclear energy over the next two decades, they retorted, which would create a total 6,000-MW capacity, gave them a vested interest in self-sufficiency, just in case Russian support was ever imperilled. But their behaviour still left many awkward questions unanswered. If this was what they really intended, why had they kept so quiet about the existence of the sites? And as the Americans legitimately asked, would they have come forward to inform the IAEA of its undeclared activities if they had not first been picked up by satellite? Tehran's silence gave a good impression of having something to hide and revealed a fundamental lack of co-operation that was criticized by the head of the IAEA, Mohamed el Baradei. This impression was reinforced by Iranian claims that they had never enriched uranium at all, a claim that independent inspectors say is quite unconvincing, since 'only after conducting tests and developing an optimized centrifuge design would a country build a pilot plant', such as the one at Natanz.[20]

Soon after this revelation, Tehran made matters worse by announcing the existence of other sites that, although once again quite plausibly intended only for a peaceful nuclear programme just as much as a military one, had for some time also been kept secret from the outside world. In a television announcement on 9 February, President Khatami announced that deposits of uranium 'yellowcake' had been discovered in the Savand region, 200 km from the central city of Yazd, and that steps had already been taken to mine them. An uranium oxide plant had also been established at Isfahan, he continued, to produce the hexafluoride and oxide that are derived from the basic yellowcake.

The question of why Iran was choosing to keep so much hidden from international inspectors in a manner that was against the spirit, if not the letter, of its international requirements continued to arise. In June, spokesmen for the National Council of Resistance of Iran, the political wing of the MKO dissident organization, claimed to have discovered evidence of two previously undisclosed uranium enrichment facilities in the Hasthgerd region near Karaj, 25 miles west of Tehran, that had been in existence since 2000. Both places, it claimed, were 'smaller, dispersed sites used for uranium enrichment' that operated as satellite plants to the much larger facility at Natanz, and both could be used as back-up sites in case of any military attack. Although the claims are to date unverified, the source had often been proved to be an accurate source of information.[21]

At the same time, the NCRI also pointed UN inspectors to another site, the Kalaye Electric Company in Tehran, where it claimed centrifuges were being assembled that could be used to test uranium hexafluoride. Although the Iranians admitted to making centrifuge components at the plant, they flatly denied either assembling them or using the end products for testing uranium, and they refused to allow UN inspectors access. Again, although this refusal did not technically violate the 1968 treaty, which allows inspectors a right of access only to sites officially acknowledged to be used for nuclear purposes, their actions confirmed the same doubts about how genuine their declared co-operation really was: as one Western diplomat succinctly put it, 'it doesn't help Iran in its claim that their nuclear programme is open, transparent and honest.'[22] Such suspicions seemed to be well founded when, two months later, IAEA inspectors were finally granted permission to enter the premises and found that the plant had been substantially rebuilt as if to cover tracks.

The CIA also asserts that several other sites are secretly linked to a covert nuclear programme. One is Sharif University of Technology in Tehran, considered by the CIA to be an important research centre for a covert nuclear weapons programme and one that was linked to a 1991 Iranian bid to import cylinders of fluoride, suitable for processing enriched material, and specialized magnets, used for centrifuges, from a factory in Thyssen, West Germany.[23]

There are other, more particular, questions that the Iranian nuclear programme has prompted but which its spokesmen have failed to answer. The head of the AEAI, Gholamreza Aghazadeh, has admitted that Iran is actively seeking uranium metal but has to date failed to explain why Iran attaches such importance to a material that has few civilian uses but which is a key ingredient for nuclear weapons, even regarded by most experts as a key indicator of the weapons programme. Small quantities of uranium ore that had been illicitly imported from China in 1991 were converted to uranium metal even though, as the IAEA inspection report claimed in 2003, 'the role of uranium metal in Iran's declared nuclear fuel cycle still needs to be fully understood, since neither its light-water reactors nor its planned heavy-water reactors require uranium metal for fuel'.[24] It was in this regard also significant that the Iranian authorities had in 1991 failed to inform the IAEA of the ore's importation, a failure the IAEA later labelled 'a matter of concern'.

The Iranians are also self-admittedly building a 40-MW research reactor at Arak that uses 'heavy water'– ordinary water enriched in deuterium, a hydrogen isotope – that is often used in particular types of nuclear reactor. But if Bushehr and all known Iranian reactors use only light water, didn't this mean that the Iranians must be building or planning a new reactor for the heavy water, one that they hadn't yet declared? In any case, spent fuel from a heavy-water reactor is usually ideal for the extraction of weapons-grade plutonium as the experience of the North Korean government, which claimed to have produced several nuclear devices from the spent fuel of its own 5-MW reactor, testified.

Iran's missile programme

The considerable efforts made by the Iranian authorities to develop a long-range missile have also raised further questions about its nuclear programme. For although Tehran has always denied that any such missile would carry a nuclear warhead, this claim is disputed by many military experts, who argue that the costs of developing the missile really make sense only if intended to do so. Martin Indyck, the Assistant Secretary of State for Near East Affairs, testified to the Senate Foreign Relations Committee on 28 July 1998 that the missile programme was clearly linked to the nuclear programme, a view endorsed by independent experts such as Gary Milhollin, a director of the Wisconsin Project, who argues that 'no country has ever built a long-range ballistic missile without a nuclear weapon to put on it. They just don't make sense otherwise. You don't use a long-range missile to deliver anything except a nuclear warhead.'[25]

The Iranians have long openly admitted their efforts to develop such a missile. On 7 July 2003, more than a year after initial trials at desert sites near Qom and Qasr-e-Bahram were reported to have failed disastrously,[26] the Iranian military successfully test-fired and officially inaugurated the Shahab 3 (S3), capable of carrying a 700-kg warhead a distance of up to 1,300 km. Although it was not powerful enough to carry a nuclear warhead, its launch sent shockwaves of alarm through Israel, which for the first time suddenly found itself within striking distance of a regime that had always voiced an implacable opposition to its existence. In the words of Defence Minister Shaul Mofaz, the Shahab's inauguration was an 'extremely dangerous' development that unmistakeably posed 'both a threat and a danger' to his country's national security.

Although the Iranian authorities boasted of the S3's inauguration to the outside world, they naturally continued to keep very quiet about how they had succeeded in developing it, claiming only that 'Iran's defence industries can produce any conventional weapons the political authorities may want, since we are 100 per cent self-sufficient in possessing the technology'.[27] Such claims were hardly taken seriously because the missile in fact blended the expertise of two countries, Russia and North Korea, that the military procurement wing of the Revolutionary Guard Corps had heavily courted ever since the S3 programme had started in the mid-1990s. Based originally on the North Korean NoDong missile, a single-stage, liquid-fuelled and single-engine missile whose details Pyongyang is thought to have leaked to Tehran in 1994, the S3 also bears hallmarks of extensive Russian modification. Its rocket engine, for instance, is based on the Russian SS4 missile that Iran succeeded in obtaining in 1998, while Russian sources have also provided Iranian technicians with high-grade steel and special alloys to provide specialized casing and shielding of its guidance systems. Iranian dissident sources have also claimed that Tehran has since signed a $7 million contract with a Russian company for the transfer of SS4 missile parts.

The immense efforts made by the Iranian authorities to acquire the hardware and expertise needed to develop the S3 had not gone altogether unnoticed by foreign intelligence. Both the CIA and the Israelis have tracked, for example, the movements of a Russian military team as it took control of a mothballed missile production facility and subsequently transported spare parts for the SS4 'piece by piece' to Iran.[28] The USA had also identified a number of Russian companies believed to be assisting the Iranian missile programme, pressing Moscow to investigate them and end the support they give. From the beginning of 1998, acting under considerable US pressure, the Russian government took a series of steps to strengthen its export-control system, cancelling some contracts between various companies and their Iranian clients and passing a new export-control law in July 1999 that gave the government considerably more legal authority to investigate and punish legal entities that were illicitly exporting material in support of overseas WMD programmes. But these efforts did not stop Iran from approaching, in violation of Russian law, smaller and more obscure companies and individuals whose goods managed to slip through a bureaucratic net that was in any case both cumbersome and cast only sporadically.

In their bid to develop a two-stage solid-fuel missile that would improve the performance of its long-range Shahab missiles, the Iranians have also approached North Korean and Chinese companies. By the summer of 2003, fifteen Chinese companies had been subjected to US sanctions for their alleged attempts to 'make a material contribution to weapons of mass destruction' that violated the terms of its Non-Proliferation Act 2000. A few of these companies had just joined the list for the first time, such as the Taian Foreign Trade General Corporation of China, the Zibo Chemical Equipment Plant of China, the Liyang Yunlong Chemical Equipment Group of China and the China Precision Machinery Import/Export Corporation. But another name on the list, Norinco (China North Industries), China's vast state-owned industrial conglomerate, was an old offender. Having started off in the weapons trade in the early 1980s, it had first been identified by US officials in 1984 as a partner in a bid to smuggle high-tech military equipment from the USA to China, while a few years later one of its subsidiaries, Rex International, was closed by the British authorities in Hong Kong after allegedly selling chemical weapons precursors to Iran. In May 2003, Washington alleged that Norinco, one of the most influential state-owned businesses in China, had supplied ballistic-missile components to Iran and imposed sanctions that were expected to deprive the company of more than $200 million in exports to the USA over the next two years.

A North Korean attempt to ship missile parts to Iran via Yemen was also allegedly intercepted in December 2002 after its cargo was successfully tracked by US satellites. Since then, North Korean components have instead been flown to Iran in Il-76 cargo planes, including dissembled Rodong missiles, which have a 1,300-km range, that were flown in from Sunan airport.[29] A North Korean firm, Changgwang Sinyong Corporation, was also sanctioned by the USA in July 2003 under the same terms as fifteen Chinese companies.

Since the onset of the US war in Iraq, American officials have also claimed that some senior Iraqi scientists have fled their homeland to Iran, selling their skills and experience to the regime's missile programme. Chief among these is Dr Modher Sadiq-Saba al-Tamimi, a Czech-educated scientist who has previously been responsible for the development of Saddam's Al-Samoud missile programme during the 1990s but who had found himself out of work after the fall of Saddam's regime.

Covert attempts to acquire nuclear materials

More suspicion about Iranian intent arises as a result of the activities of the illicit procurement network, run by its army's specially commissioned Atomic Unit, that has in recent years pursued spare parts for both its nuclear and missile programmes. Although these parts could plausibly be intended for a peaceful programme, many of them are 'dual-use' items that could be used for both military and civilian ends and there are some items from the network's nuclear 'shopping list' that are likely to be intended only for a weapons programme. As the former weapons inspector David Albright has argued, 'if you put all these things together, it's the kind of equipment you want to make to test a nuclear weapon and build a nuclear weapon'.[30] A report of the French government, obtained by the news agency AFP in August 2003, also pointed out that 'the list of Iranian purchasing attempts in the French nuclear industry and dual goods manufacturers clearly points to the development of large capacities in terms of reprocessing and spent fuel radiation'.[31]

The efforts of Iran's Defence Industries Organization, a state-owned company based in Tehran that works on behalf of the Iranian military, is central to the regime's bid to import the spare parts needed both for its nuclear programme as well as other military projects. To try to bypass the arms and trade embargoes imposed on Iran by the US and EU governments, the DIO has become adept at setting up sham companies throughout the world, although London, with strong links to both Europe and the United States, has hitherto been a particularly favoured location.

Sponsored by the IRGC and the Intelligence Ministry, the DIO has a long history of using such front companies to cover its activities. A cargo of arms that was exported by the Iranians in March 1996 on board the Iranian ship *Kolahdooz* was intercepted by the Belgian police at Antwerp and found to have been initially assembled by Jiroft Food Industries, a company affiliated to the IRGC and whose president was believed to have formerly been a serving member of the elite corps. Specially designed high-calibre mortars had been packed into food containers at the plant before being entrusted to a sea-transport company, Haml-e Varedat, whose main office was formerly located in central Tehran but which also had several subsidiary offices elsewhere in the country. The consignments were then finally registered under different names, the Mohammed Khorsand Merchant Company and Saeed Textiles, before being finally approved for export.

Since the early 1990s, many of these efforts have been focused on the nuclear and missile programmes. In 1993, the Italian authorities seized eight steam condensers, packaged and ready for export to Iran, that could have been used for a nuclear programme, while the following year reports emerged that Iranians had approached a number of German and Swiss firms to purchase the balancing machines and diagnostic and monitoring equipment that play a key role in the development of centrifuges. A British company was also contacted at this time as a possible supplier of samarium-cobalt magnetic equipment that can be used to make the top bearings of a centrifuge.[32] In November 2000, Tehran attempted to buy ten high-density radiation shielding windows from a French manufacturer and in 2002 an Iranian company based in the United Arab Emirates approached another French supplier with a view to obtaining twenty-eight remote manipulators that had the capacity to produce material with radioactive levels 'above the threshold' of the Nuclear Suppliers Group of nations committed to curbing nuclear proliferation.[33] In September 2003 US federal agents also arrested an Iranian man, Serzhik Avasappian, on charges of trying to smuggle $750,000 worth of restricted spare parts of F14 fighter aircraft to Iran in contravention of the Arms Export Control Act.[34]

Many similar operations have since been launched and sometimes only narrowly foiled. A typical operation was discovered by MI5 in July 1996 when one branch of the DIO, based in Dusseldorf, was found to have made regular payments to an Iranian businessman, Ali Ashgar Manzarpouri, in order to procure maraging steel, metal of a special strength that can be used to tip missiles and nuclear warheads, and for centrifuges required for the enrichment of uranium. The businessman had used false names to order the material from the USA and had arranged to have the delivery moved on arrival at Heathrow by lorry to mainland Europe. Before being subsequently tried and sentenced for transporting unlicensed materials he also claimed to have been regularly exporting goods to Iran's Ya Mahdi military industrial complex with the approval of Britain's Department of Trade and Industry.

Another such operation was undertaken by Multicore, a London-based company also known as AKS Industries, that sought to acquire the spare parts for Iranian fighter jets. Multicore staff had established themselves in Bakersfield, California, and purchased aircraft and missile components with $2.5 million that was paid into their US account. Always placing orders by phone and fax, and picking up deliveries only from parcel post companies like Federal Express and UPS, they were careful not to make direct contact with their suppliers in a bid to avoid arousing suspicion. Their tactics paid off and because they were representatives of a supposedly bona fide British-based company, the Iranian agents were able to export the large quantities of materials – about sixteen industrial pallets' worth of avionics equipment – that they had secretly stockpiled. Before being finally busted in 2002 after a surveillance operation by US Customs Services, the ring is thought to have tricked more than fifty US firms into shipping components into the hands of the fraudulent company.[35]

There are numerous other instances of Iranian agents making similar attempts to acquire the nuclear materials they need. One Birmingham-based company, Britannia Heat Transfer, was contacted in 2000 by a London export company that requested 500 pieces of tubing that is typically used for evaporative cooling in refrigerators and other cooling equipment but which could have been intended for either the Pakistani or Iranian nuclear projects; several British companies contacted MI5 when an Iranian-born businessman based in Glasgow made suspicious approaches to them about the purchase of high-tech mass spectrometers that can, among other uses, be used on nuclear weapons development. In 2002, a BBC investigation also claimed to have uncovered evidence, including listings in the UK government's annual report on strategic export controls, that other 'dual-use' technology, including furnaces, inertial equipment and perhaps the metal beryllium, had also been approved for export to unknown destinations.

The efficiency and success of this network has also been summarized by Albright, who has said that Iranian agents are good at seeing and exploiting weaknesses in export laws. 'Those who want nuclear weapons,' he has said, 'will assign their very top people to understand export control systems and find the weaknesses and exploit them.' The Iranians, he continues, 'understand the export control limits very well, and know that if they bought equipment above these limits it would be subject to export controls. They get round this by buying right under the limits.' Its track record is probably best judged by the fact that Iran has succeeded in 'getting together a centrifuge programme and a heavy-water production plant but certainly didn't do so from its indigenous efforts'.[36]

Has US policy aggravated the crisis?

Although all these unanswered questions about Iran's nuclear programme clearly give the outside world very strong grounds for serious concern, the sense of crisis that has recently characterized US–Iranian relations over the issue has none the less to some extent also been fuelled by sometimes questionable US reactions.

One such reaction is a tendency of some US officials to speak of their 'certainty' about the existence of a supposed Iranian nuclear weapons project instead of the mere 'likelihood' or 'probability' to which a series of unanswered questions point. By using such strong terms to describe the undoubted dangers posed by a nuclear Iran, the USA could run the same risks as those raised by its hitherto unverified claims of Iraqi WMD, overreacting in a way that alienates the international support it needs to put effective pressure on Iran.

This tendency to speak of 'proof' rather than 'likelihood' has emerged in the statements made by Defense Secretary Donald Rumsfeld, who has insisted that there is 'clear evidence' that Iran is trying to develop a nuclear warhead[37] and in the reports of the CIA, which has for the past decade been 'convinced' that Tehran is 'vigorously pursuing' the same programme.[38] Kenneth Brill, the US representative of the International Atomic Energy Agency (IAEA) in Vienna, has also spoken in the same vein, accusing Iran of 'aggressively pursuing a nuclear weapons programme'. But such terms have not been endorsed either by the EU or the IAEA, whose spokesmen have stopped short of stating that any such weapons programme exists and declared only that Iran's nuclear agenda, peaceful or otherwise, is 'a matter of concern'.[39] This view is also reiterated by the IAEA's November 2003 report on Iran's record of compliance with the obligations imposed by the 1968 treaty, which claims that 'there is no evidence that [Iran's] previously undeclared nuclear materials and activities ... were related to a nuclear weapons programme'. Their more cautious tone is also echoed by independent experts such as Hans Blix[40] and David Albright, who has spoken only of 'circumstantial evidence of a nuclear programme or ambitions', without question enough to justify international calls for far more openness on the part of the Iranians, and George Perkovich of the Carnegie Institute in Washington, who has pointed out that 'outsiders do not know exactly who makes Iran's decisions regarding nuclear weapons acquisition or what those decisions are'.[41] Similar differences had also arisen in 1995 when Zalmay Khalilzad, who had then recently left the UN National Security Council, reported that Iran had developed a $10 billion strategy for the acquisition of nuclear weapons, a claim strongly disputed by most Western experts.[42]

This same difference of emphasis also became clear in the autumn of 2003 when a new IAEA report declared that its inspectors had taken samples at Natanz revealing 'the possible presence in Iran of highly enriched uranium, material that is not on its inventory of declared nuclear material'. Although no one disputed Washington's position that any such step to enrich uranium without the IAEA's approval would amount to a serious violation of the 1968 treaty, US officials nevertheless appeared quick to dismiss Iranian claims that the nuclear equipment in question had already been contaminated before being brought into the country more than a decade before. And as US diplomats tried to rally support for their position, their position appeared prejudicial when an IAEA spokeswoman, Melissa Fleming, confirmed that the report was not conclusive and pointed out that 'it asks a lot more questions than it provides answers'.[43] The discovery of more traces of uranium a few weeks later at the Kalaye plant, where the contaminated centrifuges had been stored, certainly complicated and perhaps vindicated the Iranian claim.[44]

The vulnerability of American claims to charges of exaggeration also becomes evident from discussions of the completion date of any Iranian nuclear warhead. Most independent experts estimate that 'during the second half of this decade the Iranians could conceivably withdraw from the Non-Proliferation Treaty and start making nuclear weapons rapidly',[45] while others believe that the government hasn't as yet even given the final go-ahead for a weapons programme.[46] As Albright has argued, 'predictions of when Iran might succeed in building an indigenous capability to produce HEU or separated plutonium are fraught with uncertainty'.[47] By comparison, some US critics of Iran have sometimes given the impression of exaggerating the speed with which any such programme could be completed. Donald Rumsfeld has said, for example, that Iran will have nuclear weapons 'in a relatively short period of time'[48] and Michael Ledeen, writing in September 2002, claimed that 'the regime's leaders have told their doomsday scientists and technicians that they desperately want to demonstrate a nuclear capacity by the end of the year'.[49] Nine months later, Ledeen pushed his timetable back, claiming that 'some well-informed people now believe the regime is hoping to be able to test a device by the end of the summer'[50] and that 'the nuclear programme is on the verge of fulfilment'.[51]

Looked at from another angle, such black-and-white American terminology fails to acknowledge a subtle difference that lies halfway between the existence or complete lack of any weapons programme. Some of the 'evidence' of such a programme points not to any firm intention to develop such a warhead but instead to keeping open an option to develop such a programme at a later stage. This viewpoint is taken by some Western diplomats who have monitored the Iranian nuclear programme. 'If you look at the way in which the Iranians have tried to acquire materials, it doesn't seem to fit any actual pattern but is often much more incoherent. The most likely explanation is that they want to reach a level where they can go ahead and develop a warhead if in future the country's leaders decide that they should want to.'[52]

By using very sweeping terms to condemn Iran, US hawks not only risk sacrificing their own credibility but also unnecessarily pursuing heavy-handed policy options, such as a possible military strike on Bushehr or, as American officials have suggested,[53] an outright objection to even a peaceful nuclear programme conducted under stringent international scrutiny: in September 2003, for example, Britain had broken ranks with the USA on this issue and instead sided with a French and German offer to help Iran obtain nuclear fuel in return for the dismantling of the Natanz plant and for promising full co-operation with the UN.

But besides unnecessarily creating divisions between would-be allies, such heavy-handedness also plays into the hands of political hard-liners inside Iran who argue that the insubstantial nature of Washington's arguments reveals an ulterior motive against which all Iranians should guard themselves. For by forging an association between the Iranian nuclear programme and US diplomatic, economic or military pressure, the hard-liners are likely to stiffen a wider Iranian resolve not to be seen to cave in to international pressure. In this respect, a belligerent US diplomatic posture is open to charges of aggravating the possibility of a state of crisis between Tehran and Washington.

In June 2003, for example, as international tension over the nuclear programme reached a new height, Foreign Minister Kamal Kharrazi claimed that 'the USA has political aims vis-à-vis Iran of which the IAEA should stay clear'. And two months later, as pressure on Iran to sign up to the NNPT's Additional Protocol increased, Islamic conservatives were quick to warn their fellow Iranians that signing up would mean sacrificing their national independence to a Western 'conspiracy' that was enforced by inspectors 'acting on behalf of America, Israel and the EU', who would go around 'sticking their noses in all over the place' while helping 'the conspiracy of America, its allies and the UN against the existence of the Islamic Republic'. Some media voices even called for Tehran to withdraw from the NNPT altogether, including the conservative paper *Entekhab*, which splashed the headline 'Growing Opposition to Signature of Additional Protocol' on its front pages, and the head of the judiciary, Mahmoud Hashemi Shahroudi, who claimed on 4 August that 'the Iranian leadership, with the support of the people, will not give in to pressure and the representatives of the people and the students will resist America's aim to impose its will by force'. The IAEA's alleged interest, claimed other newspapers, was 'a calculated conspiracy aimed at overthrowing the Islamic Republic of Iran' (*Keyhan*) by 'international bullies and blackmailers' (*Jomhuri-ye Eslami*) and 'hegemonic powers'

(Iranian State TV). 'The fact of the matter,' the editor of *Keyhan* argues, 'is that all international bodies, including the UN and IAEA, in some way have to yield to the interests of the biggest power in the world, which now happens to be the United States.'[54]

Moreover, an aggressive diplomatic tone from Washington is apt to make its own accusations self-fulfilling in the same way as US allegations about Iranian intervention in Iraq and Afghanistan, since by convincing mainstream Iranian opinion of the inevitability of American antipathy, no matter what course is taken, such rhetoric gives an incentive to develop the very nuclear capabilities it is supposed to deter (see Introduction). This danger has been recognized by independent weapons experts such as Albright, who argue that 'if the US threatens Iran, then Iran may launch a crash nuclear programme whereby it could conceivably realize its capabilities in a much shorter space of time', thereby making hawkish predictions self-fulfilling.

Iranian fears of an ulterior motive lying behind US allegations of a covert weapons programme have also been exacerbated by Washington's perceived double standards. Since 1994, for example, the Tehran authorities have asked why Washington has condemned their own bid to rebuild Bushehr, having struck a $4.6 million deal to provide North Korea with light-water reactors in return for dismantling two existing nuclear facilities. And throughout Iran, and in the wider Islamic world, many repeatedly ask why the same US administrations that condemn Iran so vociferously are also so silent about Israel's nuclear capabilities. 'Why don't you make the same protest against Israel?' protested Amir Mohebian, an unofficial adviser to the Supreme Leader, with an indignation shared across the spectrum of Iranian politics. As a leading advocate of political reform inside Iran, Mustafa Tajzadeh, has argued in typical vein, 'On the one hand Israel says, "If I don't have it, I don't have security," and we say "As long as Israel has it, we don't have security."'[55] Such protests were also aired in very public fashion at a joint Iranian–Syrian summit on 9 December 2002, when Kamal Kharrazi and Syrian President Bashar Assad called for urgent international action against Israel's arms arsenal.

Surrounded and outnumbered by hostile regional forces, Israel may of course have quite legitimate reasons to possess the nuclear capabilities that it is currently widely accepted to have had since the mid-1960s.[56] But the US government has to date failed to explain why the supposed nuclear programme of a country that is a signatory member of the Non-Proliferation Treaty is more of a risk to regional stability than a neighbour that not only already possesses such a weapon but which has not signed up to the 1968 treaty. It is 'unacceptable' and 'regrettable', spokesmen for Egypt, Syria and Saudi Arabia protested before the UN General Assembly in September 2003, that 'some quarters are ignoring the Israeli arsenal of weapons of mass destruction' and 'the rejection of Israel in not joining the treaty'.[57]

Washington's case for urgent action against Iran also appears to be moderated by the fact that any efforts by the Iranian authorities to finalize such a weapons programme would be extremely difficult to hide from the highly focused eyes of the outside world. In such a scenario, the Iranians would have to take spent reactor fuel from Bushehr and reprocess it to extract plutonium, a task that requires the construction of a large and unmissable reprocessing plant. The alternative method of enriching uranium also involves the reconfiguration and testing of centrifuges that in the absence of extremely sophisticated abatement technology is equally difficult to disguise both from satellite thermal imaging and also from the international inspectors who can detect, monitor and analyse the chemical discharges from these plants. The immense difficulty of disguising such a programme, and of shielding it from a prospective military attack, is made clear from the fact that the outside world, in the words of a leading authority on the Iranian nuclear programme, 'knows where Iran's main production sites are. Natanz will be where they'll make enriched uranium and Arak is where they'll make plutonium.'[58]

Washington has hitherto also failed to explain why the Iranian authorities would not be deterred from using first-strike capabilities or pursuing any policy of nuclear brinkmanship by the prospect of Israeli or American retaliation that would be both immediate and massive. Some US spokesmen, for example, appear to have made unconvincing suggestions that unelected elites are less likely to be deterred by this mutually assured destruction than their elected counterparts elsewhere in the world: Khalilzad has argued that 'it is a particularly dangerous prospect for an Iranian government – not accountable to the Iranian people and supporting terrorists – to acquire nuclear weapons',[59] and although few do not share his concerns about such materials being transferred into the hands of third parties, any such suggestion failed to explain why unelected rulers are less easily deterred than their democratically elected counterparts. The near-hysterical scenes in some Indian cities in December 2001 and June 2002, as huge crowds shouted their enthusiasm for a nuclear attack on Pakistan, amply illustrate the limits of Khalilzad's argument.

There are also respects in which Iran, should it ever develop a warhead, would probably be a cause of less concern than some other countries that already have them in their possession. Pakistan, for example, has had a long-standing enmity with India that on previous occasions, notably during the summers of 1990 and 2002, has taken governmental fingers to the verge of pressing the nuclear trigger. And although the current Iranian regime, like most other Islamic countries, has always openly declared its hostility to the state of Israel, there is no dispute of sovereignty between the two countries comparable to the status of Kashmir, over which India and Pakistan have quarrelled since 1947 and which has sparked three major confrontations and threatened several more. Moreover, neither of the two south-west Asian countries is a signatory to the 1968 Non-Proliferation Treaty and elements of the Pakistani government, notably its Inter-Services Intelligence, have had ties with terrorist groups linked to Al Qaeda just as elements within the Iranian regime have their own protégés in the Middle East.

Iran also wholly lacks the same track record of unwarranted aggressive war that gave the USA and its allies strong grounds for concern about the alleged weapons programme of Saddam's Iraq. 'Iran has never been an aggressor against any of its neighbours,' claimed government spokesman Hassan Mashhadi, pointing out that his country had been the victim, not the perpetrator, of foreign invasions such as the Iraqi incursion in 1980 and the allies' wartime partition of Iran in 1941. Although it has always asserted its sovereignty over the Shatt al-Arab waterway, a region long disputed with Iraq, and over the islands in the Straits of Hormuz, he convincingly argued that Tehran had always seen this as a legal and diplomatic contest, not a military one: 'Iran is merely trying to claim its natural position in the region, and some countries are trying to deny it that role.' This view is also reiterated by some Western diplomats: 'The real reason why I would hate to see Tehran get a nuclear warhead is not because of any threat it poses but because it would give a huge boost in prestige to the current regime.'[60]

Instead, some of Washington's claims about the likely behaviour of the Iranian authorities, should they acquire nuclear weapons, have been open to question. Zalmay Khalilzad, for example, has argued that Iranian leaders 'have made threatening references to use a potential Islamic nuclear capability against Israel' and Michael Ledeen that 'Rafsanjani gave a speech many months ago in which he said that the moment Iran obtained nuclear weapons they would be used to destroy Israel'.[61] But the views put forward by the chairman of the Expediency Council at Friday prayers in Tehran on 14 December 2001 were far from being any statement of official government policy and instead seemed to be merely an accurate portrayal of where the balance of power would in future lie: 'If a day comes when the world of Islam is duly equipped with the arms Israel has in its possession, the strategy of colonialism would face a stalemate because the application of an atomic bomb would not leave anything in Israel but the same thing would just produce damage in the Muslim world [that can] still inflict greater costs on the imperialists.'

Another statement by the former President, made a few weeks later, referred only to the use of armed force in general but certainly not to nuclear weapons in particular: 'Developments over the last few months really frightened the Americans. That is a cost in itself. Under special circumstances, such costs may be inflicted on the imperialists by people who are fighting for their rights or by Muslims.' One speech upon which much attention has been focused, and which is sometimes quoted as evidence of Tehran's bad intent, was made by the head of the Revolutionary Guard, Yahya Rahim-Safavi, before fellow officers at Qom in April 1998. Safavi asked: 'Can we withstand America's threats and domineering attitude with a policy of détente? Can we foil dangers coming from America through a dialogue of civilizations? Will we be able to protect the Islamic Republic from international Zionism by signing conventions banning the proliferation of chemical and nuclear weapons?' But although some US commentators claimed that this speech raised 'unsettling questions about the willingness of at least some conservative hard-liners to adhere to Iran's arms-control commitments',[62] it is clear that the remarks were not only the personal views of an individual who had no role in making policy but could in any case be interpreted in several different ways. As one commentator has asked, why should the IRGC commander protest against the presidential decision to conform to international obligations if Iran's Supreme National Council had decided to pursue a covert weapons programme? And if hard-line elites within the regime really are in a position to pursue their own agenda, as the Americans allege, why did Safavi feel the need to complain, if indeed these remarks did amount to a complaint at all?[63]

Most independent experts think that such nightmare scenarios misapprehend the real reasons behind any covert nuclear weapons programme. The regime's leaders, as George Perkovich has argued, instead have in mind much more defensive and symbolic ideas:

> They intuit that the bomb will keep all outside powers, including Israel and the US, from thinking they can dictate to Iran or invade it. A nuclear weapons capability also will demonstrate the brilliance and technical prowess of the great Persian civilization. In particular, Shia Iranians may feel that the bomb would demonstrate and reinsure their

general superiority over their mostly Sunni Arab rivals. In sum, Iranian nationalists see nuclear weapons as an expression and guarantor of self-reliance, independence and, at the global level, equality with other great civilizations and powers.[64]

As Safavi claimed in December 2000, 'Iranian missiles can cause irreparable damage to either Israel or the United States', but nevertheless were still only 'for defensive purposes'.

There is at least one respect, however, in which future US policies could greatly exacerbate the risks of a nuclear crisis between Iran and the rest of the world. In the immediate or short term any active sponsorship by Washington of regime change within Iran risks creating a power vacuum in which all governmental assets are potentially at risk of being seized by whoever is in a position to do so. The scenes of anarchy in Baghdad that followed in the days after the disappearance of Saddam Hussein in April 2003 in fact illustrate a much wider danger that would conceivably place a regime's arsenal at risk of being spirited away as its authority begins to break down. Moreover, regime change in Iraq, like the former Soviet Union, also created a financial crisis that makes formerly state-employed scientists vulnerable to the approaches of countries eager to pay for their knowledge and experience. Since the fall of Saddam, the US State Department has for this reason been forced to draw up plans for a $16 million programme that aims to prevent scientists selling their skills and experience to other governments.[65]

In the longer term, another danger can sometimes arise from the possibility that regime change in any country can potentially lead to some political fragmentation, although for reasons discussed below this is most unlikely in the particular case of Iran.[66] In such a scenario the outside world would have to deal with several authorities that possess nuclear warheads, thereby making the task of drawing up, enforcing and monitoring international agreements proportionately more difficult. A comparison can clearly be drawn here with the disintegration of the Soviet Union into several republics, each of which possessed its own advanced nuclear facilities and most of which have since enforced international agreements on arms exports with sometimes only sporadic efficiency.

In this respect there is arguably an in-built contradiction in the Bush doctrine. Except in the most extreme circumstances, regime change is at least as likely to augment the risk to the United States as to eliminate it, because of the risks of creating a power vacuum in the immediate term and a political fragmentation in the longer term that only dissipates a threat.

Notes

1. See Chapter 1.
2. *Washington Post*, 23 October 2003.
3. *Weekly Standard*, 9 February 2002.
4. *Ha'aretz*, 16 June 2002.
5. *Time*, 8 March 2003.
6. *Sunday Telegraph*, 1 June 2003.
7. BBC News, 1 August 2003.
8. Statement by the Deputy Foreign Minister for Legal International Affairs, 29 April 2003.
9. Mark Hibbs, 'Bonn Will Decline Tehran Bid to Resuscitate Bushehr Project', *Nucleonics Week*, 26 November 1991.
10. ISIS Report, April/May 2003.
11. *New Yorker*, 3 December 2001.
12. George Perkovich, 'Dealing with Iran's Nuclear Challenge', Carnegie Endowment for International Peace, 28 April 2003, p. 5.
13. *New Yorker*, 3 December 2001.
14. Ibid.
15. See generally Robert J. Einhorn and Gary Samore, 'Ending Russian Assistance to Iran's Nuclear Bomb', *Survival*, vol. 44, no. 2, summer 2002.
16. Ibid., pp. 51–70.
17. AP, 13 January 2003.
18. See generally *Middle East International*, no. 644, 23 February 2001.
19. The Iranian state press agency IRNA quoted EC spokeswoman Emma Udwin on 19 February 2003: 'We understand that Iran wants to build nuclear reactors for electricity needs.'
20. ISIS Report, *Iran: Furor over Fuel*, May–June 2003.
21. See below, Chapter 8.
22. Quoted in *The Times*, 13 June 2003.
23. Quoted in Anthony Cordesmann's article, CSIS, 2 July 2000.
24. Report by the IAEA Director General on the implementation of the NPT safeguards agreement in the Islamic Republic of Iran, 6 June 2003.
25. Indyck quoted in the *Washington Times*, 29 July 1998; Gary Milhollin quoted in 'File on Four', BBC Radio 4, 24 September 2002.
26. AP, 23 October 2002.
27. Statement of Rear Admiral Shamkani, reported by BBC News, 26 May 2002.
28. *New Yorker*, 3 December 2001.
29. *Joongang* (South Korea), 15 June 2003.
30. 'File on Four', 24 September 2002.
31. AFP, 27 August 2003.
32. *Washington Times*, 24 February 1997.
33. AFP, 27 August 2003.

34. *Washington Post*, 25 September 2003.

35. AP, 10 July 2003.

36. Author's telephone interview with David Albright, 7 August 2003; 'File on Four', 24 September 2002.

37. BBC News, 26 May 2002.

38. Unclassified CIA report to Congress on the 'Acquisition of Technology Relating to Weapons of Mass Destruction', 2002.

39. *Guardian*, 17 June 2003; State Department briefing, 6 June 2003.

40. Reuters, 12 November 2003.

41. Albright's telephone interview with the author; Perkovich, 'Dealing with Iran's Nuclear Challenge'.

42. *Survival*, vol. 37, no. 2, summer 1995. But US experts disputed this view in reports published by the *Washington Post*, 17 May 1995.

43. *Guardian*, 27 August 2003.

44. *Guardian*, 26 September 2003.

45. Author's telephone interview with David Albright, 7 August 2003.

46. *Los Angeles Times*, 4 August 2003.

47. David Albright, 'An Iranian Bomb?', *Bulletin of the Atomic Scientists*, January 1995.

48. Reuters, 11 June 2003.

49. *National Review Online*, 9 September 2002.

50. 'The Moment of Truth', AEI, 30 May 2003.

51. Michael Ledeen, 'Desert Shame Redux', *National Review Online*, 30 April 2003.

52. Author's interview with Western diplomat, Tehran, 24 November 2003.

53. *Washington Post*, 25 September 2003.

54. Interview with the author, Tehran, 11 November 2003.

55. *Washington Post*, 11 March 2003.

56. See, for example, the report of Power and Interest News Report, 11 September 2003, <www.pinr.com>.

57. BBC News, 30 September 2003.

58. Albright, telephone interview.

59. Speech to the American–Iranian Council, 13 March 2002.

60. Interview with the author, Tehran, 24 November 2003.

61. *New York Post Online*, 11 March 2003.

62. Michael Eisenstadt, 'Living with a Nuclear Iran', *Survival*, autumn 1999.

63. See the essay by Farideh Farhi, 'To Have or Not to Have', published in *Iran's Nuclear Weapons Option: Issues and Analyis*, Nixon Center, January 2001, p. 47.

64. Perkovich, 'Dealing with Iran's Nuclear Challenge', p. 4.

65. Associated Press, 3 November 2003.

66. See below, Chapter 7.

PART II
Domestic Crisis

5 | Political tensions

US critics of the Tehran regime not only allege that its hard-line elements pose a threat to the stability of the outside world but also condemn the Iranian people's lack of democracy and other basic freedoms. President George, W. Bush has spoken both of his general 'commitment to helping those in captive nations achieve democracy' and of his aspiration to see 'democracy and the rule of law' established in Iran in particular, while his regional envoy, Zalmay Khalilzad, has emphasized Washington's commitment to a future Iran 'that is free, open and prosperous ... [and] in which their government adheres to the rule of law [and] respects human rights',[1] providing 'freedom, democracy and economic and educational opportunity' for all its people.[2] Colin Powell has also commented that 'the Iranian people want their freedom back ... to be free of those who have dragged the sacred garments of Islam into the political gutter'.[3] But besides provoking American antipathy, Iran's political system also has the makings of a domestic crisis, for in recent years the country's future has been fiercely contested by bitterly opposed interest groups whose struggle for political power has been fought out in fits and starts ever since the election of the reformist President, Muhammed Khatami, in 1997.

These domestic political disputes, which are essentially focused upon a struggle between unelected hard-line elements in the regime on the one hand and democratically elected representatives and their sympathizers on the other, could potentially boil over into a domestic crisis in at least two different ways. At a parliamentary level, they could lead to a stand-off between 'conservative' and 'reformist' politicians, in the way that eventuated in the run-up to the February 2004 Parliamentary elections, when the Guardian Council blocked many reformists from standing. But a frustrated reformist agenda can also threaten a crisis of legitimacy, as its sympathizers lose all hope of finding a parliamentary solution to conservative rule and instead take to the streets to effect their own solution. Such a profound loss of interest in the political system explains why Iranian conservatives, relying upon their diehard supporters, look set to win the parliamentary elections of February 2004 in the same way that they had won the council elections a year earlier.

This chapter seeks to look in more detail at what lies behind this pending domestic state of crisis and to consider some of the possible outcomes.

Democracy and the Iranian constitution

At the root of this tension between different political factions is a curious paradox that lies at the heart of the contemporary constitution. For in contemporary Iran political power is to an unusual degree wielded both by unelected theocratic elements as well as by elected institutions, just as it had historically rested with a shahdom that on paper possessed despotic powers but which in practice was dependent upon the consent of the popular masses and their representatives.

This political dichotomy not only lies at the heart of Iran's political crisis but also calls into question the sweeping terms in which the US government has condemned the Iranian regime. For despite the undoubted degree of repression within the country, it is far from clear that the regime can justifiably be typified as 'authoritarian' any more easily than it can unreservedly be called 'democratic'. The Iranian constitution instead contains elements of both authoritarianism and democracy that were mixed together in 1979 to conciliate conflicting political pressures of the moment, thereby creating what has convincingly been termed 'an ideological mishmash ... probably unmatched in the history of constitutionalism'[4] and 'a working anarchy'.[5] Its subsequent amendment, in the summer of 1989, left these essential inconsistencies untouched.

The constitution's democratic traits emerge most clearly in Article 6, which declares that 'the affairs of the country must be administered on the basis of public opinion expressed by the means of elections ... or by means of referenda', while Article 7 continues that 'in accordance with the command of The Koran – "their affairs are by consultations amongst them" (42:38); "consult them in affairs" (3:159) – consultative bodies are the decision-making and administrative organs of the country'. In practice, these general principles allow for the popular election of both a President and a parliament (Majles) that 'despite limitations on its ultimate authority ... wields enormous political, social and economic power',[6] for the establishment of a tier of local government and for a separation of legislative, executive and judicial powers. President Khatami has in this respect convincingly argued that 'Imam Khomeini himself believed in the combination of Islamic principles and the voice of the people', and that the terms of the constitution, ratified by referendum both in 1979 and 1989, showed that 'our people voted for freedom to speak, freedom to assemble, freedom to criticize – [that] are inalienable rights of the people'.

But these elected representatives compete with several other sources of political power that do not have any real popular mandate, foremost among them being the Supreme Leader, who under the terms of Article 110 has powers to 'delineate the general policies of the Islamic Republic of Iran' and to appoint members of the bodies upon which political power ultimately rests: the judiciary, the security forces and a constitutional watchdog, the Expediency Council. The Leader also exercises the ultimate authority to adjudicate on issues that would otherwise be gridlocked, such as a dispute between the elected parliament and the council: Khamenei intervened on 19 June 2001, for example, to settle just such a disagreement over the right of the Majles to launch a full investigation into governmental finances, an issue that he later affirmed did lie within parliamentary remit. He also maintains a right to step into processes of law that would otherwise be virtually autonomous, just as in July 1998 he intervened to reduce a five-year term imposed on Ghulam Hussein Karbaschi, a high official in the Servants of Construction Party who had been charged with and convicted of bribery.

Although not chosen by referendum or by parliamentary vote, the election of the Supreme Leader appears on paper to have some democratic basis because the Qom-based Assembly of Experts (Majles-e Khobregan), whose eighty-six members make the final decision, are elected by the people under the terms of Article 107. But in practice the shortlist from which the experts have to choose is drawn up by hard-line conservatives who comprise an institution that plays a crucial role in the Iranian constitution: the Guardian Council (Shura-ye Negahban).

The twelve-member Guardian Council, currently headed by Ayatollah Ahmad Jannati, acts as a constitutional watchdog by supervising electoral polls and vetting parliamentary legislation to ensure its 'compatibility with the criteria of Islam and the constitution'. These considerable powers could in theory also manifest the wishes and interests of the elected Majles, which is entitled to select six of the council's members, but in practice this freedom is also severely curtailed for reasons similar to those that restrict the freedom of the Assembly of Experts: they have to choose from a carefully selected shortlist put forward by the conservative judiciary. When drawn up in July 2001 by the head of the conservative-dominated judiciary, Mohammed Hashemi Shahrudi, this list in typical fashion included the names only of like-minded lawyers and even included two – Gholam Hussein Elham, a professor of law, and

Hussein Mir Mohammed Sadiqi, a spokesman for the judiciary – who were regarded by some as ultra-conservative.

Another reason why the power of the Majles to elect council members is curtailed, however, is that the remaining six guardians, all clerics, are hand-picked solely by the Supreme Leader. Yet only these clerics are allowed to vote on the validity of 'Islamic' issues as opposed to the 'constitutional' matters on which all twelve members can vote. The political orientation of one such cleric, Ayatollah Ali Jannati, became abundantly clear on 31 August 2001 when, together with Ghorban Ali Najafabadi, a former intelligence chief, he appeared to praise the Taliban movement in Afghanistan for the brutality of their punishments.

Appointees of the Leader also dominate the Supreme National Security Council (SNSC), the functions of which, according to Article 176, are to safeguard 'the national interests and to preserve the Islamic Revolution, territorial integrity and national sovereignty'. The vital role played by the twelve members of this body became particularly clear in October 2003 during the negotiations with EU politicians over the nuclear programme, when the Iranian position was represented not by appointees of Khatami but almost solely by the SNSC's secretary, Hojja-toleslam Hassan Rouhani. Besides acting as a national security adviser to the President and a vice-speaker of the Iranian parliament, Rouhani has since the early 1990s also acted as a leading representative of the regime and taken particular interest in promoting a newly founded defence and commercial alliance between Tehran and New Delhi.

Khomeini's arguments

In one sense, the autocratic elements within the Iranian constitution reflect the influence of the Revolution's founder and guiding spirit, Ruhollah Khomeini, who argued from the early 1940s, with the publication of *Kashf al-Asrar* ('The Discovery of Secrets'), that the human world should be ruled not by man-made decisions but by the word of God as decreed in the Koran. Khomeini's starting point was the essential belief held by all Shia Muslims that the leadership of the Islamic world was entrusted to his followers, the Imams, and that although the Twelfth Iman, the Mahdi, had disappeared in the year 874, he would by a miracle one day return to establish a new era of divine truth. But Khomeini challenged the traditional Shia suspicion of interference in temporal affairs that had been adopted by more senior clerics such as Grand Ayatollah Mohammed Hussein Borujerdi. Borujerdi's death in 1961 suddenly allowed Khomeini a new freedom to argue, much more radically, that until the arrival of the last Iman the world could be

governed by the 'guardianship' (*vali*) of a clerical elite of highly qualified scholars of Islam (*faqih*) who, as 'knowers of Islam', are uniquely
qualified to interpret the word of God as laid down in the Koran. The
radicalism of Khomeini's position became clear from his insistence that
all legislation, on every conceivable subject matter, should be derived
from the Koran and *sunna* (the traditions of Muhammad), a view that
sharply conflicted with those of other senior clerics such as Ayatollah
Shari'atmadari, who argued that the *velayat-e faqih* could be applied only
in cases when it was otherwise unavoidable.[7]

Khomeini's view that God's word had to be 'interpreted' by elites
rather than 'created' at a popular level is wholly at odds, however, with
the history of constitutional government that originated in the early
1890s, when demands for 'a national consultative assembly' comparable to Western parliaments were first published in influential Persian
journals[8] before becoming a formal reality on 5 August 1906 with the
ratification by the dying Shah, Muzaffar al-Din, of the basis of a written constitution. This document, known as the Fundamental Laws,
recognized Persia's National Assembly as 'the representative of the
people' and allowed its members 'the right in all questions to propose
any measure that it regards as conducive to the well-being of the
Government and the People' and to have the final say over all Persian
laws, decrees, treaties and loans. Another document, the Supplementary Fundamental Laws, added to this by affirming the rule of law,
the separation of powers and some basic freedoms of expression and
of association. Although the new Majles was shut down in 1911, the
five-year parliamentary experiment had laid the foundations for some
semblance of democracy in Iran.

One leading clergyman of the time who supported the Shah's attempted counter-revolution against Persia's new National Assembly,
Sheikh Fazlollah Nuri, later became a very powerful influence upon
the young Khomeini. Although to begin with Fazlollah had sympathized
with the values of the Constitutional Revolution, he had soon lost faith,
regarding the legislative sessions he attended as a misjudged attempt to
create law rather than merely interpret Koranic decrees. Because the
proper role of such a parliament, he argued, was to ratify and enforce
the Sharia laws that are properly drawn up by an absolutist government
that interprets and lays down Islamic law, the Shah's despotism was the
lesser of two evils.[9]

Viewed in these terms, the absolutism of the 'unelected minority'
that rules much of contemporary Iran clearly follows in the same tradition of a shahdom whose secular despotism, although in another sense

so different in kind from the theocracy of the Islamic Revolution, was none the less also fundamentally at odds with the democratic forces that began to emerge in Persia from the end of the nineteenth century.

The paradox of Persian political power

How then can this dichotomy between 'autocracy' and 'democracy' be best explained? The origins of the contemporary debate about who really rules Iran reveal a paradox: that political power in Persia historically belonged to rulers who were both omnipotent and powerless. For Persia had long been ruled by monarchs who, until the beginning of the twentieth century, were widely famed for their virtually unbridled theoretical power but who in practice wholly lacked both the central bureaucracy and the standing army upon which the enforcement of their decrees depended. As a result, political power was to an unusual degree sharply divided between theory and practice.

This paradox was clear in the century preceding the Constitutional Revolution when Persia had been ruled by the Qajars, a dynasty that had origins among the semi-nomadic tribes of Central Asia and whose members had come to rule Persia from the end of the eighteenth century, when Aqa Mohammed Khan, a tribal ruler, had made a successful bid for the throne. Regarding themselves as God's representatives on earth – a claim that had been made on behalf of the shahdom for at least a thousand years – the Qajar rulers had little hesitation in describing themselves in impressive terms that included titles such as 'King-of-Kings', 'Supreme Arbitrator', 'Shadow of God', 'Guardian of the Flock' and 'Divine Conqueror'. Foreign visitors to the court also regarded their rule as 'one of the most absolute monarchies in the world', free of any constitutional restraint.[10]

In practice, however, the shahdom was dependent upon the goodwill of the local *kadkhudas*, the leaders and representatives of local villages, towns and tribes, as well as the main religious leaders (*mujtaheds*) who were wary of royal claims. This meant that royal power often relied upon tactics of 'divide-and-rule' that exploited rivalries between opponents, and of cautiously treading carefully to avoid unnecessary confrontation. This was obvious to outsiders who travelled the country: a British observer noted at the beginning of the nineteenth century how 'the Qajars ensured their own safety by nicely balancing and systematically fomenting mutual jealousies',[11] finding and exploiting divisions between tribes such as the Kurds, Turkomans and Persians in the north east of the country, and the Sheikis and Mutashar'is in Tabriz province. And in 1887 the first US envoy to Persia, Samuel Benjamin, also noted that many of the country's leading *mujtaheds* claimed to have the right to unseat any authority deemed to violate Islamic law, an authority whose exercise the Shah, not surprisingly, went to immense lengths not to provoke.[12]

The conflict between these competing visions of 'absolutist' and 'democratic' political rule has erupted throughout the twentieth century, including the tumultuous days of July 1952, when Prime Minister Mohammed Reza Shah brought a longer-standing political crisis to a head by suddenly exercising his constitutional right as premier to nominate the cabinet's war minister. Wanting this political privilege for himself, Reza Shah had refused to recognize this new nomination, thereby prompting Mossadeq to resign so that 'someone who enjoys royal confidence [can] form a new government and implement His Majesty's policies'. On 21 July, however, after five days of strikes and often violent street demonstrations, the Shah had stood down, reinstating Mossadeq and agreeing to the formation of a new cabinet. Over the coming months the premier stripped the shahdom of many of the constitutional powers acquired since August 1941, powers that included official jurisdiction over the armed services and a direct channel to foreign diplomats. For the moment at least, the political initiative lay with the premier, not the Shah.

This political dichotomy means that the sweeping condemnation of the Iranian regime as 'repressive' and 'undemocratic' by Washington's Manichaean rhetoric is based upon a highly misleading premise. And if the US President and his spokesmen claim that only 'an unelected few repress the Iranian people's hope for freedom', then it is far from clear why the whole regime needs to be condemned in such sweeping terms. Phil Dibble, a deputy assistant secretary of the Bureau of Near Eastern Affairs in the US State Department, has pointed out that the USA did not differentiate between hard-liners and reformers, since 'the government as a whole must be held responsible for its actions' but added that US policy towards Iran was in this respect 'unlike some countries'. But he failed to explain why Iran in this respect deserved to be treated differently.

It is this dichotomy within the Iranian constitution that also accounts for any forthcoming state of political crisis, as democratically elected Majles parliamentarians seek to wrest political power from the hands of the unelected.

Constitutional crisis 2002–03

This conflict appeared to be reaching a climax from the summer of 2003 over the fate of two bills designed to 'respond to the aspirations of the people' by placing important political powers into the hands of elected institutions at the expense of unelected bodies. At the time of writing, however, the reformists have temporarily renounced hope of seeing their bills ratified, thereby defusing the political tension that had built up around them.

The first such bill sought to guarantee free parliamentary elections by removing the Guardian Council's prerogative of disqualifying candidates deemed unfit to stand in elections, and instead handing these powers over to the reformist Interior Ministry, which reports to the democratically elected President. The council has sometimes energetically exercised these powers, disqualifying 35 per cent of candidates wanting to stand as MPs in the elections to the Fifth Majles in 1996 and rejecting 229 of the 396 candidates for the eighty-six vacancies on the Assembly of Experts for Leadership, without specifying its reasons for doing so, in October 1998.[13] Until February 2004 this power was not used so energetically – only 11 per cent of around 1,500 candidates were barred from standing in the February 2000 Majles elections for reasons that ranged from drug-taking, a previous association with the Shah's regime, and a questionable commitment to Islam – but such a privilege still potentially allows the council to block the election of particularly able or popular candidates whose views or behaviour are deemed to pose a threat to the Revolution. For this reason it is still a prerogative strongly defended by those who wield it, such as Ayatollah Mohammed Yazdi, who opposed the bill because ending 'the Guardian Council's right of supervision is tantamount to allowing law-breakers to run in elections',[14] or Gholam Hussein Elham, head of the council's research centre, who claimed that if approved the bill would allow 'all the infidels, former Marxists and non-Iranians with acquired nationality' to enter parliament.[15] As a result the bill has been rejected by the Council for alleged discrepancies and inconsistencies against the constitution and the Shariah law of Islam.

The other proposed measure puts more power in the hands of the President at the expense of both the judiciary and the Guardian Council. On the one hand, the President would be able to neutralize verdicts – including politically motivated judgments against reformers – by wielding a power to strip judges of their office and ending practices such as trials held without jury or behind closed doors. The same bill also seeks to end the council's power arbitrarily to veto any parliamentary legislation it wishes, a right of veto it had exercised in previous years against more than fifty bills that had been passed by the Majles before being referred to the council for final approval. In theory the council's veto does not bring an immediate end to any such legislative proposals since the parliament could still refer a rejected bill to the Expediency Council which, under Article 112, arbitrates constitutional conflicts when 'the Guardian Council judges a proposed bill ... to be against the principles of *shari'a* or the constitution and the assembly is unable to meet the expectations of the Guardian Council'. But in practice such a move is most unlikely to make any real difference since all the Expediency Council's members are hand-picked by the Supreme Leader and therefore merely reflect the same uncompromising conservatism of attitude: as Ali Shakouri-Rad, a reformist law-maker, argued in 2003, there is little point in making such a referral 'because its composition is no better than the Guardian Council'.

In one sense, the origins of this constitutional crisis stemmed from the sensational results of the national elections of 23 May 1997 that were widely considered, in the words of Ayatollah Hosseyn-Ali Montazeri, to have been 'a second revolution'. A mere 25 per cent of votes were cast for the candidate of the conservative right, Ali Akbar Nateq-Nouri, who had been chosen to replace the departing Ali Akbar Hashemi Rafsanjani, and an overwhelming victory was instead won by fifty-four-year-old Hojjatoleslam Muhammed Khatami, a candidate with an openly reformist agenda, who took 69 per cent of the vote.

The new President was certainly well qualified to take up such a position. He was not only a cleric, higher in religious rank than both his conservative rival, but also held university degrees at two of Iran's leading universities, Tehran and Isfahan, and had spent time abroad to learn both English and German. He had also acquired ministerial experience during the Khomeini era, having been appointed as a Minister of Islamic Guidance in 1982, but had resigned his post ten years later after hard-liners in the Iranian parliament criticized his 'reformist' leanings. Khatami had then effectively removed himself from frontline politics, working as a head of the Iranian National Library, before being approached in 1997 by members of the centrist parliamentary party, the Servants of Construction, who asked if he was willing to put his name forward as their new leader.

The electoral platform upon which Khatami stood was unmistakeably reformist although his manifesto, like most others, revealed few specific details. In contrast to the position of his rival, Nateq-Nuri, who asserted the importance of merely keeping things as they were, Khatami argued openly for political and economic reforms that would curtail the many abuses of civil rights and the rule of law that were perpetrated by unaccountable elements within the regime and for granting ordinary people the freedoms for which they increasingly clamoured. Such a programme, he emphasized, did not challenge Khomeini's legacy but merely ensured that his message was put both fairly and effectively into practice and adapted to meet fast-changing contemporary needs.

The Iranian parliament

The 1997 election set the stage upon which the subsequent struggle between reformist and hard-liners has since been enacted by a wide variety of players. For inside Iran's 290-member Majles, political issues are debated and contested between affiliates of what are typically called, with a misleading simplicity, 'reformist', 'moderate' or 'hard-line' factions of opinion.

These affiliations represent not any formal loyalty but a complex interplay of individual opinions that are difficult to classify under any one individual label. Some conservatives like Ali Akbar Nateq-Nuri, the current speaker of Iran's parliament, have economic views that, being based on free-market principles, are widely considered to be 'progressive', whereas many political reformers, including Khatami, advocate a stronger role for the state. Others move over time from one extreme to another, such as Ali Akbar Muhtashemi-Pur, who as Iran's former ambassador to Syria was formerly a hard-line backer of the Lebanese Hezbollah militia but who since 1997 has been an outspoken supporter of many of Khatami's policies. The various labels attached to the former President Hashemi Rafsanjani, who has in recent years been cast by different commentators as ideologue, pragmatist and reformer, illustrate the difficulties of describing Iranian political allegiances with any real exactness.

But however uncertain the delineation of these allegiances, there are a number of identifiable groupings within the Iranian parliament that are divided between those who essentially advocate the need for political reform and those who seek to resist it. Named after the date in the Persian calendar (Khordad 2 1376, or 23 May 1997) when Khatami had won his first presidential victory, the Second Khordad Front represents mainstream parliamentary reformism by acting as an umbrella movement for eighteen political groupings that share a broadly similar outlook but lack any coherent strategy on many issues, particularly economic affairs. These factions include the Society of Combatant Clerics, a group led by the parliamentary speaker Mehdi Karrubi; the Organization of Mujahideen of the Islamic Revolution, headed by the deputy speaker Behzad Nabavi; and the leftist Islamic Iran Participation Front (IIPF or Mosharekat), whose leader is the president's brother, Mohammed-Reza Khatami. Headed by Gholam Hussein Karbaschi, the outspoken ex-Mayor of Tehran, the Kargozaran ('Executives of Construction') is also affiliated to Second Khordad. The 'Executives' advocate the rule of 'technocrats' who are chosen not by the people but specially selected by an administrative elite for their knowledge of economic affairs.

The shared political platform of these various parties is best defined in negative terms, as being opposed to those that lie at the other end of the spectrum of parliamentary politics, the conservatively minded Association of Militant Clergy and the Islamic Coalition Association, whose directing spirit if not organizational centre is the Supreme Leader, Ayatollah Ali Khamenei, and whose views are aired in newspapers such as *Resalat*, *Keyhan* and *Jomhuri-ye Islami*. The leaders of the Militant Clergy are Ali Akbar Nateq-Nuri and Mohammed Mahdavi-Kani, while Habibollah Asgar Ouladim heads the Coalition. Prior to the February 2004 elections, these conservatives held only fifty-four parliamentary seats out of the total of 290.

The conflict between reformers and conservatives is contested not just between different factions within the Majles, however, but also between MPs and a judiciary that has hotly contested a parliamentary privilege upon which democratic freedom is clearly dependent: the right of elected representatives to speak in the house with impunity. Since 1997 a large number of MPs have been either summoned to appear before the courts or successfully prosecuted, usually on a count of *mohareb ba khoda* ('enmity with God') that under Article 190 of the current Penal Code can be punishable by death. Two such cases have become particularly notorious. On 22 August 2001, Fatima Haqiqatju was jailed for making remarks over the forcible arrest of a female journalist that were deemed by the courts to misinterpret the words of Khomeini and insult members of the Guardian Council. Four months later, on 26 December 2001, MP Hussein Loqmanian was also sentenced for allegedly attacking the powers of the judiciary in the Majles. Other MPs have been charged with offences such as election fraud, including a deputy interior minister and a key reformist, Mustafa Tajzadeh, who on 4 March 2001 were both found guilty by Tehran's Civil Service Court, while in November 1999 the courts jailed a leading reformer of great charisma, former Interior Minister Abdollah Nouri, to a five-year term for political and religious dissent. A key ally of the President, Nouri had been widely tipped as a future parliamentary speaker, one of the most important roles in Iranian politics, and his conviction was widely seen as a hard-line bid to curb the growing reform movement.

The question of how much freedom MPs should be allowed to enjoy emerged particularly clearly at the time of student riots in June 2003 when the Tehran prosecutor announced that the judiciary would indict any MP who was found guilty of stirring up unrest. These charges were partly a response to the announcement by some Majles members, Meytham Sa'idi, Fatima Haqiqat Joo, Reza Yosefian and Ali Akbar Mousavi Hoini, of a forty-eight-hour sit-in protest against heavy-handed police treatment of students[16] and by the publication in conservative journals of the allegations of a detained student, Payman 'Aref, that some MPs had been involved in the protests.[17] Members who commit such offences risk not just prosecution but the imposition of an immediate ban on their political parties in the same way that Iran's Freedom Movement (IFM), led by Ebrahim Yazdi, was suddenly closed down amid sweeping arrests in March 2001.

Chosen by hard-line elements and bearing considerable freedom under wide-ranging laws to prosecute almost anyone they wish, the judges are the hard-liners' most effective means of holding back the reformist movement. Those with the most fearsome reputations include the head of the judiciary, Ayatollah Mahmoud Hashemi Shahroudi; Saeed Mortazavi, the Tehran province prosecutor; and Gholam Hussein Mohseni- Ejei, who was alleged to have been behind some of the 'chain murders' of specific individuals that took place in 1998/9.

Judicial harassment of the press and dissidents

It is not just members of parliament whom the courts have targeted in their bid to rein in the reform movement, but their supporters and sympathizers, particularly in the media. Around eighty papers were closed down in the three years that followed April 2000 when a new hard-line campaign against the pro-reform press began, prompted by sweeping reformist gains at the parliamentary elections in February. Speaking on 20 April, soon after the passing of a new law that redefined criticism of the constitution, Supreme Leader Khamenei openly attacked reformist papers that he claimed were subverting the Islamic revolution: 'There are ten to fifteen newspapers which undermine Islamic principles, insult state bodies and create social discord,' he claimed, 'and unfortunately some of the newspapers have become the bases of the enemy. They are performing the same tasks that the BBC Radio and the Voice of America, as well as the British, American and Zionist television broadcasts intend to perform.'

Since then judges have conducted a campaign described by critics as one of 'judicial lawlessness' that has led not only to the closing down of scores of reformist newspapers – some of which go on to reopen under different titles – but to the harassment and imprisonment of individual editors and journalists. During one typical bout of repression that began in the late spring of 2002, a regional weekly, *Shams-e-Tabriz*, was banned on 16 April, and its editor, Ali-Hamed Iman, sentenced to eight months in jail and seventy-four lashes for 'insulting religion and the Prophet', 'trying to stir up ethnic tension', 'insulting the leaders of the regime' and 'publishing lies'. The following day another pro-reform journalist, Ahmad Zeid-Abadi of *Hamshari*, was sentenced for disseminating 'propaganda against the Islamic regime and its institutions' while two weeks later, on 4 May, a leading reformist paper, *Bonyan*, was closed down 'for repeated offences' and a government-controlled daily, *Iran*, suspended after publishing an article deemed 'offensive to the sacred principles of Islam'. These moves also coincided with a particularly threatening circular issued on 25 May by the Tehran Justice Department, warning newspapers that any article favouring negotiations with the USA would be deemed a criminal offence, while Supreme Leader Khamenei at the same time argued that even mere dialogue was 'an insult to the Iranian people' that would amount to 'both treason and stupidity'. The following day the Prosecutor-General also issued formal complaints against two prominent reformists for commenting on this very issue.

During another repressive bout of judicial activity that began a few months later, a court on 11 January 2003 ordered the suspension of the daily paper *Bahar*, charged with insulting state officials and inciting public opinion against the regime: the newspaper had already been banned once before, in 2000, for 'fabricating stories and blatant lies', and had now inflamed the wrath of hard-liners after running an article about questionable stock-exchange dealings by the company Alzhra, whose shareholders included the former President, Hashemi Rafsanjani, as well as Ayatollah Yazdi, a former head of the judiciary, and Ayatollah Ahmad Jannati, head of the Guardian Council. The campaign then continued on 24 January when Iran's biggest daily newspaper, *Hamshari*, was closed down and several of its journalists were harassed after refusing to print an article from Ali-Reza Majub, the head of a government-controlled union, that replied to criticism published a few days earlier. *Hamshari* was one of several newspapers to be banned in the space of five weeks – the others including *Hayat-e-No* and *Nowruz* – during a governmental crackdown that continued on 18 February with the arrest of Mohammed Mohsen Sazegara, charged with making open criticisms of Supreme Leader Khamenei on his website and for arguing that the Iranian popular will was 'being held hostage by six hard-line clerics on the Guardian Council'. The following month a distinguished Iranian writer, Massoud

Behnoud, was also given a nineteen-month jail term on the usual charges on spreading lies and insulting Islam.

Prompted by Saeed Mortazavi, the Tehran prosecutor known as the 'Butcher of the Press' who has unofficially led the campaign to censor the press, hard-line judges have in recent months continued this crackdown. 'How can I do my job in this kind of environment?' one frustrated newspaper editor asked a Western online journal, *EurasiaNet*, 'I'm always wondering: will this next article land me in jail?' Twenty Iranian journalists were behind bars in July 2003,[18] a state of affairs that led the President of the World Association of Newspapers, Seok Hyun Hong, and Gloria Brown Anderson, President of the World Editors' Forum, to send a joint letter to Ayatollah Mahmoud Shahroudi, the head of Iran's judiciary, to express publicly concern at the treatment of journalists.

When editors are summoned to answer questions about particular articles they have published, they generally appear before special 'press courts' whose sessions, like judicial hearings for high-level officials and ministers, are generally held in secrecy before a jury of at least two judges. But the regime also has the power to arrest and detain individual journalists 'on a temporary basis' at the instigation not of the courts but only of the Prosecutor-General. One reformist journalist interviewed by the author was detained for more than a week in solitary confinement in Evin Prison on such a 'temporary basis', although others are detained for far longer under the same order.

Since 2000, arrests and harassment of journalists have been undertaken not by the police but by the Herasat. Although this agency was originally established to protect the interests of national security inside particular sections of government, it has since been greatly expanded in size and scope to carry out judicial orders against the press and is currently reckoned by some to be 'several times larger' than the particular department of the MOIS that formerly had the same responsibilities.[19]

In their bid to clamp down on reformist activities, the courts have also targeted polling agencies capable of revealing truths about public opinion that are uncomfortable to the authorities. In October 2002, for example, a judicial ruling shut down Iran's National Institute for Public Opinion, a research body that had published a poll showing around 75 per cent of the public to be supportive of diplomatic negotiations with the USA, and issued a warrant for the arrest and detention of Behrouz Geranpayeh, the institute's director. This polling organization had been set up by the reformist head of the Majles' Foreign Affairs and National

Security Committee, Ahmed Borghani, who was also arrested and accused of 'spreading lies to incite public opinion'. Two months later came the trial of pollsters Behrouz Geranpayeh, Hussein-Ali Ghazian and Abbas Abdi, all accused by the public prosecutor of making contact with 'agents associated with foreign intelligence and security services' and by one conservative newspaper editor of being 'the ultimate base of American espionage and the operations centre for a fifth column'.

One particularly notorious case of judicial harassment took place in November 2002 when Judge Ramazani of the Fourteenth District Court in Hamadan passed a death sentence, as well as seventy-four lashes and an eight-year jail term, on a forty-five-year-old liberal activist, Hashem Aghajari. Although no one expected it, the case instantly became a *cause célèbre* throughout the country.

A war veteran of the eight-year conflict with Iraq who had lost both his own leg and his brother in the fighting, and a senior member of the Islamic Mujahideen Organization who unquestionably had a strong commitment to Islam, Iran and the principles of the Islamic Revolution, Aghajari did not at first sight appear to have the makings of a dissident who had long been loathed by the political establishment. But he had none the less deeply offended senior conservatives when addressing a university audience in Hamadan the previous August. Basing his arguments on those of the Muslim reformer, Ali Shar'iati, who claimed that Islam has to be reformed in the same way as the Reformation had once cleansed Christianity and that the clergy should not be allowed to stand between the people and their God, Aghajari had asserted that good Muslims should not 'blindly follow' the edicts of their religious leaders 'like monkeys' but should instead seek a 'religious renewal' of Shiite Islam. But because these comments overtly challenge the central Shiite principle of emulation of the clergy, they immediately provoked a huge storm of controversy.

Although there was never any real doubt that the death sentence would be commuted, the Aghajari case immediately became highly symbolic of the struggle between reformers and hard-liners, partly because of the severity of the sentence, but also because the trial had been conducted behind closed doors and the defendant allowed only very limited access to his lawyers. It immediately prompted huge protests among Iranian students (Chapter 7) that led to Supreme Leader Khamenei personally intervening on 17 November to demand a speedy review of his case. But the courts seemed to resist Khamenei's intervention, dragging their heels and trying to delay or even avoid the implementation of his decision, and when the head of the judiciary,

Ayatollah Hashemi Shahroudi, declared that political expediency should not interfere with the legal process, his position drew letters of support from judges in at least two provinces. The death sentence was eventually lifted on the grounds of 'defects in investigations' while a new trial for Aghajari was prepared.

The rule of law

The reformers who struggle with the judiciary do not just seek to keep the right people out of the courts but also to ensure that no one, including those who work within government departments and ministries, is allowed to be above the law. As President Khatami has pointed out, 'Islamic freedom' means not only 'freedom of thought, freedom of expression [and] freedom of choice' but also the 'freedom [to have] comprehensive supervision by the nation over all pillars of the government'.[20]

This issue was pushed to the forefront of Iranian politics by the 'Chain Murders', a series of killings of political dissidents that began on 22 November 1998 with the murders of Dariush Forouhar, the seventy-year-old leader of the Iran People's Party, and his fifty-four-year-old wife, Parvaneh, who were stabbed to death and mutilated in their Tehran flat. Soon afterwards, on 9 December, the dead body of Mohammed Mokhtari, a dissident poet, was discovered in a Tehran morgue and two days later writer Mohammed Pouyandeh was also found dead, apparently strangled, underneath a railway bridge in one of the capital's suburbs.

By mid-January a special governmental commission set up by the President had announced that elements within the Intelligence Ministry, including Deputy Intelligence Minister Saeed Emami, were responsible and issued warrants for the arrest of those thought to be involved. Eventually, on 27 January 2001, court sentences that ranged from the death penalty to various terms of imprisonment were passed on the eighteen intelligence agents who had been formally charged with murdering the four dissident intellectuals in 1998, a number undoubtedly far lower than the true figure of those they had put to death. Emami himself escaped trial by allegedly committing suicide while in police custody.

The arrest, detention and trial of those involved was of huge symbolic importance. For although the pro-Khatami Participation Front denounced the subsequent outcome of the trials that ended in January 2001, the fact that they had taken place at all represented an immense achievement for reformists trying to establish the rule of law in a country where unaccountable political elites have often been able to do much as they pleased. Moreover, Khatami won parliamentary approval in appointing a new Intelligence Minister, Ali Yunesi, who proceeded to replace hard-line officials, including the former chief Ghorban Ali Najafabadi, and close down the various businesses that had illicitly funded the ministry and thereby allowed it effectively to escape parliamentary censure.

The scale of the reformist victory became clear to one journalist who pointed out that Iranians were:

> not used to such transparency about matters of this kind and the revelations have left them perplexed and confused. Until recently the Intelligence Ministry was spoken of only in hushed voices, in dark corners or in private places. Now newspapers ... have pounced on the story like hungry beasts. They are cornering the Ministry of Intelligence and clawing for more information and explanations. A former Intelligence Minister, Ali Fallahian, is already being implicated in the press.[21]

Despite winning such occasional victories, the reformist bid to establish the rule of law in public life currently still has a long way to go and many of their efforts to bring to heel some of the most ruthless opponents of their political struggle have so far been thwarted. In its annual survey for 2001–02, Freedom House, a human-rights watchdog based in New York, claimed that 'the state continues to maintain control through terror', adding that 'arbitrary detention, torture, disappearance, summary trial and execution are commonplace'. These dangers were made abundantly clear to the outside world in the summer of 2003 when Zahra Kazemi, a fifty-four-year-old Canadian photo-journalist of Iranian origin, died in a Tehran hospital as a result of injuries sustained in police detention. Kazemi, a contributor to the Montreal-based magazine *Recto Verso*, had been arrested on 23 June for taking photos of a protest by the families of imprisoned students outside Tehran's Evin Prison, but three days later was suddenly taken to hospital with head injures. Despite efforts by prison spokesmen to blame her collapse on a stroke, a reformist Vice-President, Mohammed Ali Abtahi, was forced to admit that her death had been caused by beatings inflicted in prison, prompting President Khatami to commission a 'rapid and comprehensive investigation' into the true cause of death.

Intellectual disputes

But the dispute between conservative and reformist opinions in Iran is not just limited to clashes in the street or exchanges in parliament but is also fought out at an intellectual level. Many of the clerics who formulate and articulate conservative viewpoints, for instance, are based at the holy city of Qom, a pre-eminent religious centre for all Shia Muslims ever since 1979, when Saddam Hussein ordered the expulsion of senior clerics from the true home of Shiite theology at the Iraqi city of Najaf. At the beginning of 2003, Qom was home not only to around 40,000 clergy but also ten Grand Ayatollahs – or 'Objects of Emulation' (*marja'-e taqlid*). Many, although by no means most, of the senior clergy are supportive of the constitutional status quo including some, like Ayatollah Mohammed-Taqi Mesbah-Yazdi, who have openly called on Iran's judiciary to adopt even tougher measures against student protesters, claiming in June 2003 that the protesters were guilty of *moraheb*. Others, including Ayatollah Mohammed Emami-Kashani, an eminent Friday prayers leader, have openly organized demonstrations against reformist bills deemed to offend Islam, such as the gathering staged by a group of clerics on 3 August 2003 at the Feizieh Seminary School, a religious school strongly associated with Khomeini, in protest at moves to incorporate into Iranian law a UN Convention to outlaw discrimination against women.

There are many other clerics in Qom and elsewhere who are, by contrast, strongly supportive of the reformers' case. Whereas hard-line clerics argue that Islamic law is a series of immutable divine decrees that can be always be universally applied, the more moderately minded argue for a more relativist approach that takes contemporary circumstances into account and makes *maslaha* – public interest – a key determinant of policy. Grand Ayatollah Yousef Sanei, for example, has been criticized by hard-liners for advocating that 'blood money' paid in compensation to the relatives of murdered women should be the same as, not less than, the sum paid to those of murdered men.

By far the most prominent intellectual influence upon the reform movement, however, has hitherto been Ali Hussein Montazeri, an Ayatollah of unrivalled religious knowledge and, as a cleric who was associated with Khomeini's political struggle since the 1950s, one of immense political experience. Montazeri had been one of the main draftsmen of the 1979 Constitution and in November 1985 was chosen to step into the shoes of the dying Supreme Leader. The subsequent appointment of Ali Khamenei in March 1989 reflected a sudden change of mind by Khomeini that was prompted by Montazeri's criticisms of the mass slaughter of prisoners a few months previously (see Chapter 7) and of the failure to allow the 'freedom of speech and freedom for political parties' for which the spurned cleric had called. But the association between the cleric and the reformist movement continued and reached a climax soon after Khatami's 1997 election victory. For amid rumours that Supreme Leader Khamenei was trying to impose his influence on the President's composition of a new government, Montazeri had made a sensational speech, claiming that the duty of the Supreme Leader was not 'to interfere in everything' but instead 'to oversee the country' and intimating that Khamenei was in any case unqualified to be a Supreme Leader and perhaps even an Object of Emulation.[22]

Since being released in 2003 from house arrest in Qom, after five years of incarceration, Montazeri has continued to venture criticisms of the existing regime, arguing that 'a government system cannot and must not be concentrated in the hands of one person' and that 'the clergy's absolute power is bad' for Iran. His work and writings, moreover, have inspired those who remained loyal to the principles of the 1979 Revolution but who argued that its ideals had since been corrupted, notably Ayatollah Yusef Sanei, an Object of Emulation, who now thinks the Guardian Council has taken too much power for itself and who has issued a number of more progressive edicts, notably on the rights of women and religious minorities inside Iran.

Like other leading reformists, such as Mohammed Mojtahid Shabestari, Mohsen Kadivar and Abdollah Nuri, Khatami's impeached Interior Minister, Montazeri does not question the Revolution's theocratic principles by arguing for any formal separation of Islam from politics. The constitution, Montazeri has always claimed, is rightly 'far removed from every Western principle', not least because it is based on an inseparability of politics and religion that allows the divine leader to lay down guidelines on all matters that concern the lives of ordinary citizens. By contrast a far more secular message is put forward by liberal philosophers such as Dr Abdul Karim Soroush, a former Khomeini ally who was educated at Tehran and London Universities and who has since held academic posts at Iranian universities. In recent years, Soroush has put forward a much more radical case than Montazeri, arguing for a much greater separation of religion from politics. His many speeches and writings continue to inspire the more radically minded reformists and have held powerful sway over at least one magazine, *Kiyan*, that has since been closed down. Other influential voices that articulate a similarly radical message include Akbar Ganji, who has also played an important role in articulating this radicalism, not least by posting online a 'Manifesto for Republicans' arguing that Islam must 'retreat from the domain of the state into the private sphere' if conflict inside Iran is ever to be avoided.

The pending crisis

The political gridlock between these different political factions has several possible outcomes. Conservative hard-liners could, for example, be forced to bow to demands for constitutional reform if popular pressure for a referendum seriously threatens law and order, or if opinion within the higher echelons of the clergy turns against a maintenance of the status quo. In particular, the repercussions of just one senior clergyman losing nerve and publicly breaking ranks cannot be exaggerated, just as political shockwaves were sent through the Iranian political establishment in 2002 when on 9 July an eminent Imam of the city of Isfahan, Ayatollah Jalaluddin Taheri, who had been appointed as a prayer leader by an exiled Khomeini in 1976, wrote a letter of resignation in language unprecedented for such a senior figure and that affirmed the worst fears of every hard-liner: 'When I remember the promises we made early in the Revolution, I tremble like a willow tree. I break into a sweat when I see some who consider the wealth of the Muslims to be their own, and who consider the country their own absolute property. Was this the pledge we gave to the downtrodden?' As he criticized 'those who are crossing the bridge of religion to reach the land of worldly possessions' and 'the gang of shroud-wearers who sharpen the teeth of the crocodile of power who want to marry the ill-tempered, ugly hag of violence to religion', he continued his assault on: 'society's louts and fascists, a mixture of ignorance and madness, whose umbilical cords are attached to the centres of power, who are unchecked and unbridled, who are neither reproached by the executors of justice nor reproved by the law, act not just as your jurisconsuls but as your philosophers, your sheriffs and rulers, your jurists and judges'. Despite the censorship of this sensational speech by the state-controlled media, which published only small segments, it was quoted in full in the private press.

The effects of US intervention

A less favourable outcome for the reformists, however, is likely to eventuate if Washington adopts an overly hostile approach towards Iran that unnecessarily polarizes opinion. Although most ordinary Iranians would welcome opening negotiations with the United States after years of isolation and sanction, few independent commentators dispute that an aggressive American approach to Iran would none the less prove counter-productive and play into the hands of hard-liners. 'The tone of arrogance has to go down as much as possible … and if that doesn't change [behaviour] I see little hope that US policy could succeed,' as Abdul Aziz Sajednia, a Professor of Islamic Studies at the University of Virginia,[23] has said; for a Western diplomat in Tehran, US aggression was 'a very crude' approach that would backfire by encouraging rival factions to close ranks, while for Sadeq Zibakalam, a professor of politics at Tehran University, 'the United States' threatening rhetoric against Iran, if anything, has actually benefited the hard-liners, because now they are appealing to the patriotism and religious sentiments of the Iranians'.[24] One reformist MP, Ali-Asgar Hadizadeh, even claimed that 'by adopting an anti-American posture, these people [Iranian hard-liners] think they can provoke a limited military attack, create a military atmosphere in the country, suppress the reform movement and take control themselves'.

Although such an appeal may perhaps not have the same resonance it once had among a general public increasingly supportive of opening dialogue with the West, it can still strike a powerful chord among people whose independence has for thousands of years been taken away or imperilled by the armies of its neighbours. These have ranged from Alexander the Great, whose followers trekked through the region after 334 BC, the Arab tribes that conquered the region and introduced Islam after 638, the Mongol hordes that swept through the region during the thirteenth century, the Ottoman armies that for centuries pushed against Persia's western borders in a bid to acquire more territories, and the Russian forces that from the eighteenth century frequently threatened to move southwards across its borders.

Such fears have long been both mirrored and played upon by politicians such as Rafsanjani, who has accused Washington of trying to 'realize an old dream that the Russian regime once had – to reach the Indian Ocean from the north', thereby emulating the Russian Czar Peter the Great who sent his armies to invade Persia in 1722 in a bid to establish a trade route to India across the Caspian Sea. Such fears also find clear expression in the Iranian constitution, Article 43(8) of which outlaws 'the foreign economic domination of the economy' in a country that had previously experienced such dominance: in 1872 Persia had been effectively sold out to a British businessman, Baron Julius de Reuter, and in 1891 Nasir al-Din Shah sold the country's entire tobacco industry for the sum of £15,000 to the British Imperial Tobacco Company, which monopolized the purchase of tobacco from Persian farmers and its retail distribution throughout the entire land.

Many of these nationalist passions were directed at the perceived exploitation of their country's natural resources, most obviously by the Anglo-Persian Oil Company. First established in 1908 to take control of the exploration and development of the region's newly discovered oil reserves, APOC was obliged to provide the Persian government with only 16 per cent of the profits it generated. By 1928 it had became clear that the company's operations were starting to stir considerable nationalist passions and the new ruler, Reza Shah, ordered his ministers to review the company's legal basis. Such nationalist sentiments spilled out into violent disorder in 1946, as protests and strikes broke out among the labourers at the company's main refinery, Abadan, and soon afterwards this discontent prompted the Majles to pass a new law that forbade the grant of any further concessions to any foreign companies and order a new review of the company's terms.

The best-known single episode of recent years that both encapsulated and aggravated deeply rooted Iranian fears of foreign intervention was the joint US–British venture in 1953 to topple Mohammed Mossadeq as Prime Minister in a desperate bid to reverse both his nationalization of the Anglo-Iranian Oil Company – Britain's main concern – and to prevent him from allowing any possible Soviet domination. Making contact with a dissident group of disgruntled royalist officers, the Secret Committee to Save the Fatherland, British and American agents were able to undermine Mossadeq's rule by bribing key officials, officers and clerics, supplying arms to rebellious tribes across the country and carrying out assassinations of his sympathizers, such as General Mahmud Afshartous, a Mossadeq diehard whose mutilated corpse was left outside Tehran to deter other officers from showing the same loyalty as his own. The joint CIA–SIS action, Operation Ajax, reached a climax in August 1953 when a mob of protesters, under the pay of the CIA's main representative, Kermit 'Kim' Roosevelt, stormed Mossadeq's residence, forcing him to resign and allowing the young Shah to return from a brief exile in Italy.[25]

Such historical experiences reveal why rumours and accusations of foreign support have always been central to Iranian politics. The political struggle between Khomeini and the Shah, for example, was fought out by allegations that the other side was allied with 'foreign agents' conspiring against the national interest: as the protests against the 'White Revolution' climaxed in the summer of 1963, Khomeini launched tirades against 'Israel and its agents' while the Shah and the head of his secret police, General Pakravan, claimed that many of the Ayatollah's followers had each been paid 'twenty-five rials to say "long live so-and-so"' by mysterious foreign sources. A few days after issuing this statement, police authorities also announced that they had discovered a large foreign spy ring and informed the press that a hitherto unknown individual, an 'Abdul Qeis Jojo', had been arrested as he entered the country from

Lebanon and was found to be carrying huge quantities of cash with which he intended to buy political support.

Washington's overtly aggressive posture has at times antagonized such deeply rooted suspicions and prompted noticeable shifts of opinion within the reformist camp. On 4 February 2001, soon after President Bush's 'Axis of Evil' speech, for example, the umbrella reformist group, the Second Khordad Front, publicly urged a new spirit of national unity that would allow Iranians to confront the US threat and any 'impudent moves by covetous foreign powers'. The perception of a foreign threat was not sharp enough, however, to smooth over the deep divisions between the various factions, and the front's statement included a well-aimed sideswipe against rogue elements within the regime: 'It should be stressed,' ran the argument, 'that in a sensitive and dangerous international situation, any kind of behaviour from rogue trends can endanger national security and the nation's interests and provide the necessary excuse to the war-mongering factions in the White House to start a broad propaganda campaign against the Islamic republic, preparing the grounds for a possible clash.'

Stronger signs of a respite between reformers and at least some elements in the conservative camp briefly emerged a few weeks later, however, as fears of US action against Iran were heightened by new developments in a long-running regional dispute over the sovereignty of the Caspian Sea. At a summit of five states on 23–24 April 2002, Iran and Turkmenistan reiterated their long-standing claim that the sea should be divided into five equal shares for each of the neighbouring countries, whereas the governments of Russia, Azerbaijan and Kazakhstan instead argued for any division to be based on the proportion to the shoreline of each country. Because this arrangement would have given their country sovereignty over only 13 per cent, many Iranians blamed this disagreement on the pressure of an American administration that, having toppled the Taliban, was now seen to be looking for new targets elsewhere.

As Washington turned up the heat against Saddam in the second half of 2002, President Khatami appeared less positive about the possibility of opening a new dialogue with the US government and instead became more mistrustful of American intentions. At meetings of the Supreme National Security Council, Khatami reportedly took a much more negative view of any such dialogue than hard-line members, whose more positive attitude was probably motivated by a wish to appease American pressure and thereby keep themselves in power.[26] And speaking at the Non-Aligned Movement (NAM) summit in Kuala Lumpur in February

2003, Khatami complained of Washington's 'position of Big Brother or, worse still, as a self-appointed master of the world' and of its 'instinct for a sense of superiority' so that 'the very security of many countries in the world is seriously threatened'.[27] This was a very different position from the one he had taken the previous October, when senior political allies of the President such as Mohsen Mirdamadi, Chairman of the Parliamentary Foreign Affairs Committee, had made open calls for a 'debate' and 'dialogue' with the USA, calls that had been immediately slammed by the Supreme Leader for their leniency towards 'so-called democracies based on lies and propaganda'[28] and by ex-premier Rafsanjani as bowing to a 'Zionism–Christianity coalition plan to bring about a big rift in Iran' and 'alienate the Iranian youth from the Revolution'.

Frustration with the political process

The most likely consequence of the struggle between conservative and reformist factions, however, is a political gridlock that prompts ordinary people to take to the streets, not the ballot box, in order to make their views known. 'The most serious threat to the country's political system is a situation where its rulers cannot justify their conduct to the people,' Khatami has argued, adding that 'if the demands of the public are not met, be sure that they will not abandon them. If they are frustrated, they will express themselves outside the system.' The President could perhaps have supported his case by pointing out how the 1979 Revolution had taken place in a country whose people had since 1965 been only nominally represented by a puppet parliament and which had since March 1975 been formally decreed by the Shah as a one-party state where only the Resurgence Party (Hezb-i Rastakhiz) was allowed to operate.

From 2001 there were increasing signs that this disassociation between the electoral system and its voters was already becoming a dangerous reality. Whereas 91 per cent of Iran's 33 million eligible voters had turned out to vote in the presidential elections of 23 May 1997 and 83 per cent for the general elections to the Sixth Majles in April 2000, this level of participation had begun to fall dramatically from the time of the next presidential vote in June 2001. Although Khatami won more votes than the 20 million he had received in 1997, a third of the electorate, numbering around 14 million potential voters, had stayed away from the polls altogether. The level of turnout was lower still in the local council elections held on 28 February 2003 when, instead of the traditional levels of around 70 per cent, less than 15 per cent participated in many parts of the country, including Tehran, the stronghold of liberal reformers.

Because conservatives effectively mobilized core support that amounted to around 7–8 per cent, they were able to make significant gains and take fourteen of the city's fifteen council seats.

It was not just indifference or apathy that lay behind this, for the level of popular interest in politics had been made clear by polling organizations like Ayandeh, which reported in 2002 that 71 per cent backed a referendum to choose a new form of government while 63 per cent were looking for 'fundamental change'. A more likely reason was that many of those who stayed away from the polls disapproved of the whole system of politics, sympathizing with the values of reformist parties but exasperated by their protracted struggle with entrenched conservative institutions. This was why opinion surveys conducted in August 2002 were showing that Khatami's level of public support had dipped to a mere 43 per cent, a massive fall from the 75 per cent approval rating he had enjoyed in 1998, and prompting the President to admit that 'there is a sort of hopelessness in our society'.

This sense of alienation from the political process is often expressed most clearly by the sentiments of Iran's student activists. Some of the protesters who took to the streets in June 2003, for example, shouted cries of 'Khatami, Khatami, resign, resign' and wrote an open letter to the President to either 'prevent turmoil before it is too late' or to 'act bravely by resigning from your post so as not to legitimize the policy of repression'.[29] Soon afterwards, one of the main pro-democracy student groups, the Daftar-e-Takhim-e-Vahdat ('Office to Foster Unity'), officially broke from the reform movement and instead addressed an open letter of complaint to the UN Secretary-General Kofi Annan. And speaking to a journalist after the demonstrations, one of the leaders of the June protests, student Sayeed Razavi-Faqih, spoke openly about what lay behind this outbreak. Following the conservative victories in the local elections of the previous February, he claimed, 'a noticeable shift in attitude had taken place' because of 'apathy' among students who no longer believed that 'reforms or elections could bring about the political changes they desire'. The reformist lobby in the parliament, he continued, 'is not effective and the parliament has not been able to implement its reformist agenda' and most students 'no longer have any ties to the elected institutions and reformers'.[30] Further consideration to this expression of popular dissatisfaction with the electoral system is given in Chapter 7 below.

There are many other unfortunate consequences of Iran's political tension. One is a state of social and economic disorder created, or unaddressed, by politicians who either are preoccupied by rivalry or who bear insufficient authority to make their proposed reforms effective. Such a scenario is considered in the chapter that follows.

Notes

1. Speech to the American–Iranian Council, 13 March 2002.

2. Speech to the Washington Institute, 2 August 2002.

3. Speech to the City College of New York, 10 November 2003.

4. Daniel Brumberg, *Reinventing Khomeini: The Struggle for Reform in Iran* (Chicago, IL: University of Chicago Press, 2001).

5. Baqer Moin, *Khomeini: Life of the Ayatollah* (London: I.B. Tauris, 1999), p. 225.

6. *Middle East Policy*, vol. VII, no. 3, 3 June 2000.

7. Asghar Schirazi, *The Constitution of Iran* (London: I.B. Tauris, 1997), p. 48.

8. Malkum Khan's article 'A Letter from Qazvin', *Qanun*, July 1890.

9. Moin, *Khomeini*, p. 19.

10. Malcolm, *History of Persia*, vol. II, pp. 303, 435.

11. John Kinnear, *A Geographical Memoir of the Persian Empire* (London, 1813), p. 45.

12. Samuel Benjamin, *Persia and the Persians* (Boston, 1887), p. 441.

13. *Middle East International*, 25 February 2000.

14. Associated Press, 2 February 2003.

15. BBC News, 5 November 2002.

16. *Aftab-e Yazd* (Iran), 29 June 2003.

17. *Keyhan* (Iran), *Resalat*, 3 July 2003.

18. *EurasiaNet*, 16 July 2003.

19. Information to the author from reformist journalists, Tehran, November 2003.

20. Speech, 3 June 2003.

21. *Middle East International*, 2 July 1999.

22. For the Persian texts of Montazeri's protests see *Khaterat-e Ayatollah Montazeri* ('The Memoirs of Ayatollah Montazeri'), February 2001.

23. Reuters, 23 June 2003.

24. Both quotes here from Mike Theodoulou's article 'Crude US Rhetoric Could Boost Iran's Hard-liners', *Christian Science Monitor*, 30 May 2003.

25. See Stephen Kinzer, *All the Shah's Men: An American Coup and the Roots of Middle East Terror* (Chichester: Wiley, 2003).

26. *The Economist*, 3 May 2003.

27. AFP, 23 February 2003.

28. *Middle East Times*, 27 October 2002.

29. CNN, 18 July 2003.

30. Interview with Kaveh Ehsani, *Middle East Report*, 15 July 2003.

6 | Social and economic malaise

At a glance, Iran looks unlikely to have the makings of a country in a state of economic crisis. Its superb natural resources of oil and gas, much of which remain largely untapped, continue to generate huge earnings, attract sizeable foreign investment and supply its industries with unlimited cheap energy. Backing on to the Gulf Straits, it is well positioned to export into the rest of the Middle East but also has easy access to the southern republics of the former Soviet Union, notably Azerbaijan and Kyrgyzstan, with which it already has well-established trade links. And with a population of around 72 million, Iran not only has a strong domestic market of its own but also possesses a talented and educated workforce comprised of a large number of university graduates – there were around 150,000 students at universities and higher education institutes in 2001 – who are ready to work for a very low wage. It is a country, as one leading Western trade delegate has argued, 'that has everything Turkey offers and a lot more besides', representing a 'massive business opportunity' for foreign investors.[1]

Nor might any state of economic crisis become immediately apparent from many of the statistics and reports of independent bodies such as the International Monetary Fund. Since the years of economic stagnation in the late 1990s, the IMF has produced some fairly upbeat analyses about Iran's condition and in June 2003 noted that its economy had over the previous three years achieved one of the highest rates of growth in the entire Middle East/North Africa region. The country's overall economic condition, said the IMF report, was 'relatively favourable', not least because its Gross Domestic Product (GDP) had grown by 4.8 per cent in the previous fiscal year, only marginally slower than the increases of 5 per cent and 5.8 per cent during the previous two years, and looked ready to continue along the same path. Although this was much lower than the sharp rate of economic growth experienced in the two decades before the 1979 Revolution, when Iran's GDP growth exceeded the rest of the Middle East and North Africa region,[2] it is a record that, nevertheless, scarcely seems to warrant any serious alarm.

The IMF also praised the direction in which the Iranian authorities were moving, singling out several of their recent reforms. These included the unification of the exchange rate on 21 March 2002, a measure that much simplified highly complex foreign-exchange transactions by replacing three officially recognized rates that each applied to different types of transaction, and a foreign-investment law that gave limited extra protection and incentives to international investors. The IMF also commended the establishment of three private banks and a reduction and simplification of the rates of tax, regulatory laws, non-tariff barriers and licensing procedures. Overall, such moves were judged to have laid the ground for further liberalization of the economy and to have boosted international business confidence in a way that became evident from Iran's successful return to world financial markets in July 2002, when the government successfully floated a Eurobond issue.

There are other superficial signs that point to the Iranian economy's good health. During the twelve months that followed the ratification of new legislation in 2002, for example, foreign investment exceeded 4 billion Rials (Rls), an increase of 70 per cent over the previous year that was sustained by the interest of major Western investors such as the Italian company MCC SpA, which agreed to put down $300 million on a vast aluminium complex, and British American Tobacco, which had also decided to invest $34 million in the production of cigarettes in Tehran.[3] Major investments also came from companies in India, which cumulatively invested $5.5 million over the same period, Germany and Turkey.

Yet this selection of upbeat judgements and statistics disguises the reality of an economy that is beset by deeply rooted difficulties. So serious is its condition that, on paper at least, it should have all the makings of a crisis that forces the regime's rulers either decisively to draw up and enforce a far-reaching programme of free-market re-forms, whatever political price they may have to pay, or else watch the economy crumble. But in practice it is probably at least as likely that the economy could limp on in the same relatively unreformed state, sustained by immediate-term measures implemented by a regime desperate to maintain its grip on power. Instead a crisis is more likely to eventuate if harsh economic conditions spark a small-scale protest that quickly spirals out of control into a major political confrontation: the social unrest sparked by sporadic fuel shortages experienced by parts of Iran in the winter of 2003–04, in spite of its natural resources, could in this respect perhaps give a glimpse of where the country's economic chaos might in future lead.[4]

Although the causes of Iran's economic failures may be complex and highly contentious, this chapter seeks to argue that the essence of the failure to find any meaningful solution to these difficulties is in large part a reflection of the country's political condition. For without freedom of speech, important viewpoints about how to solve this predicament cannot be aired, and without democracy important barriers to any such solution cannot be removed.

Some signs of economic distress

The reality of the country's economic crisis has become clear in lots of different ways. It is particularly telling, for example, that its dire condition has on occasion been openly acknowledged even by the regime's most ardent supporters. As noted in the previous chapter, the open letter written in July 2002 to President Khatami by Ayatollah Jalalluddin Taheri, a highly trusted senior cleric since the time of revolution, openly denounced 'the despair, unemployment, inflation and high prices, the hellish gap between poverty and wealth, the deep and daily growing distance between the classes, the stagnation and decline of national revenue, a sick economy, bureaucratic corruption, desperately weak administrators [and] the growing flaws in the country's political structure'. Similar despairing sentiments are privately expressed in almost every quarter of Iranian society.

But the most stark testimony to the state of Iran's economic crisis is undoubtedly the huge flow of its young people who each year leave their native country in search of a better future elsewhere. Although this exodus does not necessarily just manifest a dearth of economic opportunities – some argue that it also reflects a wider disillusionment with Iran's political system and its values – no one seriously denies that poor material prospects at home play a crucial part.

The exact numbers of Iranians who emigrate each year are inestimable – the IMF's own 'guestimate' quotes an approximate annual figure of around 160,000 from an overall population of perhaps 72 million – but the immense scale of the exodus is not in question and becomes evident in many different ways. Government ministers have voiced serious concern at what Rafsanjani has called the 'bitter and unpalatable' drain of talent that is urgently needed to rebuild Iran's own economy and whose exodus helps to create the very crisis it also reflects. The huge loss of this potential talent became clear in a report published on 2 March 2003 by *Iran News*: '109 of the total 276 scientific Olympiad prodigies in Iran have left the country to pursue their education overseas', reported the paper, adding that 'the younger generation is leaving their homeland, especially those who are bright and more well-off'. This alarming trend, it continued, gave the country's leaders 'no other choice but to create the appropriate economic, social, cultural and political atmosphere in the country so that the younger generation has enough incentives to stay in their own homeland'. In the summer of 2003, parliament responded by approving the general outlines of a bill that sought to tempt emigrant Iranians back to their country of origin by reinstating the nationality of emigrant Iranians, instead of automatically stripping them of it. And for Iranian businessmen, trying to keep skilled labour from leaving the country has become notoriously difficult: 'I can only keep my best people here for a few months before they emigrate,' as the head of one Iranian ISP has claimed, 'since I can only pay them about $500 each month. What are they supposed to do?'[5]

It is of course simplistic to conflate emigration with any lack of opportunities at home. 'There are huge opportunities in an economy that is growing very rapidly,' as one Iranian economist argues, 'but a great many Iranians just don't know how to go out and find them. Instead many have an image of Western countries where everything is given to them'.[6] In a country dominated in recent decades by a strong state sector at the expense of individual initiative, and where there is often a clear assumption that the state must 'create' jobs, such a view may well be not without foundation, but mass emigration none the less gives some reflection of the dire state of the country's economy.

There are other clear manifestations of the scale of the problem. For any visitor or resident of Tehran, a particularly noticeable symptom of the exodus is the spectacular growth in the number of foreign-language schools. One such school, Qeshm Language College, opened in the capital in the summer of 2001 with eighty students but twelve months later had enrolled 500 and was ready to open two more schools where the students would study for the Internal English Language Testing System (IELTS) exam, a compulsory qualification for those wanting to migrate to countries such as Canada and the USA, both favourite destinations for Iranian émigrés.[7]

The lack of prospects at home from which Iran's migrants are desperate to flee reflects an equation that is stated very simply but which has highly complex causes – that the rate of population growth in the country far outstrips the natural rate at which any economy can realistically provide new employment opportunities. A considerable number of the 1.8 million Iranians who turn eighteen every year will encounter great difficulties in finding work in a country whose registered level of unemployment was officially admitted to stand at 16 per cent in March 2002. In practice nearly everyone admits the real figure is much higher than this official figure, particularly among young people under thirty whose actual level of unemployment was admitted in July 2003 by the

Deputy Minister for Planning and Policy Affairs, Sadeq Bakhtiari, to be closer to 30 per cent.[8] The annual increase in available work, a figure of around 400,000 vacancies, lags well behind the 500,000-strong figure envisaged by the architects of the Third Five-Year Development Plan (FYDP), begun in 2000, and differs even more from the current annual increase of 600,000 in the size of the labour force.[9] Almost no economy, no matter how efficient and well structured it may be, can realistically absorb such a spectacular rate of growth.

This population growth manifests the 'Islamic baby boom' of the mid–late 1970s and early 1980s, which is to some extent explained by the efforts of the newly founded revolutionary order, anxious to beef up the future Islamic Republic, to encourage high birth rates. For the decade that followed the mid–late 1970s, the annual rate of population growth reached 3.2–3.9 per cent before suddenly tailing off to a relatively meagre 1.6 per cent from the early 1990s. This spectacular rate of increase accounts for the expansion of the population by nearly 50 per cent in the decade after 1976 and also means that, in contemporary Iran, around 65 per cent of the population is under the age of thirty and half are under twenty. This is a statistic that soon becomes apparent to any visitor to Tehran, the size of which has grown from just 2 million in 1970 to at least 10 million today and where young people predominate.

What, then, inhibits the rate at which work is created in the economy, thereby making, as the IMF has pointed out, 'job creation slower than in many countries in the region'?

Economic problems

Some of Iran's most important shortcomings are the same as those of most other developing countries. One vital missing ingredient in the recipe for economic success is the lack of reliable, up-to-date market data that every potential investor requires to assess risk and reward. Whereas in other countries this role is in part effectively played by government departments such as the Department of Trade and Industry, there is no comparable body inside Iran to keep investors fully informed, not least because such a role is beyond the scope of an enormous and highly cumbersome bureaucracy. 'Without this information,' as the Tehran representative of a leading Western multi-national puts the point, 'a would-be investor just can't identify the huge opportunities in the Iranian market as quickly as he needs to.'[10]

While this lack of information characterizes many developing economies, the Iranian economy bears other more particular weaknesses, the most obvious of which is its dependence upon oil. This became particularly clear after 1984, when the price of oil fell significantly and thereby allowed Iran's oil revenues to plummet from an annual average of $21 billion to a mere $6 billion in 1986. Having imported an average of $16 billion every year since 1980, this sudden downturn in the world's oil market in turn created a serious balance-of-payments deficit, one that amounted to $5 billion in 1986. Nearly two decades on, Iran still has the same vulnerability. During the 2001–02 financial year, for example, 59.7 per cent of government expenditure was financed by oil revenue that amounted to Rls 75 billion,[11] creating a trade balance surplus of $1.478 million in the first six months of 2002–03 that allowed the government to repay some of its external debts. But with oil still constituting 80 per cent of foreign-exchange earnings, such dependence also clearly makes the country extremely vulnerable to any future price fall, and is a dependence that has continued to alarm the country's leadership. President Khatami has pointed out that 'Iran lives on oil export revenues' so that 'so far as ... basic needs [are] financed through selling our natural wealth, then we will tread a wasteful and fruitless path'.[12]

This dependence partly reflects the way in which other sectors in the Iranian economy are inhibited by the adverse effects of a large-scale programme of nationalization that the regime initiated as soon as it came to power in 1979 and thereafter continued to cover all major manufacturing industries, mineral resources and the banking, insurance, media and transport and communications sectors. Despite initial attempts to liberalize the economy, state-owned enterprises (SOE) still account for around 70 per cent of the industrial sector. As the IMF reported in August 2002, 'the role of the public sector in the economy is significant, both in terms of ownership and share in GDP' (60–70 per cent), although 'the private sector is dominant in agriculture, construction and certain services' (8.02 per cent).

These weaknesses in the economy's structure were undoubtedly exacerbated by the impact of the bitter eight-year war with Saddam that began in 1980, although its importance is undoubtedly overstated by the regime. During this period the regime sought to cope with the demands of war by dramatically scaling up the role of the state, introducing a centrally administered model of resource allocation that relied upon an elaborate system of rationing, subsidies and price controls that has been only partially rolled back since the introduction of the first Five-Year Development Plan in 1989. Besides a large state sector, the conflict also bequeathed a painful legacy of debt, one that amounted to around $12 billion by the war's end on 20 July 1988. Iran had originally been able to finance its war effort from its export earnings with practically no resort to foreign borrowings, and even after five years of war its national debt stood at an insignificant $500 million while short-term borrowing was around $2 billion. But by 1985, after years of financing the war almost exclusively by cash payments to suppliers, the regime was finally forced to seek credit from international lenders. Inflation also moved sharply upwards at this time as budget deficits increased and all major economic activities suffered from the sudden decline in imports: the output and productivity of manufacturing businesses fell by about one-third between 1984 and 1988.[13]

Iran has continued to suffer from this damaging level of high inflation and its current rate, reckoned to be around 15.8 per cent during the year 2002–03, stands significantly above the world average rate of 10 per cent, having at times amounted to more than double that figure. Put into everyday practice for ordinary Iranians, this has meant that food prices are around seven times their 1979 equivalent, a figure that helps explain why ordinary consumption of bread, rice, meat and tea is estimated to have fallen by as much as 30 per cent over the same period. During the summer of 2002, outside observers for the IMF noted how ordinary day-to-day items, such as seasonal fruits and vegetables, had 'significantly higher prices than in the previous year, pushing head-on-head inflation to above 14%'. The end result for ordinary Iranians is a constant struggle to afford basic commodities as prices continually rise more than their ability to afford them, often forcing even highly skilled professionals to undertake extra jobs and work extremely long hours to make ends meet. Although such industry is quite usual among ordinary Iranians, official statistics estimate that 15 per cent of the population still live below the poverty line, although most independent economists also put the real figure far higher.

Much of this inflationary problem is a reflection of high government spending that pumps too much money into the economy. 'The growth in government spending,' as the IMF's report has emphasized, 'could lead to higher inflation and real exchange rate appreciation with further harmful effects on competitiveness.' These excessive levels of spending are reflected by some harsh economic facts. In 2002, governmental expenditure amounted to Rls128.86 billion, considerably higher than its revenues of Rls125 billion, and the measuring sticks M1 and M2 (money supply) were much more than the 18 per cent figure targeted under the Third Five-Year Development Plan, standing at 34 per cent and 30.5 per cent at the end of the financial year 2000–01, and at 19 per cent and 26 per cent by the end of 2001–02. Moreover, despite considerable efforts to rein back spending, government expenditure has increased at a much brisker pace than inflation, growing by 17.8 per cent in 2001–02 and 16.3 per cent the previous year.

Besides the inflationary pressures caused by government subsidies for the state sector, the predominance of SOEs in the economy has several other adverse consequences. Without market competition, state-subsidized industry remains particularly liable to making errors similar to those that have become particularly notorious at a giant steel works in Kordestan that originally cost $10 million to build but which, ten years after work began, is still a long way from completion. Such episodes reflect, in the words of the IMF, a clear 'lack of competition in many sectors [that] continues to weight heavily on productivity' and which is caused mainly by 'the dominance of inefficient state enterprises in economic activity and the lack of competition in the domestic market'.

The adverse effects of a strong state sector are also made abundantly clear from the activities of several semi-governmental organizations, known as *bonyads* ('foundations'), that control around 15 per cent of the Iranian economy and which are ultimately accountable only to the Supreme Leader. Although ostensibly charitable foundations, nearly all are really business conglomerates that seriously impede sustainable private-sector growth by acting as 'private mafias' whose privileged access to important licences, contracts and cheap credit has created effective monopolies that suppress competition and enjoy a tax-free status that has lost the government huge amounts of revenue. While the government of President Khatami has since 1997 made some very limited effort to roll back these privileges, they continue to distort the economy as a whole considerably.

These foundations have well-established origins in contemporary Iran, having nearly all been started soon after the Revolution by a regime that sought to use them to redistribute the 'illegitimate' wealth left behind by the 'apostates' and *saramyeh-dari-ye zalusefat* ('blood-sucking capitalists') who fled the country as the old order crumbled. In 1982 these confiscated holdings included 203 mining and manufacturing enterprises, 472 commercial farms, 101 construction businesses, 238 trading and service companies and 2,786 real-estate properties, many of which were given as a form of reward and patronage to those who were deemed to have assisted the cause of the Islamic Revolution.

Among those that hold most economic power in Iran are the Foundation of Imam Reza, the Martyrs Foundation, and the *bonyad* for the affairs of the war refugees. The 15 Khordad Foundation – which commemorates the 1963 protests against the Shah – is also another typical such institution, having been set up on 5 June 1981 at the instigation of Ayatollah Khomeini and his follower, Ayatollah Haj Sheikh Hassan Sanei. Another is the Razavi Foundation, a much longer-established organization that is ostensibly responsible for maintaining the tomb of Reza, the Eighth Shiite Imam in Masshad, but whose ownership of vast landed estates, particularly in the border regions of Turkmenistan, has prompted some economists to estimate its assets at $15 billion. Perhaps the wealthiest of all, however, is the Foundation for Mostaz'afan va Janbazan (oppressed and war wounded), which is widely recognized as the second largest commercial enterprise in the country after the National Iranian Oil Company. Headed for many years by Mohsen Rafiqdoost, a one-time head of the Revolutionary Guards whose association with Khomeini started in 1979, this particular organization employs nearly 400,000, boasts an annual turnover that amounts to perhaps as much as $10 billion and owns at least 350 companies that include the former Hyatt and Hilton Hotels in Tehran, the Zam-Zam soft drink company, an international shipping line and several companies manufacturing cement and oil products.

The Islamic regime also rewards its supporters with attractive patronage by working the predominantly state-owned banking system to its own advantage. Highly lucrative opportunities and benefit packages that are by any standards scandalous – bank employees enjoyed a 26 per cent salary increase in 2001 – have been available in all six of Iran's state-owned commercial banks, Saderat, Melli, Tejarat, Mellat, Refah and Sipah, and its three specialized banks, Keshavarzi (for the agricultural sector), Maskan (housing and construction) and Sanaat o Madan (industry and mines). Moreover, political favourites are generally offered loans much more quickly and at far lower rates of interest than are ordinary borrowers and are sometimes allowed effectively to default on their loans by having their debts 'rescheduled'. While this distortion of the market explains why the World Bank has urged the Iranian authorities to privatize their banking system, only one Iranian bank has to date been properly privatized, the Karafarin Bank, while two others, the Saman and Eghtesad Novin Banks, are only partially privatized. None can realistically compete with the street dominance of the state-run Saderat and Melli banks that run nearly 42 per cent of all of Iran's branches and whose market dominance is forcing them to struggle to compete.

The lack of a political consensus

There are many influences, however, that restrain the cause of economic reform in Iran and which have meant, in the IMF's own words, that 'the policy response has been too cautious', keeping the country at a 'point where a clear choice must be made between a strategy that continues to rely primarily on subsidies and government intervention to achieve gains in employment ... and one aimed at sustaining long-term growth and employment creation through greater efficiency and private sector-led economic development'.

Foremost among these has been a lack of the political consensus required to draw up and implement any forceful programme of economic reform. Although sympathetic to the cause of economic liberalism, President Khatami's own efforts to reform the economy have always been stultified by his political dependence upon the socialist elements of his parliamentary coalition that have in the past been much less committed to market liberalization. For this reason Khatami was forced to postpone any announcement of his economic plans until the autumn of 1998, nearly eighteen months after his election, when he put a much-watered-down 1999 budget before the Majles. Moreover, Khatami has also placated his allies by pledging his commitment to the fair distribution of wealth and appointing a proponent of state intervention to head the Ministry of Economy and Finance who maintained consumer subsidies and price controls. This lack of consensus is probably less true today than in previous years, since during Khatami's tenure of power the need for more wide-ranging market liberalization has become much more widely acknowledged, although considerable differences remain about what needs to be reformed and how it should be done.[14]

The highly contentious nature of proposals for market liberalization partly reflects the deeply rooted origins of state intervention in Iran. While some have argued that the state's dominance in Iranian life goes back to medieval times,[15] its centrality undoubtedly pre-dates the Islamic Revolution. In particular, the last two decades of monarchical power witnessed a vast expansion of bureaucracy, funded by a dramatic increase in oil revenues, that allowed the state to play a key role in the daily life of nearly every individual. Whereas in 1963 there were twelve ministries employing 150,000 civil servants, by 1977 this number had increased to nineteen such departments staffed by more than 304,000 employees. On the eve of the Revolution, nearly half of the working population in every Iranian town and city were civil servants who, for the first time in the country's history, had effectively supplanted the administrative role of local *khans* and *kadkhukas* by undertaking a considerable variety of tasks that ranged from the regulation of prices and the distribution of food and water to the building and maintenance of roads and railways.

But the strength of the state sector in contemporary Iran has also been reinforced by the way in which Islamism became merged with socialism in the years that led up to the Revolution. Although Islam is usually regarded as endorsing neither capitalism nor socialism but accepting the tenets of both, Khomeini and his followers voiced clear sympathy for the left, partly out of conviction and partly out of an opportunistic bid to win popular support in a society polarized by an immense gap between the extreme rich and very poor. 'We will deal with these capitalists, whose capital and wealth could not have become so large from legitimate sources',[16] argued Khomeini in typical vein, claiming that 'even if we assume someone has legitimate properties, the Islamic judge or *velayat-ye faqih* realizes that an individual having so much will adversely affect the welfare of us and he can expropriate those properties'.[17] It was in the same spirit that some radical but wholly unrealistic measures were attempted in the wake of the 1979 Revolution, such as the unsuccessful bid to close down the Tehran Stock Exchange on the grounds that it was an 'unIslamic' institution.[18]

One of the most important single influences in the decade before the revolution was Ali Shari'ati, a very eminent post-war cleric who in the late 1960s and early 1970s became a highly celebrated university lecturer, public speaker and author whose books became a national publishing phenomenon. In his main book, *Eslamshenasi*, Shari'ati forged an association between Islam and socialist egalitarianism and reiterated his long-held claim, originally put forward in the 1950s, that the principles of socialism had been first demonstrated by Abu Zarr, a companion of the Imam Ali, who had strongly objected to the luxuries of the early caliphs. By the time the Shah's police closed down his main speaking platform, at a forum at Ershad, in November 1972, he had undoubtedly wielded enormous influence over the public mind and played an important part in the popular association between Islam and socialist principles.

The socialist base upon which popular support for the Revolution was built became clear not just from Khomeini's promises of land, jobs and prosperity but from the influence of the left-wing Tudeh (Masses) Party upon the cause of Revolution. After its leadership was largely destroyed in a series of governmental arrests between 1953 and 1958, the followers of Tudeh, which commanded a large following amongst the country's young people, looked for a time to Khomeini as the main focus of dissent. In the later pre-revolutionary years that followed, Khomeini's followers also shared speaking platforms with the leaders of Tudeh, notably at the Resolution of the Ashura march on 11 December 1978, when at a mass rally of hundreds of thousands the

Shah's opponents decreed their economic programme in unmistakeably Marxist terminology. There should be a 'guarantee', their declaration ran, for 'the right of workers and peasants to the full benefit from the product of their labour' which would end 'the exploitation of man by man' and the 'exploitative profiteering and economic domination which will result in accumulation of great wealth on the one hand and deprivation and poverty on the other'. By demanding 'economic independence ... self-sufficiency and liberation from dependence from foreign domination', this Marxist language also blended with the deeply rooted national suspicion of foreign intervention that has been noted in the previous chapter.

In the immediate years after the Revolution, the Tudeh exerted a very strong influence over the new regime, mainly through its leader, Nureddin Kianuri. In 1979 Kianuri influenced Ayatollah Beheshti on the drafting of the constitution and was a main driving force behind Article 44, declaring that 'the state sector is to include all large-scale industries, foreign trade, major mineral resources, banking, insurance, energy, dams and large-scale irrigation networks, radio and television, post, telegraphic and telephone services, aviation, shipping, roads, rail, road and the like'. It is also possible that Kianuri instigated Article 49, which defines illegitimate sources of property ownership as usury, bribery, theft and the usurpation and misuse of endowments, criteria that can and have been interpreted very widely by the courts.

The result of this early association between socialism and the cause of Islamic Revolution has meant that many of the regime's leaders have previously had an instinctive leaning towards what has been termed 'statism-populism'. In 1994, for example, economic liberalization was condemned because of its adverse effects on the 'ordinary people' and in contemporary Iran the same attitude becomes particularly evident in the reluctance to reform the country's highly restrictive labour laws. Since its introduction in 1990, the Labour Law has put considerable restrictions upon the freedom of all employers, in the state and private sector, both to hire and dismiss employees after three months and thereby denies the economy the flexibility that all independent economists agree it needs. But reforming or abolishing the restrictions is a highly sensitive issue in a country where unemployment is rife, since the government would be open to charges of actively destroying people's jobs. For the same reason there is huge pressure on the Iranian authorities to be seen to be providing employment opportunities, pressure that has led to the adoption of a number of different initiatives, many of which are quite costly but of very questionable benefit. These include the provision of subsidized credits to small and medium-sized enterprises, the creation of retraining centres that provide new skills for those who need them, and tax exemptions on salaries of new employees. Even the strongest advocates of market reform are also forced to admit the high immediate and short-term costs of implementing any sustained implementation of reforms that would take considerable time to deliver any real benefits to the economy, as the painful experience of Russian economic liberalization from the early 1990s has demonstrated.

Such fears have probably been exacerbated by the experience of market liberalization in the early–mid-1990s when a new programme of reform was partially implemented by President Rafsanjani. Seeking to take advantage of an upswing in the oil market, one that earned an annual average of $16 billion in the first half of the decade, Rafsanjani introduced a floating exchange rate, scrapped subsidies for consumer staples and privatized some state-owned enterprises. But although the real reasons were much more complex, there was a widespread popular perception that the difficulties of implementing his programme caused a sharp upswing in inflation and a $30 billion foreign debt that forced the government to introduce austerity measures and perform U-turns, suddenly reintroducing foreign-exchange controls in May 1995. This experience has since left behind painful memories of economic reform for the general public, particularly when in 1994 the rate of inflation temporarily reached 59.6 per cent after price controls were lifted and the government subsequently raised the prices of particular goods and services in a bid to curb demand for imports and boost exports.

The lack of democracy

Governmental reluctance to implement such reforms in any lasting and meaningful way is really just a symptom of the much wider political framework of which the economy inevitably forms part. This is because, most obviously, a government that enjoys some legitimacy is clearly in a better position to meet some of the short- or immediate-term popular disquiet that its policies may incur. But because the Iranian regime as a whole – rather than just the elected government of President Khatami – clearly lacks such legitimacy, the temptation to avoid important and far-reaching reforms that may exact such demanding costs is significantly greater.

Perhaps more important, however, is the fact that the relative freedom of expression central to every genuine democracy is much more likely to allow the emergence of a consensus that recognizes the importance of such reforms, no matter how unpopular they may prove to be in certain quarters. 'In Iran there is no real idea of what the free market is and what its values really are,' one leading advocate of further liberalization, Ali Rashidi, has commented.[19] But without full democracy, the rulers of contemporary Iran have been able to inhibit the full discussion of economic affairs upon which such a consensus depends.

There are several reasons why they should wish to restrain discussion in this way. Above all, the implementation of full market liberalization effectively means devolving political power out of their own hands. In any successful liberalized economy, for example, a small number of outstandingly successful entrepreneurs inevitably emerge who would control enough financial muscle and perhaps enough prestige among the people as a whole to act effectively as alternative sources of political power and influence. A large state sector also allows the regime to command the loyalties of those it employs: many of those who attend state-organized public rallies do so because they would otherwise face dismissal from their places of work.

Such fears also inhibit international economic investment as well as domestic enterprise, and the rejection by the Guardian Council on 14 June 2001 of a long-awaited parliamentary bill aimed at providing a secure environment for foreign investment provides one such example of how such fears can hinder the effective workings of the economy. Rejecting the bill on the grounds that it would 'threaten the country's independence and territorial integrity' and could lead to 'foreign infiltration and domination of the economy', the Guardian Council acknowledged fears that are deeply rooted in a country where, for reasons detailed in the chapter above, 'the issue of foreign investment is often a very emotive one'.[20]

Another reason is a wish to protect the immensely strong vested interests that would have much to lose from any far-reaching economic reform. Whereas a democratic government derives its legitimacy from organized expressions of the popular will, an unelected authority generally depends upon the co-operation and support of elites whose loyalty can command material reward. This is the reason why Supreme Leader Khamenei has always forbidden any public discussion of the role of the *bonyads*, upon whose immensely powerful leaders he is highly dependent, and why during his term of office President Khatami has had almost no success in curbing their vast empires.

Without a proper, working democracy, many state-run organizations have therefore been able to resist any pressure for the financial 'transparency' that would allow independent bodies to inspect their dealings. State-run radio and TV networks, for example, were finally subjected to parliamentary scrutiny only in September 2002, when investigations quickly revealed a huge disparity between their actual and declared revenue, all of it donated by central government. This pressure also helps to account for the failure of the Iranian authorities to introduce genuine market reforms rather than more superficial changes. As the IMF also reported in 2002, 'in the financial sector progress in implementing reforms has been relatively slow ... progress in privatization has been limited to streamlining and clarifying the legislative and regulatory environment governing privatization, while actual privatization operations have mostly consisted of divestiture of government equity shares'.

The media are also unofficially but highly effectively restrained from discussing the financial dealings of Ali Rafsanjani, whose family acquired huge fortunes after the 1979 Revolution.[21] Those among his extensive family who are widely reputed to have particularly benefited include two brothers who have taken over Iran's largest copper mine and the state-owned television network; a brother-in-law who became a governor of Kerman province and a cousin who ran an export business with a turnover of $400 million. Rafsanjani's younger son also owns a 30-acre horse farm in a very fashionable district of north Tehran, while the family as a whole is also thought to have extensive interests in oil engineering companies, a huge construction plant that assembles Daewoo cars and private airlines.[22]

There is at least one other reason why an autocratic system of government is more likely to inhibit free-market reform than a democracy. Even if, hypothetically, a free economy posed no political threat to the existing order, Iranian parliamentarians and key civil servants are still more likely to be selected or promoted because of their loyalty to a status quo than because of their interest or experience in the matters that should really count, such as economics. Although there are of course many occasions when wholly unqualified candidates have been democratically elected as political representatives – as events in California in the autumn of 2003 amply testify – loyalty is clearly of paramount importance to any unelected regime. An example is provided by the case of Ali Rashidi, a renowned Iranian economist who has previously made two bids to enter the Majles, hoping to stand for Tehran in 1996 and for Gorgan in 2000. In spite of being a former president of the Tehran Stock Exchange and chairman of numerous highly respected research bodies and economic institutions, his candidacy was rejected on both occasions and other far less-qualified individuals selected instead. His rejection as a suitable candidate by the Guardian Council did not necessarily reflect any suspicion of the far-reaching agenda for reform that he has advocated but instead the absence of the same unmistakeable loyalty to the regime that the successful candidates could demonstrate.

US sanctions

All of these deeply ingrained economic problems have been significantly exacerbated by the sweeping economic sanctions that have been imposed on the country in recent years by the US government, although Iran is of course still able to trade with other international partners.

The current set of American economic sanctions against Iran had first been introduced in 1994 when President Clinton significantly tightened an existing embargo that had been last imposed by President Reagan on 29 October 1987. Clinton's decree took effect on 6 March 1995 with the imposition of Executive Order 12957, stopping American companies from purchasing Iranian crude oil, $4 billion worth of which had been bought in the previous financial year. They were extended after 6 May 1995, when the President had formally declared a national state of emergency between Iran and the USA, claiming 'an extraordinary threat to the national security, foreign policy and economy of the US [is] constituted by the actions and policies of the government of Iran'. The subsequent Executive Order, number 12959, was later consolidated and clarified by the administration on 19 August 1997 before being continued by President Bush on 14 March 2003.

These measures were supplemented by the 1996 Iran–Libya Sanctions Act (ILSA)[23] that allows the President discretion to impose up to two of six possible sanctions against any Western company investing more than $40 million in energy concerns in either Iran or Libya. The six sanctions of which a company could potentially fall foul under the act include a ban on its imports of goods or services into the USA; a federal government ban on the purchase of its goods and services; the imposition of a loan ceiling of $10 million by all US financial institutions; prohibiting the sanctioned entity from acting as a primary dealer of US treasury bonds; a ban on US export–import assistance; and a denial of licences that approve the export of controlled technology to the company. Although ILSA was renewed by President Bush in August 2001, it has hitherto only once been invoked when in September 1997 Clinton blacklisted a French oil consortium, Total SA, after its representatives signed a $2 billion gas contract with the Iranian regime. Even on that single occasion, the President backed down eight months later after his decree was challenged by the European Union.

There are other, more subtle, ways in which US policy has exacerbated Iran's economic crisis. The highly critical terms that successive

American governments have in recent years used to describe Iran have arguably fostered an excessively negative image that strongly discourages foreign businesses to invest. 'There's no doubt that Iran fails to attract the business interest it deserves because of the way it is portrayed in such negative terms both by the media but also from many quarters in Washington,' as one leading British trade delegate to the region has argued.[24] In particular, the tendency of the Bush administration to appeal directly to 'the people' of Iran rather than its reformist political factions has, not without justification, heightened fears of violent political disorder that would realize the worst fears of every investor. This perception has compounded the problems of Western businesses that invest in the country because, as one managing director of a British company puts it, 'we often find it difficult to persuade our British staff to make the regular visits to Iran that our company needs because many are just not sure about their personal security in such an environment'.[25]

There is another sense in which American political pressure upon the regime has compounded its economic crisis. For by fostering Iranian fears that the USA is poised to exploit any perceived weaknesses within the regime, Washington has accentuated the regime's fears of introducing even a more radical programme of market liberalization that would exact high short-term costs and thereby provoke popular unrest. Any popular demonstrations against harsh economic conditions, Iran's rulers perhaps calculate, would merely be whipped up by their American enemies and propagated as illustrative of the regime's oppressiveness and unpopularity. But the difference that this really makes is clearly negligible when compared with the much more important problems that are central to the structure of Iran's economy.

It is clear, then, that there is a very close relationship between the fate of Iran's economy and its political order. While it is of course impossible to predict how any future crisis might unfold, the following two chapters make some very tentative bids to consider some of the different ways in which such turning points might eventuate.

Notes

1. Michael Thomas, director of the Middle East Association, interview with the author, London, 27 August 2003.

2. Penn World Tables; see the chapter by Hassan Hakiman and Massoud Karshenas, 'Dilemmas and Prospects for Economic Reform and Reconstruction in Iran', in Parvin Alizadeh (ed.), *The Economy of Iran* (London: I.B. Tauris, 2000).

3. IRNA, 13 October 2003.

4. See the *Weekly Press Digest*, 8 November 2003, vol. 16, no. 46, quoting the website *Baztab*.

5. *San Francisco Chronicle*, 16 November 2003.

6. Interview with the author, Tehran, 8 November 2003.

7. BBC News, 29 May 2003.

8. IRNA, 1 July 2003.

9. IMF Report, August 2002.

10. Interview with the author, Tehran, 12 November 2003.

11. At the time of writing, $1=8,300 Rials.

12. IRNA, 2 November 2003.

13. See Sohrab Behdad's chapter, 'From Populism to Liberalism', in Alizadeh (ed.), *The Economy of Iran*.

14. See Sohrab Behdad's article in *Middle East Report Online*, 21 May 2001.

15. M. Karshenas, *Oil, State and the Industrialisation of Iran* (Cambridge: CUP, 1990), ch. 2.

16. R. Khomeini, *Payam-e Enqelab* (Tehran: Payam-e Azadi, 1982), p. 126.

17. Ibid., note vii.

18. Author's interview with former director of the TSE, Tehran, 12 November 2003.

19. Interview with the author, 17 November 2003.

20. Author's interview with Dr Azizi, Deputy Head of Melli Bank, 29 September 2003.

21. See Chapter 5.

22. See Paul Klebikov, 'Millionaire Mullahs', *Forbes Magazine*, July 2003.

23. See Executive Orders 12957, 12959 and 13059.

24. Michael Thomas, interview, 27 August 2003.

25. Author's interview with Western businessman, London, 24 October 2003.

PART III
Outcomes

7 | Popular uprising

There are several different ways in which Washington could try to engineer political change inside Iran. One is by the imposition of UN sanctions that would devastate its economy and thereby hold the regime to ransom. Alternatively it could support, overtly or otherwise, some of the armed militia movements that are in a position to pose a challenge to the regime, perhaps by means of carrying out targeted assassinations, armed uprisings or internal coups that would gravely imperil, or even 'decapitate', those who rule the country. This policy option is detailed in Chapter 8.

But US critics of the regime are also able to encourage something much more spontaneous yet potentially at least as powerful: the street protests of ordinary civilians that although perhaps entirely peaceful could conceivably bring any regime to its knees with the same dramatic power and speed as the toppling of the communist governments of Eastern Europe in 1989. For despite the great loyalty of the IRGC, whose members are tasked, under Article 150 of the constitution, with 'guarding the Revolution and its achievements'[1] and under Article 2 of its charter with stopping 'those who wish to destroy the Islamic Revolution', the question of how many fellow civilians any army is ever prepared to cut down is always open to question. The Shah had discovered this to his cost on 21 July 1952, when army officers talked of mutiny as their soldiers gunned down protesters who were demonstrating their support for the former premier, Mohammed Mossadeq, and again in December 1978 when the royal army refused to open fire on demonstrators, in some cases even joining the opposition they had been briefed to confront.[2] More recently, in August 1994, the heads of the Revolutionary Guards and the Law Enforcement Forces foresaw a similar danger when their troops quelled a rebellion at Qazvin, leaving thirty dead and 400 wounded, after regular army units had refused to intervene. Writing to their political masters, the IRGC generals warned of the dangers of 'using the armed forces to crush civilian unrest and internal conflicts'.[3]

This chapter raises several questions about such a foreign policy approach. Is it possible that such large-scale protests will take place in the future? If so would such protests thereby pose a direct challenge to the authority of the regime? And would such an eventuality in any case validate an American policy of actively stirring up such unrest?

Washington and 'popular protest'

Washington had begun to make open appeals for popular demonstrations against the regime, at the expense of reaching out to reformist politicians, from the summer of 2002. On 12 July the President urged young Iranians to 'work harder for freedom', stating that the USA would support 'the people of Iran [who] want the same freedoms, human rights and opportunities as people around the world' and advising 'their government [to] listen to their hopes'. Since then similar appeals have been reiterated by Zalmay Khalilzad, who has argued that the USA should demonstrate 'partnership and support for the Iranian people' and 'to continue to speak out in support of the Iranian people',[4] as well as by Secretary of State Colin Powell, who has advocated 'showing the Iranian people that there is a better world out there ... to put pressure on your political leaders and your religious leaders'[5] and going 'over the heads of their leaders to let them know that we agree with them'.[6] And from the offices of Washington's think-tanks, Michael Ledeen has pointed to polls that show 70 per cent of young Iranians wanting to mend fences with the outside world and argued that 'our most potent weapons are the peoples of Syria and Iran, and they are primed, loaded and ready to fire ... we should unleash democratic revolution on the terror masters in Tehran'.[7] He has also advocated:

> tangible support to the brave people who have called for a general strike. Once upon a time they could have counted on receiving money, communications equipment and moral support from Western trade unions, private philanthropies and their own diaspora. None of these has been willing to join the cause, to their great shame. But if the issue were clearly defined by all the administration's leaders, miracles might be accomplished.[8]

Many Washington voices had of course long argued in the same way for sidelining mainstream politicians. During 2002, as if bolstered by the President's earlier condemnation of Iran as a member of the 'Axis of Evil', US hawks are known to have pressed their case, arguing repeatedly that any open dialogue with representatives of the Iranian government, even with moderates like President Khatami, was futile. 'The administration,' argued Reuel Marc Gerecht, 'must not, under any circumstances, reach out to "moderate" and "pragmatic" mullahs to the detriment of the Iranian people.'[9] And Michael Rubin, a hawkish administration adviser, also urged a change in approach, pointing out that 'It is no accident that last October [2001], in the largest anti-regime protest since the Islamic Revolution, students, women, government workers, journalists and even soldiers took to the street chanting "Death to Khatami" and "we love the USA" [because] the Iranian people crave reform.'[10] Bush's 12 July declaration suggested that such hawkish views were holding powerful sway over a President who, significantly, had also just begun to adopt a much more aggressive tone towards Saddam Hussein.[11]

Iran's historic vulnerability to street power

American proponents of this approach are undoubtedly right in thinking that the people of Iran, at least as much as those of any other state in the region, have historically displayed a propensity for sudden, dramatic outbursts of violence that have posed serious threats to political stability. So Washington's premise, that a country that has hitherto often been rocked by such popular outbursts is also likely to crumble to the same pressures in the future, is in this respect a convincing one.

This propensity undoubtedly has very deep origins. The Zoroastrian religious faith, which had held sway in ancient Persia for nearly one thousand years preceding the introduction of Islam by the victorious Arab armies that stormed through the region after 638, granted extensive powers to political rulers whom its followers regarded as God's representatives on earth, but also acknowledged a right for such a ruler to be overthrown in the advent of any abuse of authority. Such ideas became deeply ingrained in the Persian mind partly because they were prevalent for so long, partly too because they were espoused by the legendary leader Cyrus as he began to forge the Persian nation after his accession to power in 559 BC.

This distinctive attitude towards authority later merged with the Shiite religion. Shiite Muslims, who currently make up around 10 per cent of the world's Muslim population, believe that the legitimate leader of the Islamic world of the Prophet Muhammad on his death in 632 was not the chosen successor but Ali, a cousin of the prophet who was over-looked as a contender. Being both better qualified and more virtuous, Ali and his son Hussein soon found followers who recognized a right of rebellion against established authority much more readily than their Sunni counterparts.

It was such attitudes that later helped to make the Shah's rule even more susceptible to popular protest. As already noted, because the shah-dom possessed only a very limited ability to enforce its vast theoretical powers, true political sovereignty traditionally lay elsewhere. Although in one sense this belonged to elected institutions, such bodies, if they existed at all, also relied upon the power of the masses to give them weight. Even as Persia's Qajar rulers were proclaiming their despotic powers in the most grandiose terms imaginable, during the latter stages of the nineteenth century, the political reality of who really ruled their kingdom was unmistakeable. Two typical instances occurred in 1886: a local *mujtahid* in Kashan quickly succeeded in removing the city's governor merely by threatening to bring huge crowds into the street unless this demand was met, while a Western visitor, William Ouseley, also recorded how the presence of agitated crowds in the streets of Shiraz almost immediately forced the local authorities to lower the price of grain.[12]

Street protest had also swung the balance of political power during Persia's 'Constitutional Revolution' when in August 1906 a sustained general strike in Tehran forced the Shah, Muzaffar al-Din, to stand down from his opposition to the establishment of a National Assembly. Soon afterwards Muzaffar was shaken by a huge demonstration of at least 100,000 agitated but peaceful protesters that prompted him to retreat further, this time guaranteeing a role for the new parliamentary body and the rule of law by placing his royal seal upon the Fundamental Laws. Alarmed by the rhetoric of secular radicals, a group of royalist sympathizers and ultra-conservative clerics conspired to undermine the new constitution by coup d'état the following year but were also thwarted by mass demonstrations in support of the revised arrangements.

A quarter of a century later, popular unrest on a massive scale toppled the regime of Shah Mohammed Reza Pahlavi. Although street demonstrations, often considerable in scale and typically violent in type, had rocked pre-revolutionary Iran from the autumn of 1977, they began to acquire highly dangerous proportions only during and after the following summer, when the number of demonstrators was swelled by the collusion of urban masses disaffected by harsher economic conditions. In July 1978 huge protests across the country forced the Shah to grant more concessions to his political critics by announcing the introduction of a new 'Western-style democracy' in which all parties, including the radical Tudeh, would be free to participate. His eventual flight, on 16 January 1979, took place against a background of months of violent protests – two million are reckoned to have marched in thirty cities three days before – and general strikes that made his own rule untenable.

The current Iranian regime has not as yet faced mass protests remotely as serious as those that challenged Shah Pahlavi, either in the tumultuous years before the Revolution or in June 1963, when his government narrowly survived violent demonstrations that were whipped up by Khomeini but brutally crushed by troops who killed hundreds of protesters. But there have none the less been occasions when sudden outbreaks of popular violence have given the regime's stability quite considerable jolts.

Some of these violent outbursts have been protests against governmental rules that were perceived to have unfairly imposed a harsh economic or financial burden. Three days of rioting in Shiraz, Shushtar Massah and Arak in 1993 that shook the newly elected Rafsanjani administration and left six dead were largely protests against price rises in a country that was then racked by inflation, while a more recent outbreak took place in Ahvaz in December 2002 among shopkeepers enraged by trade restrictions suddenly imposed by the Iranian authorities. Economic interests also account for violent rioting that took place in Isfahan in October 2001 as 10,000 textile workers protested against a parliamentary bill to close down state-run textile factories. Six died in Samirom in August 2003 during protests at the incorporation of a village, Vardasht, into a much larger municipality, while other major outbreaks of public violence have followed the defeat of the Iranian football team in qualifying rounds for the 2001 World Cup, which led to the arrest of at least 1,000 after three days of riots in Tehran. Other similar such outbreaks, although on a much smaller scale, eventuate in Iran on a regular basis.

Student protests, July 1999

By far the most serious popular challenge to the current regime, however, took place in the midsummer of 1999. For six days and nights, chaos ruled in parts of not just the Iranian capital but of twenty-two other cities, where as many as 5,000 demonstrators, many university students, took to the streets to stage often violent protest against the regime before being finally crushed by its law-enforcement agencies. Although the scale and seriousness of these protests did not remotely resemble the events of 1963, let alone 1978–79, there can be no doubt that they seriously shook the Iranian authorities.

The immediate trigger for the outbreak was the order of hard-line authorities to close down a reformist newspaper, *Salaam*, after it revealed some of the secret efforts orchestrated by Saeed Emami, a senior member of the Intelligence Ministry, to rein in the reformist press. Although few of the students who rallied to its cause had probably ever read the paper, the closure was symbolic of other recent acts of repression, including the summons and indictment of Fereydoun

Verdinejad, the reformist director of the state news agency IRNA, and the harassment of the Culture Minister, Ayatollah Mohajarani, who had helped to implement some of Khatami's reforms but who none the less had narrowly avoided impeachment for allegedly 'corrupting Islamic values'.

Some students at university campuses across Tehran had initially staged some small demonstrations as soon as news of the paper's closure was announced, but soon afterwards, on the night of 8 July, regime hard-liners struck a savage blow against them, deploying police units and vigilantes to storm a university dormitory and viciously beat some of those inside. Powerful images of these acts of violence were quickly disseminated throughout Iran and the outside world – notably an evocative picture of one particular activist, Ahmad Batebi, who held a bloodstained shirt before the camera – and as a sense of public outrage swept the country the student protesters seized the upper hand, making demands for the dismissal of the hard-line police chief, General Hedayat Lutfian, and for the law-enforcement agencies to be made accountable only to the reformist Interior Ministry. The initial wave of national revulsion gave the Iranian authorities no choice but to stand down: the President announced an independent inquiry, two senior police officers were dismissed and prosecuted, and even the Supreme Leader issued a statement deploring what had happened.

But far from being subdued by this new note of compromise, the protests suddenly gathered momentum as some enemies of the regime – many perhaps wholly unassociated with Tehran's universities – sought to capitalize upon this early victory by demanding more concessions, including ending a ban on seven other reformist newspapers and for the trials of those charged with the 'Chain Murders'[13] to be held in public. But it was at this point that much of the public became alienated from the student cause. For as large mobs stormed into the streets, forcing many Tehran shopkeepers, for the first time since the Islamic Revolution, to board up their premises against the bricks and petrol bombs that the demonstrators were using to fight pitched battles with the police, what had earlier looked like a certain moral and political victory for the radically minded students suddenly slipped from their grasp. The public, fearing a complete breakdown of law and order, lost sympathy with the protesters and the police forces were at this point licensed to use whatever means they thought necessary to restore order. Five protesters are thought to have been killed in the ensuing battles and around 1,200 arrested and hundreds imprisoned in the round-ups that followed.

The propensity of Iranian students to cause unrest had long been known. Tehran University had been the focal point for trouble in the early 1960s when the Second National Front Party organized mass protests against the Shah's political and economic programmes, forcing the authorities to close the campus. Students also played a vital role in orchestrating the disturbances of 1978–79 and the universities were later closed by Khomeini during the purges of 1980–83 to minimize the risk of popular protest. Their potential as a flashpoint against the Islamic regime also became clear in November 2002, when students organized mass protests to demonstrate against the death sentence passed against the reformist lecturer Hashem Aghajari for his alleged blasphemy (Chapter 5). These protests had begun in earnest on 9 November, hours after the sentence was made public, when more than 500 students lit fires outside Tehran University's campus, demanding the removal of the hard-line head of the judiciary, Mahmoud Hashemi Shahroudi, and shouting slogans such as 'Political Prisoners should be Released' and 'Our Problem is with the Judiciary'. Three days later the protests had not only grown significantly in size, numbering around 3,000, but had started to spread to other cities, notably Tabriz, Isfahan, Urumiyeh and Hamedan, where students abandoned their lectures to listen to rallying speeches and compile a radical 'manifesto' that called for much greater freedoms. But before the protests were eventually broken up and order restored, the students had succeeded in forcing Khatami to speak out openly against the sentence, which he declared an 'inappropriate' ruling 'that should never have been issued',[14] and had prompted the Supreme Leader to order its full review.

One feature that particularly alarmed the authorities was an increasing sign of co-ordination between protesters in different parts of the country. In a telephone interview with Radio Free Europe on 16 November, Abdollah Momeni, a leader of the nationwide student organization the Office to Consolidate Unity (OCU), talked about this newly found orchestration: 'In recent days, the unity of the students, their awareness and co-ordination in objecting to this religious inquisition against freedom of speech and this oppression of intellectuals has been excellent and we have been informed that students across the country are vigorously participating in this action.'

Six months later, on 10 June, unrest broke out again after an initial student protest against plans to privatize some universities quickly snowballed into a wider demonstration of several thousand protesters who denounced the hard-line religious establishment. These protests also broke new ground for a very different reason when eyewitnesses reported a new willingness to abuse the authorities in previously unthinkable terms, with some of the demonstrators even reported to have chanted the seditious and blasphemous cry that 'Khamenei, the traitor, must be hanged'.[15] These protests were also suppressed with the mass arrests of perhaps as many as 4,000 of those alleged to have been involved, a number that fuelled some suspicions that the riots had been deliberately provoked to give the regime an excuse to detain known trouble-makers at the universities.[16]

New influences

Such outbreaks of sudden, spectacular violence might arguably reflect a trait that lies somewhere in the Iranian national character, one that has historically been manifested at a governmental as well as a popular level. Particularly notorious waves of state executions, for example, were perpetrated in June 1981, when at least 2,500 death sentences were carried out in the wake of a devastating bomb explosion at the headquarters of the Islamic Republican Party, and again in the autumn of 1988, after an attempted invasion of Iran by the Iraq-based militants, the MKO, heightened fears of mass civilian insurrection. Thousands were subsequently put to death, not least at the bloody hands of Assadollah Lajavardi, the 'Butcher of Evin', whose taste for excessive violence had once led to his dismissal as head of the notorious Evin Prison but which now led to his reinstatement.[17]

There are, however, highly contemporaneous influences upon the people of Iran that inflame any more deeply ingrained traits. Perhaps the most potent is the Internet, the use of which has surged in popularity since it was first used in Iran in January 1993. By the beginning of 2003 around three million Iranians –around 4 per cent of the population – were reckoned to have some regular access to the Internet, a large proportion of whom belong to an age group that is also politically highly active. In 2001 Tehran also had at least 1,500 Internet cafes, a far higher figure relative to the population than that obtaining in other Middle Eastern capitals.

This growing popularity exists in spite of the considerable efforts of the Iranian authorities to repress both Internet users and providers. In May 2001, when the regime began its crackdown in earnest, more than 450 ISPs (Internet Service Providers) were closed down and in 2002 the Supreme Council for Cultural Revolution declared that any 'unIslamic' content published on the webspace of any Iranian-owned ISPs would not be tolerated. The following January a new campaign against the war with immorality was launched and led to the establishment of a new commission responsible for providing the Post and Telecommunications

Ministry with a full and up-to-date list of sites deemed to be illegal. The Tehran government has also warranted the arrest of some ISP managers, such as Mohammed Mohsen Sazegara, the editor of an allegedly 'seditious' website, and also claim to have blocked at least 120,000 individual sites, most of them of foreign origin and many pornographic, but others also the 'weblogs' that offer free news information that can easily disseminate uncomfortable truths about the regime. In recent years there have at any one time been around 20,000 or so such active weblogs on the net, one of which, published under the name Hussein Derakhshan, became particularly notorious to the Tehran authorities after receiving around 6,000 hits every day before finally being blocked.

Most of these efforts, however, have come to nothing, and the Iranian authorities, like their Western counterparts, are still powerless to stop the same content emerging elsewhere in cyberspace under a different name. Largely for this reason, use of the Internet in Iran, according to a spokesman for Pars-online, one of Iran's twelve certified ISPs, still 'remains largely unregulated' since efforts to block its material are 'not that intrusive'.[18] The sheer difficulty of censoring Internet use has meant that the regime has concentrated more on blocking opposition websites or news services, such as Radio Farda, that are funded by America.

The impact of the Internet on patterns of political behaviour is paradoxical. On the one hand it arguably distracts many people from participating in politics, allowing them an easy way of escaping from the unhappy realities of the outside world.[19] For those who are already disposed to take part in politics, however, there are at least two respects in which it can play a distinctive role. Most obviously, being a much more anonymous form of communication than phone or fax, it denies any state authority an easy way of pinning down the source and destination of a particular message and therefore gives dissidents much more scope to communicate among themselves and to publish inflammatory material that would be unthinkable on printed paper. For this reason, email communication has long been a favoured means of communication for members of many outlawed organizations throughout the world, notably Al Qaeda, as well as those inside Iran, such as the MKO.

Besides anonymity, the Internet also offers immediacy of communication, allowing political dissenters to make their own instant broadcasts to national or worldwide audiences by posting photographs or footage straight on to websites, thereby evading any efforts by the authorities to block out the scrutiny of the outside world. So should the Iranian police use excessive force during their attempt to quash any future demonstration, then photographic evidence of their actions would not have to be smuggled out of the country but could almost instantly be transmitted across the globe and win the demonstrators overwhelming sympathy and support. When on 18 November 2002 riot police sealed off an area around Tehran University by parking buses that obscured any outside view of their efforts to crush the revolt, their efforts still could not have prevented any of the students' own photographs from being posted online.[20] And during the further protests that erupted the following June, Mohsen Sazgara, a radical author and journalist, also placed pictures on his website of a violent vigilante attack on sleeping students that were instantly accessible elsewhere in the world.

Immediate, unregulated attention explains why the Internet has become a much-favoured form of communication for Iranian dissidents. In December 2000 Ayatollah Montazeri published his 600-page memoir online, venturing harsh criticisms of the regime in doing so, while Akbar Ganji, a leading pro-reform journalist, and Sayyed Ebrahim Nabavi, a dissident activist, have sought to resist their arrest and harassment at the hands of the authorities by also publishing personal accounts of their experiences in electronic format. In 2002 another leading activist for reform, known simply as Sazgara, published a strongly worded attack on the Supreme Leader on a popular Iranian website that not only received much attention within the country but which was also instantly transmitted to Associated Press.

While there are of course other ways in which the Internet can arguably inspire political violence, different types of media probably also have comparable effects. Radio messages and television images, for example, share a capacity for making everyone aware of lifestyles radically different from one's own, a capacity that, as Al Santoli of the Washington-based American Foreign Policy Council has argued, helps explain how the student rioting of June 2003 was perhaps 'driven by young people who have enough exposure to the outside world to know there is something different'.[21] For Iranians, this exposure has been provided as much by the satellite television and radio channels that have been broadcast into Iran in recent years and which prompted Supreme Leader Khamenei, speaking in August 1992, to deplore what he called 'the West's bombardment of our Islamic position with its corrupt culture'. A pejorative term, *Gharbzadegi* ('Westoxication'), originally coined in the post-war period by the Iranian intellectuals Jalal Al-e Ahmad and Ahmad Fardid, also began to re-emerge from this time in conservative rhetoric.

Much of this 'Westoxication' is propagated by the Voice of America (VOA) information service that reaches Iranian audiences from its Washington stations by short-wave radio transmissions and on television by the Telstar 12 and Eutelsat Hot Bird 3 satellites. The VOA, however, is just one part of a much wider media network that is run by the US Broadcasting Board of Governors (BBG), a US-funded initiative to bring 'truthful, objective and balanced news' to people across the world and which by 2003 sponsored broadcasts to Iran not only by the VOA but also by Radio Liberty and Radio Farda, a round-the-clock show aimed at young Iranians. In July 2003 the importance that the Tehran authorities attached to these broadcasts is measured by the 'deliberate and malicious' efforts of the Cuban government, reckoned to be acting on the instigation of Tehran, to block the Telstar 12 broadcasting of three programmes – 'News and Views', 'Next Chapter' and 'Round-table with You'– that Tehran blamed for inciting student protests a few weeks previously.

Since the late 1990s American-based radio and television channels have used satellite technology to broadcast directly into Iran, producing programmes aimed mainly at young people but potentially of interest to any of the estimated seven million Iranians who were thought to own satellite dishes by mid-2003. One of the first of these stations, the California-based Radio Sedaye Iran, began broadcasting directly to Iran in 1999 and took three years to acquire enough resources and technology to increase its initial two-hour slots to a twenty-four-hour coverage. National Iranian TV started up in March 2000 and within twelve months had acquired a huge following among ordinary Iranians devoted to its news shows, chat programmes and 'Saturday Night Live'. By the summer of 2003, it had been joined by a plethora of other channels with names such as Azadi, Pars, Channel One and Tapesh. Nearly all are based in the San Fernando valley, where their monthly broadcasting costs are currently funded by America's 600,000-strong Iranian diaspora who live mainly in and around Los Angeles.[22]

The power of television images and radio broadcasts to inspire dissent against the existing regime is in part reflected by the efforts of the Iranian authorities to suppress them. Public appeals against watching this material have been made by influential clerics such as Ali Akbar Hashemi Rafsanjani, who in June 2003 implored his fellow citizens 'to be careful not to be trapped by the evil television stations that America has established'.[23] The regime also maintains a strict ban on the ownership of satellite equipment that includes a right to impose heavy fines of between 1–5 million Rials ($120–600), despite a parliamentary bid in December 2003 – vetoed by the Guardian Council – to replace this prohibition with restrictions on what viewers were allowed to see. Partly because of the impossibility of effectively enforcing this ban on consumers who are adept at hiding their satellite dishes, the authorities have also made persistent efforts to block out broadcasts, efforts that in the summer of 2003 forced the Voice of America to switch its broadcasts from radio transmitters to satellite stations based in Washington.[24]

Most American hawks also regard the sponsorship of international media as a highly effective way of getting their message across to Iranian civilians. Senator Brownback's 2003 legislation (Chapter 1) proposes channelling $50 million towards the funding of radio and TV stations on the grounds that such media can promote democracy, while Brad Sherman, the main sponsor of a comparable bill in the House of Representatives, has argued that 'it is clear that those demonstrators now are getting information from the short-wave radio and satellite television broadcasts and are aware of the demonstrations because of that coverage'.[25] At the same time, the US administration has reportedly been drawing up plans for a $100 million 'pro-democracy website' written in Farsi for the people of Iran. While it is currently far from clear that any of these proposals will ever be put into practice, the hawkish policy of appealing to 'the people' of Iran, at the expense of reformist elements within the mainstream government, none the less raises unanswered questions.

Some difficulties of Washington's approach

The essential premise of Washington's appeals to 'the people' of Iran – that popular protest has the potential to push for far-reaching political changes – is in these respects a sound one. There are several reasons, however, why this does not validate America's policy of sidelining mainstream political reformers.

This is in part because a clear gulf exists between supporting ordinary street protesters on the one hand and an organized opposition to any regime on the other. As noted above (Introduction), without at least one outstanding leader, a degree of unity and a political programme with at least some coherence, it is highly questionable that any public demonstrations, even on a much larger scale than those of July 1999, are likely to pose any serious threat to the stability of the regime. Almost every government toppled by the street power of the popular masses has been challenged by outstanding leaders such as Ruhollah Khomeini, Lech Walesa and Mahatma Gandhi. But there is at present no Iranian equivalent to such exceptional figures, and the vital elements of an imminent political crisis brought about by mass demonstrations are plainly lacking. Even if such a figure does at some point emerge inside Iran, then there are other powerful objections to the American approach. Most obviously, any reference to 'the people' of Iran is clearly a Manichaean term that misleadingly places a very complex phenomenon under one convenient label. 'The Iranian people' are of course no more of a monolithic interest group with a distinct 'desire' and 'will' than their counterparts anywhere else in the world and are no more represented by street demonstrators than the general Western public has ever been represented by their own. The counterblast against the presidential speech of 12 July by Iran's Foreign Ministry, which condemned the USA for 'calling a few individuals the voice of the people', was in this respect entirely convincing.

Even if such an approach does succeed in bringing about the political changes for which American hawks have long called, it remains unclear why the risk of inciting violence against innocent civilians and their property is preferable to a more gradualist approach that allows the Iranian authorities temporarily to retain their grip on law and order while a new system of government is peacefully phased in. Instead the more radical US approach clearly means that those involved in any protests will inevitably pay a very heavy price because mass protests that threaten the stability of any regime are likely to provoke violent reprisals from law-enforcement agencies in the same way that thousands fell to the bullets of the Shah's army during the anarchy of 1978–79: on one particularly violent day alone, the notorious Black Friday of 7 September 1978, an indeterminable number that doubtless amounted to hundreds died in Tehran's Jaleh Square as tanks and helicopter gunships raked a huge protest with live ammunition. 'Hard-liners have used vigilante groups against student demonstrators in the past and the results were tragic,' Hanny Megally, the executive director of the Middle East division of Human Rights Watch, has said,[26] citing how these groups 'have brutally assaulted demonstrators using batons, chains and knives [and] have charged into crowds on motorcycles, causing numerous injuries ... and leading students into ambushes where they are attacked and beaten'[27] (see Chapter 8).

This objection becomes more powerful because of the tendency of such violence, no matter how it ends up in the short term, to breed more violence. When hundreds of protesters were shot by the Shah's forces at Masshad in 1935, a British consul observed that 'the massacre is not likely to be forgotten rapidly and while all this discontent will no doubt be driven underground by severe repression it might crop up again at some favourable moment'.[28] It is possible that he was proved right when, a decade later, further anarchy broke out in some cities, notably Masshad and Abadan, and more demonstrators were shot dead. Some have argued that the quelling of the popular uprisings of 1891 and 1963 merely repressed and aggravated feelings that were later manifested during the 1905–09 Constitutional Revolution and the 1978–79 Islamic Revolution: 'The son of Reza Khan,' Khomeini had chillingly but prophetically warned as protesters fell to the bullets of the Imperial Guard in June 1963, 'has dug his own grave and disgraced himself.'[29] There is also no doubt that the countdown to the Islamic Revolution was accelerated by the killing of at least six protesters by the Shah's forces at Qom on 7 January 1978, a massacre that prompted vast numbers to venture into the streets to pay their respects to the dead in traditional acts of mourning and thereby prompted further rioting.

Not only is a more gradualist approach more peaceful, but it also allows time for the drawing up of a new political alternative to the existing order. Just as critics allege that the White House concentrated brilliantly on battlefield strategy to topple Saddam but still overlooked how to govern a new Iraq, so too does an appeal to 'the people' of Iran appear to concentrate only upon the immediate objective of destabilizing the existing regime but ignore the difficult task of drawing up a coherent and appealing picture of a future Iran. By contrast, the alternative approach of reaching out to political reformers within the existing structure of government, as President Clinton's administration had sought to do, gives scope for just such a picture to emerge gradually. Moreover, the anarchic aftermath of post-Saddam Iraq shows clearly enough that not only would the welfare of ordinary people suffer but that the reputation of the outside powers – in Iraq's case the United States and Britain – that had helped to orchestrate regime change by force would also be blackened.

Looked at from another angle, Washington's appeals to 'the people' also stray perilously close towards an incitement to anarchy and violence. This is partly because there is no material difference between civil disobedience and anarchy, and partly too because earlier protests, although initially peaceful, have easily spilled over into violent disturbances. On a theoretical level, this approach is highly dubious: making appeals to individuals to take the law into their own hands against an established order appears questionable, for the reasons mentioned above, in a country where such views can be readily channelled into a system of limited democracy. But on a more practical level, any outbreak of violence is in any case likely to inhibit the cause of reform by allowing hard-liners to identify the protesters' cause not with the terminology of 'freedom', 'liberty' and 'human rights' of which Washington habitually speaks but with the breakdown of law and order. By invoking such fears among the Iranian people as a whole – fears that are undoubtedly held almost universally in a country with relatively recent memories of revolution – conservatives would force mainstream reformers to condemn the rioters and instead side with the hard-liners who defend the status quo and control the law-enforcement agencies.

It was for this reason that in July 1999, as the student protests spilled violently off the university campuses and into the streets, Ayatollah Khamenei emphasized the threat they posed not to the Revolution and its values but to law and order: in a speech on 13 July he denounced the 'riotous behaviour' of those 'who aim to damage public property', 'engender violence', and 'cause discomfort', and instead appealed not to any guardians of the Revolution to resist them but instead to 'the dear forces responsible for law and order'. The strongly defensive note that he had been forced to adopt after the 9 July dormitory incident also vanished, as the Supreme Leader continued by alleging: 'Officials in the government, especially those in charge of public security, have been emphatically instructed to put down the corrupt and warring elements with insight and power and, no doubt, those who have invested hope in the mischievous acts of these disgraced elements will be disappointed.'

Foreign support

The other appeal made by hard-liners to rally public opinion on to their side was the familiar accusation of 'foreign involvement' with the demonstrators. On 14 July Khamenei implored his fellow Iranians not to 'permit the bandits and counter-revolutionaries to allow domination by the criminal USA over Iran', while other conservatives, such as the parliamentary speaker and SNSC secretary general Hassan Rouhani, also warned vehemently of the dangers of 'foreign interference'. In an apparent dig at Turkey, whose Prime Minister, Bulent Ecevit, had on 13 July expressed his sympathy for the protesters, Rouhani had also added, 'We expected the reaction from the USA and the Zionist regime [Israel] but certain other countries are making a mistake by lending their support.'

This powerful appeal illustrates how the Bush line has risked hindering the cause of reform by allowing Iranian conservatives to tar protesters with the brush of foreign involvement. The same tactic also became more evident as soon as the June 2003 student protests erupted, when the Supreme Leader accused the USA of orchestrating the demonstrations and referred to the protesters as 'emissaries of the enemy', adding that 'the enemy openly supports these adventurers ... therefore the entire people, especially youth and officials, must remain vigilant'.[30] Rafsanjani also condemned the riots in similar terms, claiming 'the failure of the recent unrest in Iran is a further disgrace to the USA',[31] while for Tehran's Police Chief, Brigadier-General Morteza Talaie, the troubles had been caused by 'those who once used to serve Saddam Hussein and America... and who are now inciting people by means of television broadcasts funded by the Americans'.[32]

Interviewed by the *Middle East Report*, a student leader of the June 2003 protests also reiterated this danger:

> recent US positions have seriously complicated the position of the reform movement in Iran. Some reformers are highly sensitive to the issue of the territorial integrity of the country. The aggressive US postures encouraging internal disturbances ... will stir a strong reaction among liberal and nationalist-religious forces [and] a US military attack or a threat against the country's territorial and national integrity will create a strong nationalist reaction [that] Iranians will not forgive.[33]

US hostility 'allows the hard-liners to argue that there is an external threat and they must crack down in the name of national unity', argued Kevah Ehsani, editor of the reformist paper *Dialogue*,[34] whose words seemed to be borne out by the spate of arrests of reformist journalists in the wake of the student demonstrations in June 2003. And as President Bush voiced his support for the protesters, the Iranian Supreme Leader and other conservatives wasted little time in castigating them. For Khamenei, speaking before a crowd of several thousand in the southern city of Varamin, the USA was trying to turn disaffected people into 'mercenaries', while Intelligence Minister Ali Yunesi argued that the protesters were 'incited by extremists outside the country'. Such sentiments were also widely echoed on the pages of the country's state-run newspapers, and are widely reiterated by some European diplomats in Tehran: 'Washington would have done much better just to kept quiet during the protests and let things take their natural course,' as one senior diplomat has argued, 'instead of making things much more difficult by being seen to support the demonstrators.'[35]

SANAM: misjudging its importance?

Other similar question marks also hang over another putative American bid to stir up popular protest inside Iran – a possible association between Washington and an organization that claims to represent much popular opinion in the provinces of east and west Azerbaijan, where some degree of regionalist sentiment exists. For as American pressure on Iran increased after May 2003, the spotlight of international attention was suddenly thrown on the Southern Azerbaijan National Awareness

Movement (SANAM),[36] whose leader, Dr Mahmud Ali Chehregani, has reportedly met Pentagon officials to discuss the possibility of instigating a popular rebellion against the regime and to make some basic assessment of what would follow.[37] But the real objection to supporting the movement is not just that its exact aims and methods are either unclear or highly questionable, but that any such support would give the movement an importance that it does not deserve.

This reflects a disparity between the influence that the movement, like the MKO (Chapter 8), has acquired in Washington and the real following it has inside Iran. On the one hand, Chehregani has won some significant levels of support and sympathy among his various international audiences, especially those of Capitol Hill where he held fifty meetings in just eleven months during 2002–03. In the words of Patrick Long, a former departmental chief of the Pentagon's Defence Intelligence Agency, he is viewed by many people in Washington as an 'appealing' figure who has been particularly championed by Senator Brownback.[38] By contrast, however, SANAM is almost unheard-of inside Iran and there is no evidence at all that Chehregani commands any real following there. Although he was voted into the Majles as a representative for Tabriz in 1995, he stood as an independent candidate who voiced only very vague sentiments about 'Azeri interests'. His rhetoric is thus generally more of interest to American academics and politicians than it is to those whom it directly concerns.

This disparity does not at first sight seem obvious, since Chehregani has spoken in pleasing and sincere terms of his interest in 'human rights, total equality and justice'. He has also made an appealing case for more Azeri rights and argued that the Iranian regime, anxious to assert that 'the noble nation gives priority to unity over factors which might divide it',[39] has effectively banned the use of the Azeri language in schools, replaced the traditional names of towns and places, demolished buildings symbolic of its national past – notably an ancient amphitheatre at Shiru Kurshid – and deliberately underplayed the real number of Azeris in the country, which he reckons to be closer to 35 million than the official estimate of 14 million. Chehregani and his followers also point to the harassment and imprisonment of Azeri political activists who argue for the enforcement of Articles 15 and 19 of the Iranian constitution, allowing for 'the use of regional and tribal languages in the press and mass media, as well as for teaching of their literature in schools' and for 'all people of Iran, whatever the ethnic group or tribe to which they belong, to enjoy equal rights'.

There can also be little doubt that there is some limited degree of

Azeri mistrust and ill-feeling towards what is perceived as discrimination on the part of Tehran. This perhaps becomes clear, as SANAM claims, from the large public turnouts at various gatherings held to commemorate distinctly Azeri history, notably at Babak Fortress, in Kalibar in eastern Azerbaijan, built in commemoration of the Persian rebel Babak Khorramdin, which is today highly symbolic of the region's national past. More importantly, calls for Tehran to give proper recognition to Azerbaijan's distinctive interests have also recently been expressed in an open letter by Azeri academics and parliamentarians that complained of 'dust covering our civil rights', mainly by suppressing the Azeri language and failing to offer the people proper parliamentary representation, and similar complaints are frequently raised in the Tabriz press, such as an editorial in the daily paper *Payam-e No* on 9 June 2000 which complained that of the three Azeri ministers in Khatami's cabinet, only the Minister of Industries, Qulam Reza Shafei, was of any real importance.[40]

Such sentiments, however, are somewhat removed from the demands made by Chehregani and his followers for the establishment of a modern and secular Azeri state within a federal system in Iran. His preferred option, he typically states, would be to effect 'a federal structure resembling the United States, where Azeris can have their own flag and parliament',[41] 'a compact federated republic inside Iran' and 'a federalist form that respects the rights of Azeri Turks'. Although he has also added that 'we support the territorial integrity of Iran and do not seek unification with the Republic of Azerbaijan or Turkey', from other statements it also becomes clear that the SANAM leader envisages 'radical changes' that stray perilously close to what in effect would be an outright separatism: 'Our aim is to create a democracy in which autonomy will be granted to southern Azerbaijan. We want Tabriz to become the capital of our autonomy, which will have its own government, parliament, state attributes and army.'[42]

Chehregani and his lieutenants are also forced to admit that the establishment of what is, in effect, very close to an independent Azerbaijani state could conceivably open a Pandora's box within Iran. 'I cannot predict what will happen', the movement's leader has admitted, when southern Azerbaijan is eventually 'awakened', adding that 'if there is no interference from Europe and America then Iran will gradually split into different independent states and Azerbaijan will gradually go its own way' as 'the Baluchis, Arabs and Turkmens follow'.[43]

If there is no evidence that any of these sentiments are shared by even a sizeable number of Iranian Azerbaijanis, there is even less reason to suppose that they would support the use of violence to make them a reality. Chehregani, however, has remained ambivalent about the tactics his movement will use, speaking only of his wish to 'provoke' his fellow Azerbaijanis into action against the Tehran regime. But he has refused to rule out violence, claiming that 'tolerance and patience might wear thin in one or two years and we may have to resort to violence',[44] and adding:

We give priority to peaceful protests. If that doesn't work then we will go to public demonstrations, strikes and civil disobedience. We will do our best not to get involved in any military action. Our struggle will not be armed struggle but if we are provoked because the Tehran regime sheds our blood then we will consider using any method that will be available to us.[45]

The radical tradition of Iranian Azerbaijan

This is not to say, however, that the basic premise of any possible American support for Chehregani's movement is unsound. For because radical ideas and organizations have since the days of the Constitutional Revolution often been played out largely in Iranian Azerbaijan, there are good historical reasons to assume that the disintegration of the present regime could begin with stirrings in the same region.

This tradition in part reflects the region's linguistic differences with the Farsi-speaking population of Iran, a differentiation born of the influence of the Mongol invaders who in the Middle Ages had discouraged the use of the Persian language in these regions and instead allowed the Azeris to use their own Turkic-based native tongue. But although linguistic differences often nurture differences of attitude and loyalty, this does not explain the radical Azeri tradition: there are also other regions in Iran where clear ethnic and linguistic divisions have not historically generated a comparable radicalism of spirit, such as the estimated 1.35 million Turkmen population that is concentrated in the north-eastern provinces of Khorassan and Golestan. Instead, a more convincing reason lies in the foreign influences that have seeped southwards through northern Azerbaijan. Although formally separated from the Iranian province under the terms of the Russo-Persian treaties of Gulestan (1813) and Turkmanchay (1828), an open border and the use of a common Azeri language have allowed ideas, commerce and people to move with ease. During the Second World War, for example, Iranian Azerbaijan was well within range of a Soviet radio station at Baku that was specially set up to broadcast inflammatory messages against the 'Persian chauvinism' of the Shah's rule.

Another difference lies in the much greater degree of urbanization in this region than in the rest of the country: by 1945, the region was populated with twelve major towns and cities, each with a population of at least 100,000 – compared with just five in the province of Isfahan. These relatively concentrated Azeri masses, the product of a much higher regional rate of population growth than that found elsewhere in the country, were therefore particularly susceptible to distinctive messages that appealed to their material interests.

The radical leanings of some elements among the Azeri masses became evident at the onset of the Constitutional Revolution in 1906, as tens of thousands protested at the Shah's refusal to ratify the proposed Supplementary Fundamental Laws that would have guaranteed a role for a new national assembly and equality before the law. There was a particularly strong adverse reaction in the regional capital, Tabriz, where a crowd of at least 20,000 vowed to remain on strike and threatened to 'separate Azerbaijan from the rest of the country unless the constitution is immediately ratified', and where two years later, on 23 June 1908, the first protests took place against a royalist counter-coup in Tehran intended to annul the new constitution.

Half a century later, in October 1945, a small number of radical Azerbaijani nationalists instigated an armed uprising that led to the establishment of a new, independent 'People's Republic of Azerbaijan' with its own 'distinct national identity', while Soviet troops readied themselves to prevent Iranian military reinforcements from entering the region to suppress their revolt. The new republic did not last long, however, and its leaders sued for peace in December 1946 as the Iranian army moved against them. A subsequent Soviet bid to establish a communist republic was foiled when the Iranian government, acting under strong US pressure, approached the new UN Court in The Hague to force a Soviet withdrawal.

In the autumn of 1979, soon after the Islamic Revolution, other dramatic events followed this radical tradition when Ayatollah Kazem Shari'atmadari, the leader of the Muslim People's Republican Party, incurred Khomeini's displeasure by challenging both the principle of *velayat* and the validity of a referendum that had been put forward to the people of Iran. To show their support for his protest, some of Shari'atmadari's fellow Azeris, who regarded him as a *Marja'-e Taqlid* (Object of Emulation), seized a radio station in Tabriz while some of his party members organized a mass demonstration in the city centre. But as hundreds of thousands of protesters took to the streets of Tabriz, clamouring for Shari'atmadari to declare a jihad, a holy war, against

Khomeini, the Ayatollah lost his nerve and backed down, allowing the Revolutionary Guard to crush the rebellion.

Separatism within Iran?

But despite this radical tradition, Chehregani's ideas are still at odds with a strong identity that most Iranians have with their country, rather than just their region. At one level this is because, as a national entity, Iran has very much deeper historical origins than many of its Arab neighbours, such as Iraq and Jordan. With the accession of the Safavid dynasty in the sixteenth century, Persia became a unified dynastic state centred upon not just its ruler but also a shared language and a common Shiite religion that was institutionalized by the kingship in 1501. Since that time, the country has maintained a considerable ethnic diversity that also includes Kurds and Baluchis in the north of the country, Qasqais in the south, Turkmens in far north east, and Arabs in the far south-west district of Khuzistan.

In the two other regions where regionalist sentiment is strongest, Iranian Kurdistan and the far south-eastern district of Sistan va Baluchistan, there is similarly no evidence of any real popular appetite for separatism. Although many Kurds continue to complain of wide-ranging and high-level discrimination[46] that is perhaps based on the Sunni beliefs held by a majority of the Kurds, Kurdish regionalism no longer has the force it possessed during and before the 1980s. When, at the 1997 presidential election, the radical Kurdistan Democratic Party of Iran (KDPI) called on the Kurdish population to abstain from voting, their demand was largely ignored and, amid a high turn-out, a large number of votes were cast for Khatami. This blatant disregard of their demands forced the KDPI to change tactics at the Majles elections of February 2000 and instead urge the Kurds 'not to remain indifferent' to the democratic process, claiming that the 'liberation movement of the population' had made the elections worth contesting. And after years of unrest orchestrated largely by the KDPI, Iranian Kurdistan has since 1999 been officially declared by Tehran to be 'secure' from any real risk of secessionist violence.

Besides relaxing the grip of their security forces on the region, the Tehran authorities have also allowed its Kurdish population more freedoms than before. Clerics suspected of separatist tendencies are no longer harassed and permits for the performance of Kurdish plays and music are granted. The Kurdish language is now used more than at any other time since the Revolution, including in several newspapers now printed and among schoolchildren, while the presence of thirty Kurdish deputies in the 290-strong parliament has also helped to undermine claims of discrimination. The loyalty felt by most Kurds towards Tehran is probably best captured by this statement of a Kurdish representative in the capital:

> Every Kurd wants to see himself reunited with his brothers in an independent Kurdistan. But this is only just a dream. In practice independence from Iran would only be an absolute last resort if we are simply denied the same opportunities in the job market and the same lever of economic investment as everyone else. If only we had that, then we will certainly remain loyal Iranians.[47]

When viewed from an international perspective, the possibility of any popular clamour successfully pushing for an independent Kurdistan appears just as remote. Faced with such demands, a central government in Tehran would come under very strong political and perhaps military pressure from all its regional neighbours not to give way to any nationalist sentiments. As one former Western ambassador to the region has argued, 'Not only would the Iranians fiercely oppose such a prospect, but the Turks would be absolutely against it and the international community would also be very alarmed.'[48] A resurgent Kurdish nationalism would also be viewed as a possible provocation for military intervention by the Turkish government, which has always also been haunted by fears of Kurdish separatism within its own borders, and therefore almost certainly be quickly stamped out by Tehran.

Regionalist sentiment is probably weaker in Kurdistan than in the far south-western province of Baluchistan, where an even stronger Sunni population has long harboured resentments at the perceived discrimination practised by a Shia regime. In a region that is probably the most poverty-stricken in Iran, allegations that Baluchis are routinely denied the same employment and educational opportunities as Iranians from the country's other regions generally strike a powerful chord. Moreover, such claims scarcely appear without foundation, since very few of those within the higher ranks of the country's administration and armed services can readily be considered to be of Baluchi origin.

Such resentments have hitherto been strong enough to create the occasional law-and-order problem in the region. In February 1994 serious riots broke out among a local population that alleged a systematic plan by Tehran to alter the ethnic balance in the major Baluchi cities of Zahedan, Iranshahr, Chabahar and Khash, where the Iranian army had relocated some local people to make room for outsiders. Although the Tehran authorities have also frequently claimed that local trouble in the area is caused by common criminals, their occasional references to 'insurgents' have sometimes intimated something more serious. In October 2000 General Abdul Mohammed Raufinejad, a senior IRGC commander in Zahedan, claimed that 'the enemy has opened a new front against the Islamic Revolution' by sponsoring violence in the region, while in December 2003 reports surfaced of a rebellion near the Pakistani border that had been sparked by the shooting of a ten-year-old boy but which was never officially admitted by the Iranian authorities.[49] Warnings have also been issued by the Ministry of Intelligence of organized efforts to set local Shia and Sunni populations in the region against each other.[50] But any real pressure for autonomy is still widely considered to be most unlikely, and even as such sentiments peaked in the late 1970s, during a low-level tribal insurgency against the Shah's regime, it was in practice a remote prospect.

Instead of seeking to stir up popular rebellion, another option for American policy-makers is to sponsor an armed organization that can conceivably pose a more targeted challenge to the Tehran regime. One such group, the MKO, is looked at in more detail in the next chapter.

Notes

1. On 14 July 2003, following the student protests, IRGC spokesman Brigadier-General Massoud Jazayeri affirmed that 'the Revolutionary Guards will continue to defend the lofty value system of the Islamic Revolution in the military, cultural, political and social domains'.

2. *Washington Post*, 19 December 1978, reported that in the preceding few years troops had refused to open fire on demonstrators in Qom, while in Tabriz more than 500 soldiers joined the opposition.

3. *Middle East International*, 9 September 1994.

4. Speech to the Washington Institute, 2 August 2002.

5. CNN, 8 June 2003.

6. *Washington Post*,15 June 2003.

7. *The Spectator*, 12 April 2003.

8. 'The Moment of Truth', AEI, 30 May 2003.

9. *Weekly Standard*, 18 February 2002.

10. *Daily Telegraph*, 9 April 2002.

11. *New Yorker*, March 2003

12. Hamid Algar, *Religion and State in Iran 1785–1906: The Role of the Ulama in the Qajar Period* (Berkeley, CA: UCLA Press, 1969), p. 57.

13. See Chapter 5.

14. Radio Free Europe, 14 November 2002.

15. 'Tehran Protesters Call for Khamenei's Hanging', *Guardian*, 13 June 2003.

16. These allegations were made to the author by a number of Iranian journalists, Tehran, November 2003.

17. Amnesty International has documented 3,000 victims, although says that the real number went much higher.

18. CNN, 18 July 2003.

19. *San Francisco Chronicle*, 16 November 2003.

20. Reuters, 18 November 2002.

21. BBC News, 19 June 2003.

22. *Washington Post*, 26 June 2003.

23. Friday prayers, Tehran, 12 June 2003.

24. *Washington Post*, 3 July 2003.

25. *Los Angeles Times*, 18 June 2003.

26. <www.hrw.org>, 22 November 2002.

27. Letter to Ayatollah Khamenei from Human Rights Watch, 19 June 2003.

28. Foreign Office 371/Persia 1935/34-18997.

29. Hamid Ruhani Ziyarati, *Nehzt-e Emam Khomeini* (Tehran), vol. 1, p. 377; quoted in Baqer Moin, *Khomeini* (London: I.B. Tauris, 1999), p. 95.

30. *Jomhouri-ye Islami* (Iran), 14 June 2003.

31. *Keyhan* (Iran), 2 July 2003.

32. *Jomhouri-ye Islami* (Iran), 21 June 2003.

33. *Middle East Report*, 15 July 2003.

34. *Washington Post*, 15 June 2003.

35. Interview with the author, Tehran, 26 November 2003.

36. The acronym GAMOH (Guney Azerbaycan Milli Oyan Herekaty) is sometimes also used.

37. Pacific News Service, 6 June 2003.

38. *Daily Telegraph*, 23 June 2003.

39. Supreme Leader Khamenei, Friday prayer sermons at Tehran University, 17 December 1999.

40. See *Comparative Studies of South Asia, Africa and the Middle East*, vol. XX, nos 1 and 2 (2000).

41. Speech to Johns Hopkins University Central Asia–Caucasus Institute, 9 April 2003.

42. *Baku Echo*, 3 June 2003.

43. Telephone interview with the author, 1 August 2003.

44. Speech to the Centre for Strategic and International Studies, 2 July 2000.

45. Telephone interview with the author, 1 August 2003.

46. *Gulf News*, 22 November 2002; author's interview with Kurdish representatives, Tehran, 22 November 2003.

47. Author's interview with Kurdish representative in Tehran, 22 November 2003.

48. Interview with the author, 22 September 2003.

49. IRNA, 29 October 2000; *World Net Daily*, 5 December 2003.

50. Hojjatoleslam Ali Yunesi, speaking at Iranshahr, 25 November 2000.

8 | Dissidents

As US–Iranian tension heightened in the early summer of 2003, no one seriously advocated a full-scale military invasion of Iran by the huge armed US force that had just overrun the Iraqi army. Even a much more limited strike against particular targets, such as the Bushehr reactor or the military headquarters where Iraqi 'terrorists' were allegedly briefed, has always been considered a measure of last resort.[1] Instead, a strategy that carries far fewer political and military risks is to support an armed dissident organization inside Iran that can pose a targeted and well-organized challenge to the stability of the regime.

Such an organization can challenge an established political order in several different ways. It could undermine confidence in the regime by assassinating any number of its key members, just as Khomeini's rule was dealt a heavy blow on 28 June 1981 by a massive bomb that killed his party leader, Ayatollah Beheshti, and several cabinet ministers, and just as the Shah's rule had been badly shaken in January 1965 by the assassination of Prime Minister Hassan Ali Mansur, gunned down on his way to the parliament building in Tehran by members of the radical Coalition of Islamic Societies.

A militia group can also integrate its firepower with popular insurrection to powerful effect, perhaps by using guerrilla tactics to provoke a heavy-handed police response that could then stir up huge public anger: the two-day Tabriz uprising of February 1978, for example, when a huge crowd overran the city before being finally crushed by the Shah's helicopters and tanks, was provoked by the killing of just one teenage protester who had been shot by a nervous policeman. Or it could deploy its weapons to provide street protesters with limited armed cover from the law-enforcement bodies tasked with breaking up their demonstrations, just as on 20 June 1981 armed MKO guerrillas had fought pitched battles with the Revolutionary Guard in the streets of central Tehran as 500,000 protested against Khomeini's new regime. Occasional, spectacular acts of violence against carefully chosen targets also potentially inspire a much wider revolt in the same way that hit-and-run guerrilla attacks by the Fedayeen-e Khalq ('The People's Warriors') had in the mid-1970s struck a powerful chord among Iran's growing number of radical activists.

The issue of supporting armed militia movements to mount such challenges has become hotly contested as a result of Senator Brownback's legislative proposals to promote regime change in Iran, for although the Iran Democracy Act would bankroll exiled opposition groups for peaceful means, its sponsor has intimated that its terms could be amended to fund covert military operations against Tehran.[2] But, as this chapter seeks to argue, it remains far from clear how successfully any US administration could pursue such a course, partly because the only existing militia group operative inside Iran, the MKO, makes a highly unsuitable ally, and partly because the strength of the Iranian security apparatus will place considerable obstacles in the way of both the MKO or any newly emergent organization.

Should Washington strike up a deal with any unsuitable party, then it risks alienating wider support among would-be sympathizers who will ask, with justification, whether such an organization offers Iran and the outside world a better future than the existing regime. Moreover, such sponsorship easily plays into the hands of Iran's rulers, who can point to the double standards of a US administration that argues for democracy and human rights while supporting an organization that violates them. But the possibility that the USA might provide backing to just such an ill-qualified militia movement suddenly came to the fore in the wake of the fall of Saddam Hussein's regime in the spring of 2003, when allied forces moving through Iraq overran the bases of an armed dissident organization of several thousand Iranian exiles, the Mujahideen-e-Khalq Organization (MKO), 'The People's Army', that had been waging a long-term guerrilla war against the Tehran regime from the sanctuary of Saddam's Iraq.

Washington and the Mujahideen-e Khalq (MKO)[3]

The US administration was immediately confronted with a hard choice. It could close down both the camps and the organization, which had for many years been closely linked to Saddam Hussein's regime and which has been blacklisted by the State Department as a terrorist organization since 8 October 1997. On the other hand, it could potentially take the organization under its wing, using its resources to exert political pressure on the mullahs by effectively waging a guerrilla war against them.

Some US hawks have openly advocated this latter course of action. Daniel Pipes and Patrick Clawson, for example, writing in the *New York Post*, have claimed that, 'because Iran's mullahs irrationally fear the MKO, maintaining the MKO as an organized group in separate camps in Iraq offers an excellent way to intimidate and gain leverage over Tehran. To deter the mullahs from taking hostile steps [against the USA], it could prove highly effective to threaten US meetings with the MKO or providing help for its anti-regime publicity campaign.'[4] Not long afterwards, on 6 June, the New York weekly *Forward* quoted a well-connected former CIA and State Department official, Larry Johnson, as saying that inside the Pentagon 'the Office of Special Plans has been willing to reach out to the MKO and use them as a surrogate to pressure Iran'.

There had in fact been some signs of a new interest in the organization from some quarters in Washington just before the beginning of the military campaign against Iraq. At a press briefing on 10 March 2003 the President's spokesman, Ari Fleischer, had discussed the Iranian government's earlier admission that it was, after all, pursuing its own uranium-enrichment programme. But because the enrichment plants had been exposed by the MKO's network in Iran, Fleischer took the unprecedented step of praising this blacklisted terrorist organization by adding that Tehran had 'admitted the existence of these facilities only after it had no choice, only because they had been made public by an Iranian opposition group'.

Any suspicions this statement raised were reinforced as the allied campaign in Iraq got underway. Fulfilling their earlier promise to 'give no quarter' to the group, US warplanes 'bombed the heck' out of the MKO, striking two of its camps on 10 and 11 April in raids that the group claimed had killed eighteen and wounded forty-three. Yet this aggression was superficial since well-connected British sources pointed out that these attacks had in fact caused 'only a handful of casualties' and had targeted largely deserted camps even though the Khalq's militia had by this time already played an important role in Saddam's war effort, taking particular responsibility for his anti-aircraft defences in various towns and cities[5] and engaging US troops in several firefights.

Only as the war moved into its concluding stages were some of these initial suspicions confirmed. On 17 April, Brigadier-General Vincent Brooks announced from his headquarters in Qatar that while the MKO had been targeted 'for some time', the coalition was in the process of securing 'some sort of agreement that would be a ceasefire and a capitulation'. Five days later, on 22 April, both sides were still talking of 'negotiation', 'ceasefire' and 'ongoing action' while Brooks added that 'there's discussion that's ongoing to determine exactly what the condition and what the status will be and how we'll handle them'. He failed to reveal, however, that a ceasefire had already been struck on 15 April that allowed the militia to retain its arms.

Exactly what lay behind this decision is unclear. Allied commanders on the ground may perhaps have argued that to disarm thousands of soldiers would amount to an unnecessary distraction from the much more demanding duties with which they were then faced, notably the imposition of law and order upon a state of anarchy and chaos. It is also possible that they even envisaged deploying the MKO's militia in some basic peace-keeping role if this task proved too onerous for their own severely stretched resources. But whatever the real reason, such a decision would not have been possible without a high-level nod of approval from the same people within the Pentagon who share the Khalq's deeply rooted enmity towards the Tehran regime and who have at times almost certainly viewed the organization, despite its official status as a terrorist movement, as a possible future ally.

The ceasefire agreement certainly did not mean that any formal decision about the movement's future had been taken. It was a reflection, at most, only of a debate within individuals and departments of the US adminstration between those who envisaged a future role for the MKO, similar to that of the Northern Alliance against the Taliban in Afghanistan in 2001, and those who were sceptical of either the need for any such role or of the movement's suitability. Officially, of course, there was no suggestion of any ulterior motive and Douglas J. Feith, the Under-Secretary of Defense for Policy, said soon afterwards that allegations of any such debate were a 'characterization [that] was not accurate', adding that the Pentagon's position continued to be that the group 'is a terrorist organization'.[6] But reports of dissension continued to emerge. 'There are some who see the overthrow of the [Iranian] regime as the only way to deal with the danger of Iran possessing a nuclear weapon,' a US official told one British newspaper, '[and] the idea is to destabilize from within'.[7]

Whether it was because the more dovish elements within the administration won the argument or because of the embarrassing spotlight of international attention that the ceasefire agreement attracted, the White House backtracked soon after the 15 April deal and announced three weeks later, on 8 May, that further negotiations between MKO commanders and US General Roy Odierno had led to the terms of the original ceasefire being revised. The group would, after all, be required to disarm, handing over its weapons to the US army and withdrawing its personnel, again under American supervision, to their headquarters at Ashraf, outside Khales, some 120 km from the capital Baghdad. Some weeks later, on 15 August, American officials acted on the instruction of the State Department and closed the US offices of its political wing, the National Council of Resistance of Iran (NCRI).

Yet even this revised agreement has not as yet spelt the end of the MKO. Its militia were initially allowed to retain their light arms and the exact circumstances under which they might be allowed to gain access to their weaponry remained unclear. Four months after the disarmament, State Department officials complained that the Pentagon had not only allowed its members to retain their weapons but also granted them a freedom of movement from their camps that allowed them to continue with their military operations against Tehran. At the same time, a senior military commander in Iraq, Lieutenant General Ricardo Sanchez, also indicated that the group had not been disarmed and could also move at will[8] while in the United States soldiers of the 82nd Airborne were reportedly providing security for some of the movement's militia, who were also described by some American soldiers as 'patriots'.[9] Moreover, even if, in its worst-case scenario, the movement continues to bear a terrorist label, it is still in a position to reinvent itself by changing its name, leaders and slogans in a chameleon-like bid to find new supporters. Pentagon hawks are also in a position to sponsor not the movement as a whole but individuals within its ranks, or breakaway factions, who bear particular influence.

This is why a decision on 10 December 2003 by Iraq's new Governing Council to expel the MKO from its bases in Iraq did not threaten to deliver a deadly blow against the movement. The announcement also failed to give details of how and when the MKO's militia would be disbanded and did not specify if it had the backing of the US authorities, which controlled the Khalq's fighters. The plan, as one European diplomat told the *New York Times*, was unrealistic and designed to 'please the Iranians and annoy the [US-led] coalition in Iraq'.[10]

Military effectiveness

The essential appeal of the group to some Washington figures is based on the fact that there is simply no other serious armed opposition to the Tehran regime inside Iran. For Americans who are arguably more likely than many Europeans to over-emphasize the importance of an 'armed challenge' to a government at the expense of a more diplomatic approach,[11] the MKO remains, in the words of Bob Torricelli, one of their main congressional supporters, 'the only game in town'.[12]

To a limited degree this effectiveness reflects the resources that the organization has previously based at its six main camps in Iraq. Although the exact strength of the movement has never been clear, not least because of the uneasy distinction between 'combatants and non-combatants', prior to 2003 its 3,000 or so militia possessed an armoury of thousands of light arms, tanks, artillery pieces and even Soviet-made M-8 helicopters that was reportedly of poor serviceability and, as remnants of the Iran–Iraq War in the 1980s, outdated in any case. Instead more important is the network of sympathizers that the movement has over recent years established inside Iran, particularly Tehran. While comprised of only a small number of individuals, this network has previously provided MKO militia with safehouses where they were able to carry out military operations and to store weaponry that the movement has successfully moved in significant quantities across the border from Iraq. A favourite crossing point has been in the region between Kermanshah and Ilum, further south: in a typical exchange, one that took place on 8 January 2000, three Khalq members were intercepted and killed by units of the Iranian army as they moved materials over the border and headed for Tehran.[13] This network has allowed the MKO to execute occasional, spectacular acts of violence against the regime that were commissioned in Iraq and Paris and communicated to Tehran by coded radio intercepts received on long-range transmitters.[14] In recent years, they have included the assassinations of the former head of Iran's prison service, Assadollah Lajevardi, in 1998 and of Lieutenant General Ali Sayyed Shirazi, a deputy chief of staff in the Revolutionary Guard, on 10 April the following year.

It is just such tactics that could appeal to some in the Pentagon, where other guerrilla organizations have hitherto found friends and allies precisely because of their ability to inflict immediate casualties on the enemy of a particular moment, and this potential attraction explains why the movement or its remnants – particular individuals or cells currently affiliated to it – could in future conceivably elicit sympathy from Washington even if the actual organization continues to remain outlawed.[15]

Such military potential means that the MKO, or any successor organization that may emerge, might one day find the American backing, covert or otherwise, that it desperately needs if it is to have any political future. But this would not be in the interests of either Iran or the United States, and would in all likelihood discredit any American attempt to rein in or destabilize the Islamic Republic.

What's wrong with US support for the MKO

One central difficulty of backing the MKO is that it will open Washington to charges of shortsightedness, of supporting the group only to undermine the existing regime while overlooking the longer-term consequences of such a policy. In the light of American experiences in contemporary Iraq, where Saddam's rule was brought to a sudden end before firm plans for a new order were drawn up, such accusations clearly have particular force.

This short-termism is unmistakeable because the MKO harbours values and attitudes that scarcely seem compatible with the values of its putative American sponsors. The MKO has espoused Marxism, for example, from the moment of its inception in 1965, and still continues to retain its clear vestiges: the constitution of the National Council of Resistance that was drawn up in Dortmund in 1995 makes vague references to helping 'the workers, farmers and multitude of toiling masses' and revolutionizing existing Iranian laws to assist 'the true owners of the fruits of their labour'. Its left-wing origins also became evident from the influence of the writings of Che Guevara and of South and Central American guerrilla groups on the military tactics that it later deployed against the regimes of both the Shah and the mullahs, and from the testimony of a former KGB chief in Tehran, Vladimir Kuzichkin, who revealed in his memoirs that the movement had also acted as a valuable source of information for Moscow. Only the movement's self-declared feminism could conceivably strike a chord with some Western audiences, a feminism that emerged for no apparent reason after Rajavi's marriage in 1985 to Maryam Azodanlu, whose election as co-leader was trumpeted as a great triumph – an 'ideological revolution'– for Iranian women.

Although its 1995 Charter emphatically declares its commitment to 'general elections and suffrage', 'equal political and social rights' and an end to 'all forms of discrimination', the group's commitment to American values of 'freedom' and 'democracy' has also long been questioned by those who have pointed to a complete lack of genuine democracy within both the MKO and its political wing, also outlawed, the National Council of Resistance of Iran (NCRI). This matters because, if lacking, the group falls foul of the same contradiction as the Unita movement in Angola, which during its thirty-year conflict with the government in Luanda always proclaimed democracy but which was in fact a personality cult of its leader, Jonas Savimbi: the group's resumption of the civil war after losing the national election in 1992 demonstrated that a political party cannot seriously claim to value democracy for its country if it does not practise democracy itself. Moreover, the suppression of democracy within any political movement clearly entails a further violation of human rights – such as the harassment of members who fail to toe the party line – that makes its support by any Western government politically highly dubious.

Allegations of a personality cult of its leaders, Massoud and Maryam

Rajavi, at the expense of democracy have been made not just by defectors but also by respected journalists who have visited its military camps in Iraq and who have witnessed first-hand the brainwashed impression given by its members: in particular, a *Wall Street Journal* reporter visited MKO camps in 1994 and wrote of forced indoctrination, children being held 'hostage' from their parents and shocking violence. Since the early days of the revolution, wrote Peter Waldman, the MKO had 'become an authoritarian personality cult' that few dared to question. 'Some adherents who challenge the infallibility of the *rahbar*, or guide, as Mr Rajavi is called,' continued Waldman, 'are beaten and jailed ... and some members who ask to leave Iraq ... are put in solitary confinement for months.'[16]

Waldman pointed to the claims of a former member, a veteran of sixteen years' affiliation with the MKO, that in a move reminiscent of the Reverend Moon, the MKO's leaders had ordered all married fighters to divorce: 'Rajavi said we must forget everyone else,' claimed the defector, 'and love only him.' Rajavi's third marriage, moreover, was compared in his official writings to the Prophet Muhammad's own wedding in the Koran, praised as an act given by 'the light of God' and as a 'divine gift' to mankind. These and other claims have since been reiterated by French police chiefs, who have called the group 'sect-like', and by the independent monitor, Human Rights Watch, which has published the testimony of MKO members who have tried to leave the organization but who 'were first obliged to make a taped confession of having been a spy for Iran'.[17]

Besides being intolerant of criticism within its own ranks, the movement has acquired a particular notoriety for intolerance of its outside critics. The leaders of a Dutch organization for Iranian exiles, the Peyvand group, claim that their Arnhem offices were burgled and vandalized on 18 August 1998 and 28 March 1999 by members of the MKO, of which the Peyvand has long been critical. And in the German city of Bremen in January 1999 its members came within a whisker of killing an Iranian broadcaster and writer, Dr Ali Nourizadeh, who had often ventured criticisms of Rajavi's leadership:

> I was touring Europe, speaking and lecturing about the Chain Murders that had been taking place in Iran when I received an invitation to speak on the subject before 'The Association of Iranian Refugees in the City of Bremen'. I hadn't heard of this organization but agreed to talk to them all the same. Soon after I began to speak, however, around fifteen members of the audience, all sitting in the same row, suddenly became

abusive and then started to move threateningly towards me. Before I had time to react they had thrown something in my face and had begun to beat me ... the police told me later they had filled balloons with paint and thrown them at me and were all ready to kick me around the head when I fell down. It was only the intervention of an accomplice who fended them off that gave the police enough time to arrive and break off the attack, saving my life. It turned out afterwards that the gang all had specially designed metal studs on their shoes to kick me with when I'd fallen and that the ringleader was well-known to the police as a thug from Baghdad. The 'Association' that I was invited to address was also a complete sham designed to lure me into a trap.[18]

There could be no better illustration of the MKO's lack of interest in democracy and human rights than its past links with the regime of Saddam Hussein. So close was the association that any future alliance with Washington would, for this reason alone, prompt justifiable criticism that the USA is sacrificing all of its dearest-held principles in a bid to realize immediate goals.

Although its supporters have argued that the association between Saddam and the MKO was one of mere convenience – like the relationship between the USA and Iraq in the 1980s – this is misleading since the relationship was both deep and enduring. Rajavi had first come into contact with Saddam in 1982, visiting Baghdad from the Paris home he had set up after fleeing the Khomeini regime the previous year. And from 1986, when he was forced to leave France by a nervous Mitterrand government and headed instead for Iraq, the MKO militia effectively acted as a wing of Saddam's army, attacking Iran on the orders of Baghdad during the final stages of the eight-year war in the summer of 1988 and later working alongside the Republican Guard during major offensives against Kurdish militia in 1993 and 1996.[19] According to several high-level defectors, notably a former deputy leader, Nooruz Ali Rezvani, the organization later helped to deceive UNSCOM inspectors by hiding banned Iraqi weapons at its main camps, located mainly to the north east of Baghdad, and obstructed the efforts of inspection teams to visit them. In January 2003, such reports later prompted a thirty-three-strong UN team to raid an MKO base, situated at Abu Ghraib, 40 km west of Baghdad, although nothing was reportedly found.[20]

Not surprisingly, Saddam regarded the MKO as a mere extension of his own army and according to one Clinton official, speaking to the *Wall Street Journal* in 1994, even 'looked on the Mujahideen as more loyal than some of his own army units'. Using revenue generated from a UN 'Oil-for-Food' programme, the Iraqi leader was prepared to spend lavishly to fund a new base for the movement at Fallujah, 40 km west of Baghdad, that covered an area of 6.2 square miles and housed as many as 3,000 members.[21]

The most bloody and notorious chapter in the long story of the MKO's affair with Saddam, however, came during the 1991 Shia uprising when its tanks and APC undoubtedly helped to suppress the rebellion and take mass reprisals against thousands of innocent civilians in the most brutal manner imaginable. Its role in this episode has been independently verified by organizations such as Amnesty International and respected journalists who viewed first-hand the bloodbath that followed.

'Terrorism'

Because the MKO's role in suppressing the 1991 uprising showed clearly enough that its leaders had no real qualms about using violence against innocent civilians, the events of that bloody episode therefore also reveal much about the movement's designation as a 'terrorist' organization by both the US State Department in 1997 and the European Union, which followed suit in 2002. For however unclear the definition of the term may be, a militia that draws innocent blood, either by deliberately targeting civilians or instead by inflicting 'collateral damage' against them, is extremely hard to defend against charges of 'terrorism'.

American hawks anxious to overlook the Khalq's terrorist status have of course downplayed its use of violence in 1991. Daniel Pipes and Patrick Clawson, for example, have argued that: 'it used terrorism decades ago ... [but] for the past fifteen years the MKO has been organized as an army, and its only violent actions have been directed against the Iranian regime. Unlike Hezbollah ... the MKO attacks specific regime targets. Unlike the PLO ... the MKO really has foresworn this barbaric tactic.'[22] This mirrored the group's official line, voiced by spokesman such as Mohammed Mohaddessin, who has long claimed that its active operations 'target only military targets', not civilians, 'and can't therefore be reasonably termed "terrorist"'.

But the history of the MKO's operations inside Tehran reveals few qualms about causing civilian casualties, even if most of these attacks have targeted only military buildings and installations, mainly close to the border or inside the capital. During a sudden spate of bombings in Tehran during 2000, for example, a number of civilians were killed or injured. On 4 February an attack on the office of President Khatami, intended to disrupt the twenty-first anniversary of the Islamic Revolution, left one official dead; on 13 March a series of mortar explosions in a residential area near the Revolutionary Guards' headquarters in north Tehran injured four, although it remains unclear if these were civilian casualties; and on 8 May another six were injured by mortar fire near Tehran's police HQ. On 15 July 2000 around twenty mortar bombs exploded in Tehran's Seyed Khandan district, close to the Intelligence Ministry, ostensibly in retaliation for the previous week's 'suppression' of student demonstrations; on 22 October came another mortar attack on Seoul Street in what Iranian TV called an 'indiscriminate' attack on a Tehran sports complex adjacent to a garrison of the Revolutionary Guard; and on 24 October a massive explosion erupted at an ammunition dump near Masshad, home to the Iranian Army's 77th Division, for which the MKO claimed responsibility although its cause has never been properly ascertained.

Even if the MKO could boast a clean track record inside Iran, it is more likely that this would be a consequence not of any principled objection to the infliction of 'collateral damage' but of the very limited effectiveness of the small cells that operate inside Iran and which are ruthlessly pursued by the Iranian police (see below).

Any lingering doubts over the organization's qualification as a 'terrorist' movement were partly dispelled after 16 June 2003 when the French authorities, acting on the orders of Judge Jean-Louis Bruguière, deployed thousands of armed police backed by armoured vehicles and helicopter gunships to launch a massive raid on the MKO's Paris offices that were situated in the Auvers-sur-Oise region and a number of other sites to the north and west of the capital. After the raid, the head of France's counter-intelligence agency, the DST, announced that the movement had been planning attacks on Iranian embassies in Europe, was seeking to make Paris into its headquarters for such operations and had published an illegal newspaper, *Mojahed*, that posed 'a risk to the public order because it incites its readers to murder the main leaders of Iran who are likely to make an official visit to France'. The DST chief also claimed that the group had sought to 'proceed with the physical elimination of former members of the movement collaborating with the Iranian intelligence services'.[23] In France, continued the report, the MKO 'conducts many activities that have a clandestine ... and unlawful, even criminal, character' and the raid was therefore justified because the Khalq was fundamentally a 'criminal association that was aimed at preparing terrorism acts' and 'financing a terrorist enterprise'. Some have cast doubt on these assertions, however, alleging that pursuing such a course would have been reckless to the point of self-destruction.

Allegations of bribery

A final reason why US support for the MKO would imperil its cause against Iran, rendering it vulnerable to charges of hypocrisy and short-sightedness, is that such sponsorship would easily be perceived to be the product as much of financial lobbying as a genuine pursuit of the American national interest. For one reason why the movement has in the past won considerable sympathy on Capitol Hill has been its ability to buy political support.

The influence of this financial power has been investigated by a Washington-based journalist, Kenneth Timmerman, who has pointed out that many of its main supporters in Congress have received 'campaign contributions' from the NCRI. These supporters include Robert Torricelli, a Democrat from New Jersey, who is said to have received around $136,000, while Gary Ackerman (D-NY) and Representative Robert Ney (R-Ohio) have also accepted $4,000 donations that were later exposed by an under-cover FBI agent before being published by Timmerman. The movement's willingness and ability to buy influence in Washington have also become evident from its purchase of expensive media space in the American press, such as its full-page advertisement in the 15 January 2003 edition of the *New York Times*, bought for around $104,000 and registered against the name of a fictitious sponsor.[24] The June 2003 Paris raids, during which cash hordes of around $8–9 million were seized, also revealed the movement's full financial muscle.

How, then, had the MKO acquired such considerable resources? According to one defector, who had for a time served as a member of Maryam Rajavi's bodyguard:

> At the end of each month an Iraqi army lorry, under heavy guard, would arrive at the particular place where Maryam Rajavi was staying. The truck carried crates of Iraqi currency that were quickly offloaded. I also had indications from conversations I heard and from the currency I saw that there were substantial donations from Saudi Arabia, Bahrain and Kuwait …The organization was also very good at setting up sham charities inside Western Europe to acquire money before moving it out of the country, often to Dubai, where much of its investment has been concentrated. At the heart of this financial operation was a figure called Mohammed Tarighat Ma' Farid, known in the organization simply as 'Yasser'.[25]

These assertions were later backed up by French police, who alleged that an undisclosed number of Saudi and Yemeni patrons had helped to bankroll the movement.[26] German domestic intelligence officials also confirmed in November 2003 that before being closed down by the Landesamt für Verfassungsschutz (LV), Hamburg's intelligence department, sham charities such as 'the Iran Refugees Aid Society' had raised considerable funds for the NCRI from the large population of Iranian exiles in Bremen and Hamburg.

There are, of course, other reasons why the MKO's supporters have acquired such influence in the USA, not least through their success in conflating opposition to the existing regime with support for their own movement. Since there is no formal opposition, other than the MKO, that lies outside the mainstream of Iranian politics, it is alleged, anyone who opposes the current Tehran regime must necessarily support the Khalq. This was the approach advocated as early as 1993, when the movement first found sympathizers on Capitol Hill and the Khalq's Washington envoy, Mohammed Mohaddessin, was introduced to Congress members by Representative Robert Andrews as 'someone who has studied and learned the principles of democracy and the rule of law'. By the following year it had already found a small but growing number of sympathizers who voiced their support in similar terms: in 1994 James Traficant, an Ohio Democrat, called Rajavi 'the best chance for democracy in Iran', while for Democratic Senator Howell Heflin, of Alabama, the group simply represented 'all those who truly believe in freedom and human rights' inside Iran. Over the decade that followed, a growing number of sympathizers continued to conflate opposition to the Tehran regime with support for the MKO: a typical statement in 2001, made at a press conference organized by Gary Ackerman and Ileana Ros-Lehtinen, claimed that 'it is only our support for the Iranian people's aspirations for fundamental change and the democratic goals of the National Council of Resistance that can contribute to the promotion of peace, human rights and stability in this part of the world'.

The MKO has helped to forge this perception by making allegations – some reliable, some wholly unproven – about Iran's nuclear programme (Chapter 4). It was significant that in July 2003, soon after the crackdown by the French authorities had put the movement under a highly unfavourable light of media attention, the NCRI's Washington spokesman, Alireza Jafarzadeh, held a news conference to announce the movement's discovery of an undeclared Iranian nuclear complex at Kolahdouz, north west of Tehran. Although he provided no clues to his sources, Jafarzadeh claimed that the 40,000-square-foot site, under the control of an IRGC general, Javad Rabbani, housed hidden centrifuge equipment that was used to test the uranium-enrichment complex being set up at Natanz. This hidden site, he continued, would also allow the nuclear programme to proceed in the event of any military attack on Natanz. Some months later, the NCRI also accused Tehran of concealing a suspected atomic weapons site at Isfahan on the eve of a visit by the head of the UN's nuclear watchdog.

But there can still be no doubt that financial power plays a key part in explaining the movement's considerable political support, the full extent of which became clear when in November 2002, as US pressure on Saddam Hussein mounted, more than 150 congressmen and -women signed a petition that urged the White House to end the group's blacklisted status. The strength of this support reflected not just the number of supporters but their influence on some of those among them, including Ileana Ros-Lehtinen (R-Florida), the chairperson of the Central Asia and Middle East Sub-Committee in the House of Representatives, who later wrote in the April edition of *The Hill* that the MKO merited strong support because it is 'assisting us in the War on Terror'. Another such supporter has been John Ashcroft, Bush's Attorney-General and, to the embarrassment of the White House, also a top commander in the War on Terror, who became involved with the group during his career as a senator. Ashcroft had become a well-publicized supporter of the MKO after issuing a joint statement of solidarity for the movement at an NCRI rally outside the UN building in New York in September 2000, and after petitioning Janet Reno, the then Attorney-General, to release a leading NCRI spokeswoman, Mahnaz Samadi, from the custody of the US Immigration and Naturalization Service.[27]

Effect on Iranian politics

A final reason why any US sponsorship of the MKO would prove self-defeating is that it would play into the hands of hard-liners who would try to rally the political nation behind their struggle with a movement that is profoundly unpopular with the Iranian people. 'You're talking about a really popular movement,' one of its Washington spokesmen, Alireza Jafarzadeh, may claim, but nearly all independent observers inside Iran agree that the MKO has long been regarded as a mere puppet of their arch-enemy, Iraq. A report presented in August 2000 by the Dutch government to the EU Council, which had to decide whether to replicate Washington's decision to condemn it as a terrorist movement, declared that 'the MKO seems to have virtually no following in Iran', not least because it was 'severely discredited' by its Iraqi association, and it is also significant that the group's representatives are forced to turn back to the early 1980s to illustrate any real popular feeling for the movement.[28] If it is hard to justify the MKO's claim to be 'freedom-fighters' who are 'liberating' a population, then it is also easy to envisage Iran's hard-liners capitalizing upon the movement's unpopularity should it ever pose a perceived threat to the Islamic Republic.

This in part manifests the continuing bitterness harboured by many Iranians against Iraq, whose ties with the MKO have always been widely known. The antipathy between the two countries reflects not just a historical rivalry between Arab and Persian, or any more general suspicion of all foreign intervention, but the bitter impact of the extremely bloody eight-year conflict between the two countries. Although the number of casualties on both sides remains inestimable, millions of Iranians were undoubtedly killed and a far greater number maimed and injured. Iranian antipathy became particularly bitter during the 'War of the Cities' that began on 28 February 1988, when Iraq launched its first attack against the Iranian capital, more than 550 km from the nearest Iraqi soil, with newly developed long-range ground-to-ground missiles. Over the next five months the Iraqis launched 189 similar missiles against Tehran, causing not just thousands of casualties but also fuelling a lasting bitterness among the city's large population, then around seven million strong.

If considerations such as these do dissuade the White House from backing the MKO or any affiliate association, then there are at present no other armed opposition movements to which the USA could turn. Any effort to create such an organization from scratch, moreover, would face major obstacles from Iran's efficient security apparatus.

The lack of armed opposition to the regime

If they should look for any other established armed opposition movement to execute regime change inside Iran, then Washington hawks have few names from which to choose. Some such organizations, for example, have previously harboured an even greater emnity towards the USA and its values than to the Iranian leaders they opposed. This was true of one shadowy armed dissident group that mysteriously emerged in the late 1990s before being finally crushed by the security forces – the Mahdaviat, named after the Twelfth 'missing' Imam and led by Hassan Milani, the grandson of Ayatollah Mohammed-Hadi Milani, a Shiite leader who died before the 1979 Revolution.

Comprised of Iraqi Shia dissidents who regarded the Iranian government of the newly elected reformist president Muhammad Khatami as too liberal and straying dangerously from the values inculcated by Ayatollah Khomeini, the organization orchestrated a number of military attacks against key targets. Although the group was only very small in number, its leaders and sympathizers were well connected with the Iranian government and were therefore able to inflict a number of well-aimed blows on the regime that potentially presented a serious challenge to its stability. These included an assassination attempt on Ali Razini, the head of the Tehran justice department, who was left crippled in January 1999 by a car bomb, while the following year a plot to assassinate Mohammed Khatami, Akbar Rafsanjani and Muhammad Yazdi, the former judiciary chief, was narrowly foiled by police who later alleged that the group had set up storage facilities for a small but potent armoury of weapons and ammunition, stolen from military stores, which it planned to use against Sunni minorities and thereby 'sow religious discord' inside the Republic.[29] The leaders were captured by the police in 2000.

A few organized militia groups have also on occasion appeared along Iran's eastern border, although they have rarely posed any significant threat. During the mid–late 1990s, for example, the Taliban regime in Afghanistan gave sanctuary and light arms to a small but determined group, the Ahl-e-Sunnah Wal Jamaat, that recruited Sunni militants from the Iranian regions of Khorassan and Sistan, as well as disaffected elements from among its Turkmen, Baluchi and Afghan minorities. The group was initially given refuge in Kandahar, but Iranian diplomats allege that the group was later moved, at the request of the Taliban authorities, to Herat where they were better positioned to carry out sabotage inside Iran. Because the Tehran authorities became convinced that the group was strongly backed by the elements of the Pakistani intelligence service as an anti-Iranian organization, the militia's presence helped to fuel Iran's existing antipathy to the Taliban and almost certainly prompted their more proactive role in the war after 1998.[30]

Based along Iran's western borders are the remnants of another armed movement, the Kurdistan Democratic Party of Iran (KDPI), that currently poses no significant threat to its stability. The KDPI was defeated as a serious military force in July 1996, as major military offensives by at least 2,000 Iranian soldiers backed with heavy artillery and airstrikes pushed its insurgent forces back from their positions along the border with Iraq and struck their main bases at Qala Diza and Koi-Sanjak, 65 km across the border. Although the KDPI still has a number of armed followers, perhaps amounting to several hundred, who unofficially launch occasional hit-and-run attacks against Iranian targets, the group has been effectively controlled both by the PUK (Chapter 3), upon which Tehran has exerted considerable political leverage, and by small but effective militia groups, such as the Iraqi Kurdish Hezbollah, that have effectively waged Tehran's war by proxy.[31] Since 1997 this hard-hitting response has forced the KDPI officially to 'reject all acts of terrorism and ... planting bombs in public places' and Abdullah Hassan-Zadeh, the movement's secretary-general, instead makes only vague references to his peaceful pursuit of 'Kurdish rights' rather than the use of violent means to replace the Islamic Republic with a democratic, federal and secular state.[32]

This is not to say that the KDPI might not one day stage a comeback if there is a perceived power vacuum in Iran into which nationalist forces could conceivably step. Similar reversals of fortune have been staged by the two main Kurdish parties, the PUK and KDP, that quickly gained strength in the early 1990s even though both had been decimated by the military onslaught unleashed against them in 1988 by a vengeful Iraqi leader who suspected his own Kurdish population of complicity with the Iranians. Moreover, the KDPI has historically also staged its own comebacks. Originally a strong party on its formation in 1945, it was destroyed in 1966–67 by the Shah's major offensives but was reconstituted after 1973 at the instigation of a new leader, Mustafa Hedjri. It unofficially won a measure of autonomy from the revolutionary regime in the early 1980s after its forces resisted the advances of the Revolutionary Guard, already severely stretched by the demands of fighting the Iraqi military, and forced them to withdraw from Mahabad, Sanandaj and Kamyaran.

For American hawks seeking to destabilize the Iranian regime by covert military means there is, then, virtually no existing armed organization other than the MKO to which to turn. Any other existing dissident movement, or any new one that Washington might seek to conjure, would face a formidable enemy in the security services that are entrusted with the task of tracking down and eliminating internal organized armed dissent.

The Iranian security apparatus

Few independent observers question the efficiency of the intelligence departments that have hitherto been tasked with the suppression of organizations such as the MKO. Although responsibility for such actions falls to several such departments, ranging from the police and paramilitaries to the Revolutionary Guard, much has also been undertaken by the Ministry of Intelligence (MOIS or Ettela'at).[33]

Until 1999 the MOIS department that was specially briefed with the task of dealing with the MKO and a few other armed dissident organizations operating within Iran's borders was the Nefaq ('Hypocrisy') wing, one of the biggest of the ministry's nine departments. After the major reorganization prompted by the scandal of the Chain Murders,

Nefaq was rebranded as the 'Department against Counter-Revolutionary Forces', although it retained its offices and staff of several hundred full-time employees in central Tehran and thousands of paid informants.

The department has been particularly effective in bribing MKO members to leave the organization and in locating and approaching its defectors, often when leading new lives in the West, to obtain information about the movement. In January 2001, information from such quarters prompted Intelligence Ministry agents to raid an MKO hideout in central Tehran, seizing an unknown amount of equipment after fierce gunbattles during which six MOIS agents as well as an unknown number of Khalq members were killed.[34]

In its bid to curb domestic dissidents, the ministry also works closely with elements of the Law Enforcement Forces (Entezamat), created in 1990 by a merger of the municipal police, the gendarmerie and the revolutionary committees, although the Ministry of 'Construction Jihad' (Jihad-e Sazandegi) is technically also part of the security forces because it is authorized to use force in rural areas during emergencies. Headed by Mohammed Baqer Qalibaf, who is appointed by the Supreme Leader, the particular responsibilities of the 300,000-strong LEF include the monitoring by Special Branch officers of public demonstrations, where dissident groups have previously made bids to recruit members and disseminate literature, while within its ranks is a special intelligence unit, currently headed by Mohammed Ramezani, that also monitors domestic unrest.

The LEF has recently been particularly active in the border regions of Kordestan and Khuzestan, stepping up both the surveillance and arrest of suspected dissidents in the second half of 2002, probably because the pending turmoil in neighbouring Iraq threatened to spill into Iran. On 5 November 2002, Mustafa Jula and Ali Kak Jalil, two members of Komala, a Kurdish offshoot of the Iranian communist party (CPI), were reportedly executed in Marivan, and on 20 March 2003 Mohammed Golabi, another Komala member, was hanged. Spokesmen for the KDPI claimed that six supporters were executed in the second week of October alone.[35]

LEF agents have also led the crackdown on the members or perceived sympathizers of Chehregani's movement SANAM: on 2 July 2003, according to the independent media watchdog, Reporters Sans Frontières, Payman Pakmehr, a former correspondent for several banned papers, was attacked by four men who tried unsuccessfully to force him into a car before leaving him behind unconscious. The attack came hours after Pakmehr had given a radio interview to an international radio station that described preparations for an annual gathering at Babak Fortress that has become highly symbolic of Azerbaijani national feeling.[36]

The members of the LEF are not generally believed to have any particularly strong ideological ties to the regime, but there is no reason to question their professional commitment to the tasks they are given. Although there are eyewitness reports that 'the LEF intervened on behalf of the students to stop vigilantes attacking them' during the June 2003 student protests, for example, these reports are dismissed by others who are probably much more familiar with the way in which the LEF operates. 'Since the uprising of July 1999, the police have worked out much more effective ways of dealing with further protests,' as one such source has argued, 'and they won't have reined back vigilantes out of sympathy but in case such an attack provoked even more unrest and made things much worse'.[37]

In many situations of domestic unrest, the efforts of the LEF to restore order would also sometimes be reinforced by the state's vigilantes, groups of young men who carry out some of the regime's dirty work either because of their commitment to the Revolution's ideology or in desperate financial need of its sponsorship. For the hard-line authorities, the logic is simple: by claiming that these groups are self-appointed guardians of the Revolution who won't hesitate to 'enter the scene' if there are 'domestic threats that attack the essence of the system', they can intimidate and crush any rebellion while plausibly denying responsibility for the violence that then ensues. Because these vigilantes are also ostensibly 'volunteers', the regime can also claim that popular feeling is on its side.

These vigilantes not only embark on sudden, sporadic campaigns of enforcing public 'morality' that usually involve physically attacking young people who attend social gatherings deemed to be 'unIslamic' but also help to crush the large-scale protests that periodically erupt in Iranian streets. In July 2000 students who were marking the first anniversary of the earlier demonstration were attacked by vigilantes using knives, chains and bottles to break up their meeting. Again on 8 December 2002, another gathering of 1,500 pro-reform students at Amir Kabir University in Tehran was broken up by around 300 militia, some of whom allegedly threw pepper into the eyes of some of the students. Six months later vigilantes also launched a vicious attack on the Hemmat dormitory of Allameh Tabatabai University in Tehran, a focal point for further unrest.

There are reckoned to be around fifteen such vigilante groups, some of which are unofficially designated to monitor specific 'threats' such as those posed by student organizations or by women who are felt to be ignoring 'Islamic virtues' by refusing to wear a headscarf. Chief amongst them are the Bassijis ('Mobilization') forces that are headquartered in Azadi Street in West Tehran and which have acted as an arm of the IRGC since their formation in 1979 as 'an army of 20 million' to protect the Revolution. During riots that took place in the winter of 1994, around 115,000 members of both battalions of this paramilitary organization were mobilized to help restore law and order, and Bassij members have since been reportedly well trained in riot control, receiving new equipment and training to undertake such tasks.[38]

Other paramilitary groups include the Fedayeen-e Islam, a much smaller group that was condemned in July 1999 by Interior Minister Ali Yunesi for its violent activities against student protesters, and the Ansar-e-Hezbollah, headed by an editor of the pro-conservative weekly paper *Yalossarat* and bearing a reputation for ferocious violence. Plain-clothed members of this group, the Lebas Shakhs-iha, were also particularly active in suppressing the student riots of June 2003. All of these different groups are known to have active sympathizers and informers throughout particular hotbeds of unrest, such as a lecturer in the politics department of Tehran University who is 'widely known to be the chief Hezbollah representative and informer on the campus'.[39]

Although these various groups have independent structures and different leaders, all of their affiliates share the same loyalty to the principles of the Revolution and report directly to high-ranking members of the security forces and their sympathizers: Hamid Ostad, a vigilante leader in Masshad, claimed that 'we operate under the command of the Supreme Leader'. Others swear allegiance to particular individuals or cliques, such as those based at an ultra-conservative religious seminary in Qom, whose leading ideologues include Ayatollah Mesbah-Yazdi, a member of the Assembly of Experts.

By using their notoriously heavy-handed tactics, the vigilantes followed a long tradition in a country where politics has long been played out by use of force in the streets (Chapter 7): Mohammed Reza Shah, for example, had employed two gang leaders of southern Tehran, Nasser Jigaraki and Shah'ban Ja'fari Bimokh, against his rival Mossadeq during the 1953 coup and again, ten years later, against the huge crowds that Khomeini led in protest at the Shah's 'White Revolution' that heralded a series of economic and social changes. Soon after the Islamic Revolution, Khomeini and his followers had set up Hezbollah, then led by Hojjatoleslam Hadi Ghaffari, to intimidate and disrupt the rallies of the Islamic Revolutionary Party's opponents who then posed a serious threat to the regime's stability. Bearing an unswerving loyalty to Khomeini, and whipped up by their hatred of the 'foreign conspiracies' of the

USA, Israel and the remnants of the old regime that were alleged to be plotting against the Revolution, its followers clashed particularly bitterly during the turbulent two years of 1980–81 with the Mujahideen-e Khalq Organization (MKO), fighting street battles in the towns of the Caspian coast that had traditionally been strongholds of the political left. Over the next few years, as their numbers were swelled by veterans of the ongoing war with Iraq, the vigilantes also turned their attention to patrolling residential districts of Tehran to demand stricter adherence to 'Islamic morals'.

Although their key role lies in the use of physical violence against demonstrators, these hard-line groups also help to negate the impact of dissident protest by staging well-timed counter-protests, such as the rally of 15,000 Bassij militiamen outside the former US embassy in central Tehran on 24 November 2002 that denounced 'arrogant American politics'. Similar mass rallies were also held at the height of the student riots in July 1999 as hundreds of thousands responded to Khamenei's call for 'the government and the security forces', as well as the Bassiji militia, 'to repress corrupt and counter-revolutionary elements'. Footage of this huge crowd that marched through Tehran on the night of 13 July was broadcast live to the country on state television.

But should any violent disorder require the trained use of firepower, rather than just strong-arm tactics, however, then individual units of the 120,000-strong Revolutionary Guard would be called upon as the regime's main line of defence. Since the end of the war with Iraq in 1988, there have been growing indications that the IRGC has been trained more specifically for conducting internal security tasks rather than supporting the regular Iranian army in conventional battle. This trend was accelerated after the disturbances at Qasvin in 1994, when a new 8,000-strong Special Guards Unit of the Islamic Revolution was reportedly created to deal purely with the threat of civil unrest,[40] and became unmistakeably evident at one military exercise in June 1995, when a large number of IRGC members trained for urban warfare scenarios in a 400-square-kilometre area in the Neinava Region, south of Tehran. The Revolutionary Guard also continues to hold regular exercises in riot control with the Bassiji reserve forces.[41] Although IRGC members are believed to have voted for Khatami in large numbers in earlier presidential contests, there is no specific reason to question their loyalty to the regime in the event of any future domestic crisis.

The regular armed forces, which are trained, organized and equipped more to deal with external threats than domestic challenges, are the regime's final line of defence. The regular army, headed by General

Hassan Firuzabadi, is estimated to total between 220,000 and 225,000 active servicemen, organized into thirteen divisions. Three of these are for armoured units, two for mechanized forces, five for general infantry and there are individual units for Commandos, Special Forces and Parachutists. These regular forces are led by officers trained at the Tehran Military Academy and at other quarters that offer more specialized courses, including bases at Shiraz, for infantry and armour; Tabriz, for signals; and Isfahan, for missiles and army aviation.[42] This regular conscript army is also backed up by a further 300,000 reservists.

Even for an established, organized and well-funded armed opposition, it is clear that the obstacles to any successful military operation against the Tehran regime currently remain formidable.

Notes

1. *Financial Times*, 18 June 2003.

2. Ibid.

3. The acronyms MEK or PMOI (People's Mujahideen Organisation of Iran) are sometimes also used.

4. *New York Post*, 20 May 2003; see also <www.danielpipes.org/article/1100>.

5. *The Times*, 7 February 2003.

6. *New York Times*, 9 May 2003.

7. *Sunday Telegraph*, 1 June 2003.

8. *Washington Post*, 11 September 2003.

9. *Knox News*, 23 September 2003; *Washington Post*, 9 November 2003.

10. *New York Times*, 10 December 2003.

11. See Chapter 1.

12. 'Ashcroft's Baghdad Connection', *Newsweek*, 26 September 2002.

13. See generally *Jane's Intelligence Review*, September 2002.

14. Author's interview with MKO defector, formerly a commander of operations inside Tehran, July 2003.

15. See Chapter 1.

16. *Wall Street Journal*, 4 October 1994.

17. *Washington Post*, 21 June 2003.

18. Interview with the author, London, 2 September 2002.

19. *EurasiaNet*, 19 June 2003.

20. AP, 15 January 2003.

21. <http://usinfo.state.gov/regional.nea/iraq.iraq1991>.

22. *New York Post*, 20 May 2003.

23. AP, 25 June 2003; *Le Figaro*, 23 June 2003.

24. The 'Colorado Iranian–American Community, 19,857 E. Lindale Place, Auror, CO 80013'.

25. Author's interview with ex-MKO member, June 2003.

26. *Baltimore Sun*, 5 July 2003.

27. *Newsweek*, 26 September 2002.

28. Author's interviews with NCRI/MKO representatives, London, July–September 2002.

29. BBC News, 25 November 1999.

30. *Far Eastern Economic Review*, 5 August 1999; see Chapter 3.

31. Radio Israel, 1 March 1996.

32. *Financial Times*, 2 May 2003.

33. Also known by the acronym VEVAK (Vezarat-e Ettela'at va Amniat-e Keshvar).

34. BBC News, 29 January 2001.

35. Amnesty International, 3 March 2003.

36. RSF, 4 July 2003.

37. Author's interviews with eyewitnesses to the June 2003 unrest, Tehran, November 2003.

38. *Jane's All the World's Armies*, June 2003.

39. Information to the author from a dissident source, Tehran, November 2003.

40. Anthony Cordesman, *Iran's Military Forces in Transition* (Westport, CT: Praeger Press, 1999), p. 135.

41. See generally ibid.

42. See generally *Jane's All the World's Armies*, June 2003.

Conclusion

The wider regional significance of any future state of crisis in Iran is not hard to see. On the one hand, the country's possible political implosion would clearly threaten the dissemination of weapons, migrants and narcotics on a vast scale that could potentially destabilize much of the surrounding region. On the other, a more peaceful conclusion will offer immense business opportunities for international companies that would bring not only much-needed investment, employment and wealth for millions of Iranians but also cheap energy for the outside world. A stable, moderate Iranian government would also much improve prospects for peace in the Middle East and could make vital contributions to the rebuilding of Iraq and Afghanistan.

But the tensions within and around the country also have a much wider importance because they raise other issues and questions that are highly pertinent to the contemporary age. The demographic pressures that currently push Iran towards political crisis, by creating a conflict between a young population that shares none of the common memories and experiences that have formed the mindset of the minority that wields power, are essentially the same as those that have helped to create similar problems elsewhere in the world. In Kosovo, Northern Ireland and Israel, the perceived ancestral rights of the Serbs, Ulstermen and Jews to their homelands are put at risk by the much faster birth rates of the Albanian, Irish Catholic and Palestinian populations who also have their own claims to the same lands. In some countries, sudden but spectacular demographic growth has already wreaked political havoc, notably in Algeria where the 80 per cent of the population that is under the age of thirty remembers nothing of the struggle for independence that ended in 1962 and has instead taken to the streets in violent protests for democracy. In other places, demographic trends may in future produce social unrest on a hitherto unforeseen scale, including in Western states that are currently experiencing particularly rapid birth rates among their own Muslim populations.

The flight of huge numbers of some of these young Iranians to more promising destinations also prompts many questions about the global phenomenon of mass migration. While the impact of refugees upon their new homelands is much debated, the impact on the places they leave behind has remained largely overlooked. One possible effect, for example, is an increasing radicalization of populations, as the flight of the more moderately minded leaves behind the more fanatical, diehard factions of all sides. Traits of just such a phenomenon have already been noted in the Middle East, where one Western observer has noted that 'in the long term it sometimes seems as if it will just be the fundamentalist settlers left to confront their opposite numbers in Hamas, with fewer and fewer secular moderates remaining to keep the crazies on both sides from each other's throats'.[1] Could this mean that migration from Iran will also lead to more of the violent clashes that in recent years have already erupted on a near-perennial basis?

Such street violence has in any event also raised many other important issues, such as how much influence new technology – the potent visual images broadcast by the Internet and on satellite television – really exerts over human behaviour. At a time when experts and commentators the world over continue to hotly debate just such an influence, they could do worse than look to Iranian street protests in their bid to reach a firm conclusion. Because there are indications that the student protesters have been incited by the images and messages from dissident sources both within and outside their own country, does this mean that the Iranian model might herald a new era in which such popular protests, prompted by contemporary forms of media far more potent than those they replace, will become much more the norm? And just as in the 1970s an exiled Khomeini turned Iran's technical innovations against the regime that had created it, orchestrating revolution by use of a telephone network that the Shah had gone to great lengths to commission, and just as the 9/11 hijackers used the West's own modern forms of transport to 'stab us in the eye', could man's new forms of communication be turned against his own self, as powerful images on the Internet, already perceived by many as synonymous with human depravity, help to incite violence, crime and disorder?

In another sense, however, Iran's alleged sponsorship of suicide bombings in the Middle East also reveals the limits of modern technology. As Rafsanjani has commented, 'one Palestinian by going to paradise can send 300 Israelis to hell. This is more powerful than atomic bombs.'[2] The former premier's observation appears highly relevant at a time when the superbly equipped modern-day US army has shown the same vulnerability to the street masses of Iraq and to the determined efforts of perhaps only a small number of individuals who since the fall of Saddam have been waging a war of attrition using devices that are deemed 'not very sophisticated … made in a garage with a welder or a battery with a handful of wire'.[3] Such simplicity of tactics and methods, it appears, holds the key to the future of the battlefield as much as the wide variety of 'smart' weapons of which the Americans have in recent years much boasted.

American rhetoric on Iran also raises uncomfortable questions about the idealistic values Washington has proclaimed to embody and has sought to disseminate, chiefly its faith in democracy. While no one seriously denies the value of democracy – no matter how much dispute there may be about the exact form it may take – the US administration has generally appeared to regard it more as an article of faith rather than, as Churchill once so famously proclaimed, the 'least bad' system of government. The transformation of Iraq into a working democracy, Condoleezza Rice has argued, 'is the only guarantee' that the region 'will no longer produce ideologies of hatred that lead men to fly airplanes into buildings in New York and Washington'.[4] President Bush also argued that democracy is a path to peace, arguing in the context of Palestinian politics, for example, that 'without this outside support for terrorism, Palestinians who are working for reform, and long for democracy, will be in a better position to choose their new leaders. True leaders who strive for peace, true leaders who faithfully serve the people.'[5]

But to have such faith in the intrinsic value of democracy, instead of seeing it as a mere starting point to a better future, prompts obvious questions. Is not any direct relationship between democracy and peace questionable if some of the world's most bloody and arguably 'unnecessary' wars – among them the First World War and Vietnam – have been waged by democratic nations? And while the United States has admirably preached the value of democracy to others, is it well qualified to do so when its own political system is notoriously determined, as the story of the MKO illustrates, by those who pull financial strings? It is in this regard significant that one of the leading advocates of regime change in Iraq, Richard Perle, was not only an unelected and unaccountable adviser of great influence, but one who in 1993 was reported to have taken substantial payments from an Israeli weapons manufacturer and who a decade later, on 28 March 2003, was forced to resign from the chairmanship of the Pentagon's Defense Policy Board because of financial scandal.[6] The British government's own position is also not untouched by irony, since it has declared its commitment to democracy and human rights in Iran at the same time as handing more political power to unelected bodies, notably a judiciary at home and a bureaucracy in Brussels, while having also acquired considerable notoriety for its own 'culture of spin', designed to manipulate the free and fair workings of democracy.

It is plain, then, that there are many reasons why Iran deserves considerable attention from the outside world. But are there also any constructive measures that the West can take to reduce the risks of domestic and international confrontation?

The way forward

As a starting point, Western governments should draw a clear distinction between Iranian domestic issues on the one hand and issues that more directly affect the outside world on the other. In terms of defusing the political and economic pressures upon Iran in a way that benefits the cause of democracy and human rights, it is highly questionable that there are any real measures that the West can take. For at least as much as their counterparts in any other country, Iranian politicians generally deeply resent criticism and interference by the outside world in their own internal policies and are very much more likely to ignore international protests than bow to them. But because few Iranians would ever question the obvious legitimacy of the West's concern for its own security or for the stability of Iran's regional neighbours, there is instead a strong case for arguing that Western pressure should be concentrated on these issues.

It is in this context that the European Union's policy of 'critical engagement' should be viewed. This approach was initiated by the EU in 1995 and has since been endorsed by the European Union's General Affairs Council, which continues to declare its 'continued support for the process of reform in Iran and in this context ... its willingness to strengthen relations between the EU and Iran'.[7] But despite considerable diplomatic efforts, this approach has not achieved any of the real benefits to domestic reform for which its supporters have always hoped. Even the example that its supporters cite as evidence of its effectiveness, the official ban in December 2002 of the stoning to death of some convicted criminals, is misleading since this particular punishment was very rarely practised in modern Iran in any case: there were two such cases in both 2001 and 2002. 'The truth about critical engagement,' as one senior Western diplomat has admitted, 'is that it's achieved almost nothing in terms of advancing the cause of human rights and political reform, and for every step that we have gone forward there have been at least as many other steps back.'[8]

Some liberal humanitarians could of course plausibly counter-argue that the continuation of such an approach would be justified if there is no prospect of change inside the country. In Iran, however, for reasons that have already been discussed, such changes are inevitable and

Western governments can therefore allow Iran's own internal dynamics, engineered by profound demographic changes, to bring about the reforms they wish to see. When such a crisis point is eventually reached, they are in a position to moderate and curb some of the excesses that may very well eventuate.

By contrast, 'critical dialogue' can be strongly defended as the best approach to generate Iranian co-operation on the nuclear issue, the Middle East peace process and the rebuilding of Iraq and Afghanistan. The clearest indication that this is the best approach emerged on 21 October 2003 when the Iranians took most commentators by surprise by striking a deal that was made possible through negotiation and diplomatic pressure. If Iran had been isolated by all governments, not just by Washington, then there would have been no opening where the agreement could emerge.

This is not to say that there is no room for the harder line that Washington has always taken when dealing with Iran, and many Western diplomats argue that the present combination of European dialogue and this harsher American stance is probably the best approach towards the current Iranian regime. 'It's good to have both a good cop and bad cop,' in the words of one European representative in Tehran, 'so that the Iranians can never be quite sure what's in store for them. Too much aggression gives them no incentive to compromise, while too much leniency will make them think they can have it all their own way.'[9] Certainly the mere threat of UN-imposed economic sanctions against Iran, as the USA has sought to impose in retaliation for any violation of its nuclear obligations, is enough to make even the most diehard conservative in Tehran think twice about any misdemeanour: even a very brief embargo on the exportation of Iranian oil would devastate its economy.

But there is also considerable scope for the USA to change the way in which it deals with Iran in future. While Washington has never been slow to condemn the Iranian government, it remains to be seen if future US administrations will be equally quick to promise and deliver rewards in return for Tehran's co-operation and compromise. The US government could, for example, give details of the circumstances under which existing economic sanctions could, perhaps gradually, be lifted and also raise the spectre of potentially offering Iran membership of the World Trade Organization (WTO). Earlier Iranian bids to join the WTO have previously been blocked by both Israel and the United States, even though membership would promote the cause of reform by demanding a major overhaul of the regime's economic and political institutions in a way that would further challenge the hard-liners' grip on power.

There are other measures that the USA can arguably take, but which to date have not been addressed. Washington can ask if its economic sanctions would be better directed not at Iran as a whole but instead targeted more specifically at the extensive overseas investments that many of the regime's leaders are known to hold in Western banks. Obviously any such measures would much more effectively penalize the material interests of those who can make decisions about their country's future instead of the ordinary civilians, who clearly exert no comparable political leverage.

There are also ways in which America can reduce the level of mistrust with Iran, thereby creating a more positive climate in which threats of economic and military force, as described above, could still be made but probably much more effectively than hitherto: if the Tehran regime, instead of thinking that Washington is implacably opposed to any and every course it takes, has more faith that any new notes of compromise will be rewarded then it will of course be more willing to strike them.

One such step that the USA could take to improve its relations both with Iran and the wider Islamic world would be to withdraw, or at least considerably scale down, some of its military presence in the surrounding region. Since 9/11 the number of American military bases throughout the republics of the former Soviet Union has proliferated and currently includes around a dozen US military outposts in Kyrgyzstan, Pakistan, Tajikistan and Uzbekistan, and another three in Afghanistan. Moreover, the US military has staged joint military exercises in sensitive regions close to the Iranian border, notably with Azerbaijani troops in the strategic oil-rich Caspian Sea on 14 August 2003. But in a unipolar world in which America maintains an unparalleled military dominance, it is arguable that these bases do less to serve any constructive purpose than to symbolize US 'hegemony' and rally the anti-American cause in the same way that the presence of US troops on the 'holy soil' of Saudi Arabia has previously acted as a rallying point for Al Qaeda. By dramatically scaling down such a presence, Washington would alleviate Iran's serious and well-founded concerns for its own security and much reduce the level of mistrust between the two countries.

Although such measures might considerably defuse international tension, it nevertheless still remains impossible to predict where Iran's future lies. It may be that the best-case scenario, hoped for by every independent observer, will eventuate as the mullahs, recognizing the futility of clinging remorselessly to power, perhaps unexpectedly hand over the reins of the political order to democratic forces, thereby allowing a new political order to emerge, perhaps painlessly.

But because Iranian politics have long possessed a capacity to surprise, as noted above (Introduction), it is also possible that the current regime will continue to defy all predictions and remain in power for far longer than currently seems likely. Just as during the turmoil of the immediate post-revolutionary years, or at particularly dramatic moments of the war with Iraq, there were times when the regime's days seemed numbered, so it is possible that a new conservative government, even if given only a very dubious mandate by a low electoral turnout in the February 2004 elections, could still succeed in staving off opposition with a series of populist measures and incentives and thereby maintain its grip on power. The same tactics were used with good effect during 2002, for example, when a particularly acrimonious teachers' pay dispute that had spilled into violent disorder in the streets was defused by the offer of financial subsidies.

In any event, at the time of writing few scenarios seem to be beyond the realm of possibility. A US or Israeli military strike, an organized insurrection or mass street protests have all also been aired as possible outcomes of the country's different tensions. But whatever does in fact eventuate, there can be little doubt that Iran will not be far from tomorrow's headlines.

Notes

1. William Dalrymple, 'Disappearing Christians', *New York Review of Books*, 25 September 2003.

2. *Financial Times*, 14 June 2003.

3. US military briefing on a bomb used by insurgents against US forces, quoted in Mark Danner's article, 'Delusions in Baghdad', *New York Review of Books*, 18 December 2003.

4. *Washington Post*, 26 August 2003.

5. Speech to the AEI, 26 February 2003.

6. Perle accepted a $1.5 million payment from the US telecoms company, Global Crossing, at the same time as trying to overcome Pentagon objections to the company's sale to a Hong Kong tycoon.

7. EU General Affairs Council Conclusions, 17 June 2002.

8. Interview with the author, Tehran, 14 November 2003.

9. Ibid

Select bibliography

Abrahamiam, Ervan (1982), *Iran Between Two Revolutions*, Princeton, NJ, Princeton University Press.

Alizadeh, Parvin (2000), *The Economy of Iran: Dilemmas of an Islamic State*, London, I.B.Tauris.

Bararan, Mehdi (1984), *Inqilab-e Iran dar Dow Harakat*, Tehran.

Behdad, Sohrab (1995), *Iran After the Revolution: Crisis of an Islamic State*, London, I.B.Tauris.

Benjamin, Samuel (1887), *Persia and the Persians*, Boston.

Briant, Pierre (2002), *From Cyrus to Alexander: A History of the Persian Empire*, Eisenbrauns Press.

Brogan, Hugh (1999), *The Longman History of the United States of America*, London and New York, Longman.

Brumberg, Daniel (2001), *Reinventing Khomeini: The Struggle for Reform in Iran*, Chicago, IL, University of Chicago Press.

Bulloch, John and Harvey Morris (1989), *The Gulf War: Its Origins, History and Consequences*, London, Methuen.

Clark, Jonathan (1994), *The Language of Liberty*, Cambridge, CUP.

Cordesman, Anthony (1999), *Iran's Military Forces in Transition*, Westport, CT, Praeger Press.

Cordesman, Anthony and Ahmed S. Hashim (1997), *Iraq: Sanctions and Beyond*, Boulder, CO and Oxford, UK, Westview Press.

Freedman, Lawrence (2000), *Kennedy's Wars*, Oxford and New York, OUP.

Hiro, Dilip (2001), *Neighbours, Not Friends: Iran and Iraq after the Gulf Wars*, London and New York, Routledge.

— (2000), *Iran under the Ayatollahs* (reprinted by) Excel Press, New York,.

Kagan, Robert and William Kristol (2002), *Present Dangers: Crisis and Opportunity in American Foreign and Defense Policy*, San Francisco, Encounter Books.

Karshenas, Massoud (1990), *Oil, State and the Industrialisation of Iran*, Cambridge, CUP.

Katzman, Kenneth (1993), *The Warriors of Islam: Iran's Revolutionary Guards*, Oxford, OUP.

Kinnear, John (1813), *A Geographical Memoir of the Persian Empire*, London.

Kinzer, Stephen (2003), *All the Shah's Men: An American Coup and the Roots of Middle East Terror*, Hoboken, NJ and London, Wiley Press.

Ledeen, Michael and William Lewis (1981), *Debacle: American Failure in Iran*, New York, Alfred A. Knopf.

McNamara, Robert S. (1995), *In Retrospect*, London, Random House.

Moin, Baqer (1999), *Khomeini: Life of the Ayatollah*, London, I.B.Tauris.

Roosevelt, Kermit (1979), *Countercoup: The Struggle for Control of Iran*, New York, McGraw-Hill.

Schirazi, Ashgar (1997), *The Constitution of Iran. Politics and the State in the Islamic Republic*, London, I.B.Tauris.

Thomas, Ewan (1995), *The Very Best Men: Four Men Who Dared: The Early Years of the CIA*, New York, Simon and Schuster.

Wiesehofer, Josef (2001), *Ancient Persia from 550 BC to 650 AD*, London, I.B.Tauris.

Woodward, Bob (2002), *Bush at War*, New York, Simon and Schuster.

Articles

Albright, David, 'An Iranian Bomb?', *Bulletin of the Atomic Scientists*, January 1995.

Behdad, Sohrab, 'Khatami and His "Reformist" Economic (Non-) Agenda', *Middle East Report Online*, May 2001.

Calleo, David P., 'Power, Wealth and Wisdom', *The National Interest*, No. 72, Summer 2003.

De Bellaigue, Christopher, 'Who Rules Iran?', *New York Review of Books*, 27 June 2002.

Einhorn, Robert J. and Gary Samore, 'Ending Russian Assistance to Iran's Nuclear Bomb', *Survival*, Summer 2002.

Eisenstadt, Michael, 'Living with a Nuclear Iran', *Survival*, Autumn 1999.

Gelb, Leslie H. and Justine A. Rosenthal, 'The Rise of Ethics in Foreign Policy', *Foreign Policy*, May/June 2003.

Hibbs, Mark, 'Bonn Will Decline Tehran Bid to Resuscitate Bushehr Project', *Nucleonics Week*, 26 November 1991.

Kemp, Geoffrey, 'How to Stop the Iranian Bomb', *The National Interest*, No. 72, Summer 2003.

Lind, Michael, 'The Texas Nexus', *Prospect*, April 2003.

— 'The Christian Zionists', *Prospect*, July 2003.

Perkovich, George, 'Dealing with Iran's Nuclear Challenge', Carnegie Endowment for International Peace, 28 April 2003.

Samii, A.William, 'The Nation and Its Minorities', *Comparative Studies of South Asia, Africa and the Middle East* vol. XX, nos 1 and 2 (2000).

Tarekh, Ray, 'Iranian Options', *The National Interest*, no. 73, Fall 2003.

Index

effects of, 138–42; Manichaean view of the world, 30; relations with China, 96; relations with Israel, 20–1; rhetoric on Iran, 125, 215; support for MKO, 195–9; view of nuclear development in Iran, 95–6; vulnerability of army, 214 *see also* sanctions against Iran

US–Iranian relations, 1, 7, 10–11, 113, 119, 217–18; crisis of, 106–14; tension in, 190

US State Department, 64, 114, 194, 199; *Patterns of Global Terrorism*, 43, 58–9; report on Iran, 91

Universal Declaration of Human Rights, 38

universities: closure of, 171; privatization of, 171

University of Allameh Tabatabai, Tehran, attack on student dormitories, 208

University of Tehran, 171

uranium enrichment, 192, 202

urbanization, 184

Uzbekistan, 3, 14; US presence in, 218

Vahedi, Ahmed, 76, 77

Vajpayee, 17

velayat-ye faqih, 155, 184

Verdinejad, Fereydoun, 169

Vietnam, 32

Vietnam War, 26

Vitol, 15

vigilante forces, 208–9

Voice of America, 174–5, 176

Waldman, Peter, 197

Walid, Mahfouz Ould, 60

War of the Cities, 204

War on Terror, 2, 36, 43, 49, 203

Washington, George, 30

weapons of mass destruction (WMD), 9, 37, 102, 103, 107

weblogs, 173

Western influence, 1

Westoxication, 174

Westphalia, Treaty of, 38

White Revolution, 2, 209

Wilson, Woodrow, 29, 31

Wolfowitz, Paul, 8, 18, 27

Wolfowitz doctrine, 28

women, rights of, 13

World Bank, loans to Iran, 22

World Cup, rioting associated with, 169

World Trade Organization (WTO), attempt by Iran to join, 217

Wurmser, David, 21

Wurmser, Meyrav, 24, 27

Yazadi, Ebrahim, 130

Yazdi, Ayatollah Mohammed, 126, 131

Yazdi, General Beg, 56

Yazdi, Muhammad, 205

Yeltsin, Boris, 97

Yemen, killing of Al Qaeda suspects in, 64

Yosefian, Reza, 130

Yunesi, Ali, 59, 135, 180, 209

Zaanganeh, 55

Zadeh, Karim, 77

Zadeh, Morteza Mohsen (Sa'eed Chub-Tarash), 47

Zakeri, Hamid Reza, 60, 75

Zam-Zam company, 153

Za're, Kamal, 77

Zarqawi, Abu Mussab Al, 61

al-Zawahiri, Ayman, 61, 62

Zeid-Abadi, Ahmad, 131

Zibakalam, Sadeq, 139

Zibo Chemical Equipment Plant, 103

Zolqadr, Mohammed Baqer, 44, 60

Zoroastrian faith, 14, 167

al-Zubeidi, Mohammed Hamza, 82

Zudir, Abu, 60